Tradition and Modernity in the African Short Story

Recent Titles in
Contributions in Afro-American and African Studies

Tradition and Modernity in the African Short Story

AN INTRODUCTION TO A LITERATURE IN SEARCH OF CRITICS

F. Odun Balogun

CONTRIBUTIONS IN AFRO-AMERICAN STUDIES,
NUMBER 141
Henry Louis Gates, Jr., *Series Editor*

GREENWOOD PRESS
New York • Westport, Connecticut • London

Copyright Acknowledgments

The author and publisher are grateful for permission to reprint material from the following:

Extracts from *Girls at War and Other Stories* by Chinua Achebe are used by permission of Chinua Achebe.

Extracts from *Fixions* (1978), *The Uniformed Man* (1971), and *Thirteen Offensives Against Our Enemies* (1973) by Taban lo Liyong are used by permission of Taban lo Liyong.

F. Odun Balogun, "Characteristics of Absurdist African Literature: Taban lo Liyong's *Fixions*—A Study in the Absurd," *African Studies Review* 27, no. 1 (March 1984): 41-55. Used by permission of the African Studies Association and the editor of *African Studies Review*.

F. Odun Balogun, "Achebe's 'The Madman': A Poetic Realisation of Irony," *Okike* 23 (1983): 72-79. Used by permission of Dr. Ossie Enekwe, editor of *Okike*.

F. Odun Balogun, "Taban lo Liyong's *Fixions* and the Folk Tradition," in *Studies in the Novel*, ed. Samuel Asein and Albert Ashaolu (Ibadan, Nigeria: Ibadan University Press, 1986), 165–81. Used by permission of Ibadan University Press.

Library of Congress Cataloging-in-Publication Data

Balogun, Fidelis Odun, 1946–
   Tradition and modernity in the African short story : an
introduction to a literature in search of critics / F. Odun Balogun.
     p. cm.—(Contributions in Afro-American and African
studies, ISSN 0069–9624 ; no. 141)
  Includes bibliographical references and index.
  ISBN 0–313–27637–4 (lib. bdg. : alk. paper)
  1. Short stories, African (English)—History and criticism.
2. Africa in literature.   I. Title.   II. Series.
PR9344.B35 1991
823'.010996—dc20   90–42616

British Library Cataloguing in Publication Data is available.

Library of Congress Catalog Card Number: 90–42616
ISBN: 0–313–27637–4
ISSN: 0069–9624

First published in 1991

Greenwood Press, 88 Post Road West, Westport, CT 06881
An imprint of Greenwood Publishing Group, Inc.

Printed in the United States of America

∞™

The paper used in this book complies with the
Permanent Paper Standard issued by the National
Information Standards Organization (Z39.48–1984).

10 9 8 7 6 5 4 3 2 1

With Love to You:
Ebun, Temi, Nike, Odun Jr.

Contents

Preface

The motivation for commencing the study of African short stories a decade ago was provided by the sharp contrast I had observed between Africa, on the one hand, and Europe and the United States, on the other hand, regarding the treatment of the genre of the short story. While the genre was, and is still, popular in all three continents—being widely written and read, it was only in Africa that literary scholars had completely ignored its existence. The extent of the incorporation of the short story into the academic curriculum would provide a useful illustration of the seriousness with which Euro-American scholars regarded the short story.

The philology faculty of the Leningrad State University, Leningrad, USSR, where I studied, had two special seminar courses, one on the Russian short story and the other on the Soviet short story. It was at these seminars that I discovered both the greatness of the short story as an art form as well as the seriousness with which it was studied by literary scholars. This was how I came later to choose doing my doctoral dissertation on two decades of Russian Soviet short stories as a graduate student at the University of Illinois, Urbana, USA. Here, too, I witnessed the same level of seriousness in the attention paid to the short story. Eager to further deepen my knowledge of the genre, I went outside my major department, Slavic Languages and Literatures, to audit the undergraduate courses on the American, the English, and world short story masterpieces offered by the English Department.

Thus, my task as a scholar was obvious when I returned to Nigeria and discovered that critics had completely neglected the genre of the African short story that was, and is still, quite popular with writers and readers. This book is therefore an attempt on my part, as well as a challenge to other critics, to help end the relegating of the African short story by undertaking a thorough and systematic study of the genre.

The two-part structure of the book is born out of the desire to provide as complete a picture of the African short story as is possible in one study. While the first part gives a panoramic view of the whole field, the second part zeroes in on two representative African short story writers and provides microscopic details on their themes and artistic methods. The choice of Taban lo Liyong's stories to represent modernist trends in African short stories is an obvious one because there are not many experimental African short story writers who have been as prolific or successful as he. By contrast, the selection of Chinua Achebe's stories as representative of traditional practice in short story writing in Africa may be contentious in view of the fact that short stories by other eminent writers such as Alex la Guma, Ama Ata Aidoo, and Ngugi wa Thiong'o could equally have been chosen. Thus, the selection of Achebe's stories is arbitrary, but at the same time careful scrutiny shows that his stories have an edge over those of others when the details of craftsmanship are considered. While the traditional short story patronized by the majority of African short story writers is realistic in form and easy to understand, the modernist African short story, which is in the minority, is experimental and complex. These distinctions are discussed in greater detail in chapters 6 to 12.

The issue of tradition and modernity as discussed in this book goes beyond the dichotomy between styles. It also entails a presentation of the themes that it has become customary, traditional, to find in African short stories as indeed they have been found in all the other genres of African literature. Traditional and modern African economic, political, religious, and social cultures as they relate to precolonial Africa, colonialism, neocolonial independence, apartheid, indigenous and imported religions, and others, are critically examined by African short story writers with the aim of helping their various societies evolve authentic and ideal modern African cultures. Thus, there is also a thematic and cultural dichotomy between the criticized past and present cultures of Africa, on the one hand, and the envisaged, ideal modern cultures for Africa, on the other hand. This dichotomy is present in all the chapters but is more poignantly evident in chapters 2, 6, 8, and 11. Hence, even the chapters that are preoccupied with the dichotomy between the traditional realistic and the modern experimental styles are discussed within the framework of the thematic and cultural dichotomy between a rejected culture and a desirable one.

To make sense of the uncountable single stories involved in Part 1 of this study as well as the many stories in the individual collections in Part 2, I had to adopt the integrated mode of analysis. This method has the obvious advantage of revealing the general principles behind the artistic execution of the stories as a body. It is the best way to establish the essential elements in the thematic and artistic preoccupations of the authors concerned. There is, however, an obvious disadvantage in a synthesized study of this nature. Emphasis is on the general unifying principles underlying theme and style rather than on the peculiar characteristics of the theme and style of individual stories. In other words, the peculiar, the individual, is sacrificed for the common, the general, in a blended study. A story loses its individuality and becomes important only to the extent that it helps to establish the basic qualities in a collection or in a genre.

There is a tendency to overrate the story that boldly exhibits thematic and stylistic elements common to the collection. On the other hand, a story that happens to emphasize traits, which in themselves may be of unique significance but are marginal to the underlying principles of the collection, gets underrated. True, a marginal story (marginal in the sense just expressed) may get full credit in an integrated study if it is a strikingly successful story; in which case, it gets treated as a deserving exception. Ordinarily, however, a marginal story never gets the attention it really deserves and its true qualities may never be fully discovered.

For the writer, every story is unique and important. No writer wants to repeat himself or herself by composing a story that is just like the last one written. Good short story writers strive for originality and perfection in every attempt; and although they may not be successful, the effort guarantees uniqueness for every story. Consequently, even the stories that are most similar always have significant distinguishing characteristics.

One would expect that in short story cycles that emphasize unity of theme, character, setting, and symbolism, the individual story would lose its significance as a separate entity. The contrary is the case, however, as has been shown by story cycles such as Ivan Turgenev's *A Hunter's Sketches*, James Joyce's *Dubliners* and Sherwood Anderson's *Winesburg, Ohio*, to mention only three. Even in these works where thematic and artistic unity were uppermost in the minds of the writers, all the authors took pains to ensure that each story in their collection had artistic independence and could exist on its own outside of the collection. In fact, most of the stories in Turgenev's cycle, for example, were originally published as separate stories between 1846–76 and it was only afterwards that they were gathered into a collection. Also, the first recognition of the cyclic structure of *Dubliners*, published in 1914, occurred thirty years after its publication. Thus, even in a story cycle, the artistic independence of the individual story is still primary in spite of the great concern for overall unity. As Forest L. Ingram says in his book *Representative Short Story Cycles of the Twentieth Century*, "Every story cycle displays a double tendency of asserting the individuality of its components on one hand and of highlighting, on the other, the bonds of unity which make the many into a single whole" (19).

The ideal approach, therefore, to the study of short story collections, whether they constitute story cycles or not, is to analyze each individual story in detail. While such a method is obviously impossible for Part 1 of this book, it was the approach originally adopted for Part 2. However, I soon discovered that each story was so rich in themes and artistic qualities that in no time I had amassed such a wealth of material that it became quite clear that justice could only be done by devoting a separate chapter to each story. This was, unfortunately, beyond the scope of the study. Hence, in spite of its shortcoming, the integrated method has been adopted.

However, to demonstrate the advantage of the detailed study of an individual story and, more importantly, to share with readers the aesthetic satisfaction I have derived each time from reading what seems to me not only the best story by Achebe but also one of the best stories in the twentieth century, a separate chapter has been devoted to the analysis of "The Madman." While such a detailed study of every single African short story might not be feasible or even advisable, there is no alternative to a thorough examination of the themes and art of every important African short story writer. Thus, this book, which is further handicapped because it is limited to short stories in English from Africa south of the Sahara with only occasional mention of stories outside the region, is only an introduction. It is hoped, however, that despite its shortcomings, the book will achieve its objective of drawing critical attention to the vibrant genre of the African short story by highlighting aspects of its social and aesthetic values.

Here I wish to thank the following institutions and people who made it possible for me to carry out this study. The University of Benin, Nigeria, provided the initial grant to begin the research and also released me and paid my fares for a semester of overseas research leave in 1983. Professor Charles C. Stewart and Professor E. G. Bokamba were instrumental in my securing funds, office accommodation, and secretarial services as a visiting research scholar at the African Studies Center, University of Illinois, Urbana. I received invaluable assistance from the Africana librarian of the University of Illinois, Dr. Yvette Scheven, and her staff. The manuscript was typed under very demanding conditions twice by my wife, Ebun, and once by Sunday Ogiesoba of the Department of English and Literature, University of Benin. My colleague, Dr. Abdul R. Yesufu, read a number of chapters and offered useful advice for improvement.

There is additional ground to thank my wife for her cooperation and forbearance while I worked on the manuscript and spent the family's lean resources to complete the research.

Finally, I wish to acknowledge my children—Temi, Nike, and Odun Jr.—for tolerating my impatience whenever they came into the study.

Abbreviations

For convenience, the short story collections cited are abbreviated as follows:

AC	*African Creations*, ed. Emmanuel N. Obiechina
AS	*Africa South: Contemporary Writings*, ed. Mothobi Mutloatse
ASS	*African Short Stories*, eds. Chinua Achebe and C. L. Innes
CT	*The Collector of Treasures* by Bessie Head
DGH	*Debbie Go Home* by Alan Paton
EW	*On the Edge of the World*, ed. Stephen Gray
F	*Fixions and Other Stories* by Taban lo Liyong
GAW	*Girls at War and Other Stories* by Chinua Achebe
LT	*Lokotown and Other Stories* by Cyprian Ekwensi
M	*Miracles and Other Stories* by Kole Omotoso
MAS	*Modern African Stories*, ed. Charles R. Larson
MASF	*Modern African Stories*, ed. Ellis Ayitey Komey and Ezekiel Mphahlele
MMAS	*More Modern African Stories*, ed. Charles R. Larson
MVA	*More Voices of Africa*, ed. Barbra Nolen
ND	*Night of Darkness and Other Stories* by Paul Zeleza
NSH	*No Sweetness Here* by Ama Ata Aidoo

PASS	*Pan African Short Stories*, ed. Neville Denny
Q	*Quartet: New Voices from South Africa*, ed. Richard Rive
RC	*Restless City and Christmas Gold* by Cyprian Ekwensi
S	*Saworbeng* by Kofi Aidoo
SCSA	*Stories from Central and Southern Africa*, ed. Paul A. Scanlon
SL	*Secret Lives* by Ngugi wa Thiong'o
SMFS	*Some Monday for Sure* by Nadine Gordimer
TF	*The Feud* by R. Sarif Easmon
TS	*Tribal Scars* by Sembene Ousmane
UM	*The Uniformed Man* by Taban lo Liyong
VOZ	*Voices of Zambia*, ed. Mufalo Liswaniso
WD	*The Will To Die* by Can Themba
WN	*A Walk in the Night* by Alex la Guma
WTD	*Of Wives, Talismans and the Dead* by I.N.C. Aniebo

PART I

A GENERAL SURVEY OF
AFRICAN SHORT STORIES

1

The African Short Story: A Literature in Search of Critics

The most significant study of African short stories as a body until now has been a 1978 conference paper by Helen O. Chukwuma, appropriately titled "The Prose of Neglect." Although excellent single short stories, individual author collections, and multiple author anthologies have continued to be published by Africans since her paper bemoaned the unjustifiable neglect of the critical study of African short stories, critics of African literature have done very little to correct the situation. Yet it is not that other scholars like Charles E. Nnolim, notably in his article, "The Critic of African Literature: The Challenge of the 80's" (56), have not re-echoed this concern. It could also not be that the critics were unaware of the fact already accepted as self-evident since the nineteenth century by Euro-American scholars that the short story is a significant major genre of literature. The genre remains vibrant today especially in the United States and the Soviet Union, where it has contributed noticeably to the development of the national literatures, and serious writers and scholars have continued to hold it in high esteem. It is true, of course, that in these countries the patronage of the short story had tended to fluctuate in the level of its seriousness from one literary epoch to another, but there was hardly a time when the genre suffered a near-complete critical neglect as it now experiences in Africa.

Highly commendable in this regard, therefore, are the efforts of a few scholars who have been trying to sensitize the African literary public to the importance of the genre of the short story through conference and journal papers.[1] These efforts are nonetheless miserably little when compared to the volumes of criticism that have been written during the same period on topics relating to the other genres of African literature. Hence, scholarship in the genre of the African short story has remained primarily at the level of a few journal articles, book reviews, and introductory remarks in anthologies.[2] On those rare occasions when book chapters are reserved for the study of the stories by novelists who have also extensively published short stories, the latter are invariably treated as mere appendages to the novels.[3] There is as yet no single book-length study of the genre; conference sessions devoted to its examination are few and far apart; and undergraduate and postgraduate courses based entirely on the genre hardly exist in African educational institutions.

One of the factors that account for the low esteem in which the short story is held by some critics relates to the fact that the genre, as one observer says, is a "paradoxical form" patronized by both beginners and accomplished writers (Bergonzi 251). Indeed, the greater percentage of the stories that we read in African newspapers and popular magazines are written by the former group. Editors in these media, unlike their counterparts in scholarly journals and creative writing magazines, care little for the quality of the stories they publish. Thus, a substantial quantity of the stories printed in Africa are undoubtedly of poor quality.

However, the more decisive factor in the neglect of the short story in Africa is the difficulty of publication. As with poetry, publishing short stories or extended critical studies on the genre, especially when these are written by unknown authors, is risky business for publishing houses, which like all business establishments fear financial loss. What is strange, however, is that scholars have turned themselves into financial watchdogs for publishers in the process of reviewing manuscripts for publication. Here, for instance, is an amazing argument advanced by a scholar to discourage a university press from publishing a book-length study of African short stories in which special attention is paid to the stories of Chinua Achebe and Taban lo Liyong:

The appeal of the subject will be mostly at the tertiary level and within a very limited circle of Achebe devotees. The audience is unfortunately limited and even for a regular honours degree class *Girls at War* is mostly taught as a peripheral text and in very few institutions in Nigeria. *Fixions* and lo Liyong's other works are hardly familiar texts to most students and indeed teachers of modern African Literature, and I am not sure there will be a significant change in the reception of lo Liyong's works largely because of the artificiality of his so-called experimental forms.[4]

One would have expected that a scholar who recognizes the fact that there is a limited audience for a significant genre of literature would also see it as his or her first duty to help create an environment condusive to the promotion of an expanded audience. Similarly, one would also have thought that such a scholar would know that the promotion of critical scholarship is foremost among the things required to create a broadened audience for the genre in question. But the most disturbing aspect of these comments is the academic ignorance of the scholar that the comments expose. Obviously, the scholar has little regard for short stories and does not think that African short stories in general and the short stories of Achebe and lo Liyong in particular deserve to be treated any better than as "peripheral texts" by students and teachers of modern African literature. Yet, Achebe and lo Liyong are not only good short story writers when judged by even the harshest of standards, but are also writers who between them typify both the traditional as well as the modern trends in African short story writing. While one may excuse this scholar for not being enthusiastic about lo Liyong's experimental short stories—though no genuine scholar can really be indifferent to experimental fiction—one finds it difficult to explain away the abysmal ignorance of an African literature scholar who argues that the circle of Achebe devotees is a "very limited" one.

To fully grasp the implication of this assessor's report as far as the fortunes of the short story in Africa are concerned, we have to remember that it was written by a scholar deemed to be qualified by a university, not a commercial, press to comment competently on issues relating to African literary scholarship. But the saddest aspect of the issue is that this scholar is by no means an exception. Few African literary scholars have shown an awareness that the critic of the novel is not necessarily qualified to judge the short story without first getting intimately acquainted with the peculiar characteristics of the genre. Few critics are conversant with the specifics of the practice of short story writing in Africa today, let alone aware of the genre's comparative state of existence in contemporary Euro-American and other literatures. In short, it is often wrongly assumed that a critic does not need any special knowledge to discuss the short story.

If this state of affairs continues to prevail in African literary criticism, prospects for the development of the African short story are indeed bleak. Scholarship in the short story will remain marginalized by uninformed criticism. Furthermore, since no form of literature can flourish without the nourishment of informed critical analysis, short story writing in Africa itself will continue to lack a vital ingredient of growth and will ultimately suffer a deterioration in artistic quality. Indeed, the fact that major African writers no longer patronize the short story today, unlike they used to do when they were developing artists, is already indicative of the low level of esteem in which our writers already hold the genre. This is in sharp contrast to the practice in Europe and the United States, where established writers continue to write short stories. One of the best short stories in the world—"The Death of Ivan Ilych," for instance, was written by Lev Tolstoy as an elderly man.

Certain critics, however, would not be alarmed even if the short story were to go into extinction. This is because such critics entertain a fundamental doubt concerning the usefulness of the short story as a literary enterprise meant to have aesthetic as well as social values. K. H. Petersen, for instance, is of the view that the short story is an "amorphous" genre that has neither a unified content nor a thematic purpose (Petersen and Rutherford 61, 63). Another critic argues that "the short story, in its present condition, seems to be unhealthily limited, both in the range of literary experience it offers and its capacity to deepen our understanding of the world, or of one another" (Bergonzi 256).

The claim that the short story is of little artistic value and human relevance is of course erroneous and hence it is everywhere contradicted. Hallie Burnett in her book *On Writing the Short Story*, for instance, repeats Frank O'Connor's affirmation that the short story can reveal the truth in "a way that the novel [even] with its wider canvas cannot achieve" (8). Granted that one may not completely accept O'Connor's judgment, anyone who is familiar with the short stories of the great masters like Tolstoy, Feodor Dostoevsky, James Joyce, Ernest Hemingway, Achebe, Ngugi wa Thiong'o, Alex la Guma, and Sembene Ousmane would know that the potential of the short story to enrich our knowledge of man and of the world is enormous. In fact, what Georg Lukàcs says about the value of the novella, which he describes as the "forerunner and rearguard of the great forms," can equally apply for the short story:

It does not claim to shape the whole of social reality, nor even to depict that whole as it appears from the vantage point of a fundamental and topical problem. Its truth rests on the fact that an individual situation—usually an extreme one—is possible in a certain society at a certain level of development, and, just because it is possible, is characteristic of this society and this level. . . . With this reservation, one can say of contemporary and near-contemporary fiction that it often withdraws from the novel into the novella in its attempt to provide proof of man's moral stature.(8–10)

Thus, there can be no doubt as to the social relevance of the short story even if we discount the comparison with the novella and base our judgment on the earlier evoked valid claims of writers like Frank O'Connor and the evidence of the great masters such as Tolstoy, Dostoevsky, Anton Chekhov, Joyce, and Hemingway. And with regard to artistry, critics have long affirmed that the short story is second only to poetry in its mastery of language and technique. The reason that Edgar Allan Poe, for instance, highly esteemed short literary compositions like poetry and the short story (brief tale), which he considered similar in terms of value, was that they promoted greater artistic coherence than was possible in the longer compositions like the novel (romance).[5] This is still true today; and as a modern critic accurately observed, "The compression, intensity and momentary vision of the short story have prompted many practitioners and readers to compare the form to poetry" (Julien 85). In fact, anyone reading stories like Achebe's "The Madman" (GAW 1–10) or Mango Tshabangu's "Thoughts in a Train" (AS 156–58), which are excellent examples of prose-poems, will realize that there is no limit to the artistic perfection attainable in the genre of the short story.

It is obvious, therefore, that there is no justifiable excuse for the critics of African literature to continue to ignore the genre of the short story, the more so because some African short story writers have been among the most consumate practitioners of the genre in the twentieth century. This for instance, was what Emmanuel Obiechina, a respected African critic had to say concerning the social relevance and artistic quality of the short stories in *African Creations: A Decade of Okike Short Stories*:

All the stories in the anthology share some common qualities which deserve to be mentioned: each of them is a good story, conceived and executed in the round, original in its perception of human life, values and experiences and authentic in the expression of the nuances of human emotions. Each is featured not because it is an African story, but because, within it, African life has discernible significance, African feelings are explored with seriousness and the yearnings and aspirations of individual Africans are described with becoming sensitivity. Each of the stories is a work of art. Each carries a comment on life, exposes a slice of experience or probes the conscious and unconscious layers of human action. Above all, each enclosed short story attempts, as in a short race, to achieve its effect with considerable economy. Some of the finest writing in the field of African literature is to be found within this *Okike* collection of short stories. (vii–viii)

Thus, the challenge of the short story to the critics of African literature is an obvious one. Some short story writers have managed so far to produce excellent works despite the absence of the much needed critical input by African scholars. This is a matter of coincidence and individual talent. If, however, Africa is to realize her full potential in the writing of short stories, critics of African literature must initiate immediately the much delayed dialogue between them and the writers of short stories. To be a help rather than an impediment in this enterprise, however, the critic must first properly school himself in the peculiar demands of this genre of fiction.

NOTES

1. Notable examples among African scholars are Peter Nazareth, Charles E. Nnolim, Chimalum Nwankwo, and contributors to the 1981 short story critical anthology *Cowries and Kobos* such as Helen Chukwuma, E. P. Modum, Ian Munro, and A. U. Ohaegbu. Among non-African scholars, the most significant are Elizabeth Bell, Donald Carter, Carol M. Eastman, Kathleen B. Fatton, Aileen Julien, Elizabeth Knight, Jack B. Moore, Philip A. Noss, Carolyn A. Parker, and the contributors to *Cowries and Kobos* such as Donald Cosentino, Don Dodson, Rodney Harris, Bruce King, Kirsten H. Petersen, Anna Rutherford, Neil Skinner, and Norman Stokle. This author's contributions are also noted in the bibliography.

For the complete bibliographical information on the items in these and all subsequent notes, see the Works Cited section.

2. The more important of these introductions are by Neville Denny, M.J.C. Echeruo, Ellis A. Komey and Ezekiel Mphahlele, Charles R. Larson, Taban lo Liyong, Lewis Nkosi, Emmanuel Obiechina, and Paul A. Scanlon.

3. Typical examples are Ernest Emenyonu's *Cyprian Ekwensi* and G. D. Killam's *The Writings of Chinua Achebe*.

4. This is an extract from a 1986 reader's report prepared by a scholar who assessed the manuscript of an earlier version of this book for Obafemi Awolowo University Press (formerly University of Ife Press).

5. See Edgar Allan Poe's two essays "Twice-Told Tale" and "The Philosophy of Composition" (Davidson 440–55).

2

A Thematic Survey of African Short Stories

It is, of course, futile for anyone to attempt a comprehensive analytical survey of all the themes treated in African short stories for the simple reason that African stories are too numerous and each story handles either a different subject or a common subject from a different perspective. What is offered here, therefore, is at best only a summary discussion of the most dominant themes and the more striking angles of their representation. Hence, the themes relating to art, religion, traditional culture, urban life, colonial and postcolonial politics, apartheid, and what I call the universal ironies of life that are analyzed here can only be representative, not conclusive.

THE THEME OF ART

It is apposite to commence our discussion of thematic preoccupations in the African short story, itself a form of art, with its treatment of the theme of art. This is not because the theme is a common one—it is in fact amazingly untypical—but because it enables us to perceive how the African short story writer as an artist views art. In the few instances when art becomes the focus of attention, the writer has invariably combined a realistic setting with an idealized vision of art and the artist. Our examples, which come predominantly from South Africa, usually depict the artist as a deprived, sensitive black man struggling for survival in a negative environment. He is usually idealistic and he sustains life that is far from being satisfactory with the sheer strength of his idealism, but sometimes he succumbs to despair and suicide when he is frustrated by his philistine society.

In Mtutuzeli Matshoba's "To Kill A Man's Pride" (AS 103–27), for instance, no individual artists are isolated for attention but we are shown a group of mostly migrant black workers who escape into art to make an otherwise unlivable life bearable. After enduring racial discrimination and abuse, hard labor, risky work conditions, and gross underpayment at the apartheid factories, the migrant laborers return to the men's hostels, where conditions are so dehumanizing that the inmates name them "our Auschwitz," after the Nazi concentration camp. Here the men gather at regular intervals during the week to infuse meaning into their deprived lives by sharing companionship in the arts of music, singing, and dancing. After remarking that "song was the only solace of those lonely people," the narrator describes the nature and impact of their songs:

When they sang, it was from the core of their souls, their eyes glazed with memories of where they had first sung those lyrics; and interruptions were not tolerated. Sometimes I was so moved by their music that I yearned to join them, and because I did not know the songs I sailed away in my mind for paradises that I conjured up, where people sang their troubles away. . . . I went away feeling as if I had found treasures in a graveyard. (AS 123)

The art of music is also at the center of Kaizer Ngwenya's story "Dreams Wither Slowly" (AS 54–57), in which the hero-musician prefers to lose family, friends, job, and even life rather than succumb to the philistine demands of his materialistic society to prostitute his musical talents. This musician, named Benny, is determined to remain faithful to his musical genius and he labors hard to find a way "to deliver the unique sound which lay boiling like lava inside him" (AS 54). Benny's idealistic devotion to his art is all the more impressive—even if ultimately tragic—for the fact that he would have remained popular, rich, and successful if he had agreed to use his musical gifts to satisfy vulgar public taste. Rather, he aimed at "an audacious bop approach than at commercial stuff. He wanted to be as jazzy as Charlie Parker" (AS 54). In the adamant pursuit of his idealistic goal, Benny lost his wife, children, friends and employment as well as the opportunity to realize his musical dream and in the end he committed suicide. Benny's suicide seems naive and unwarranted under the circumstances presented in the story but then the author hardly wants us to read the story at the literal level. Benny is more like the author's symbolic depiction of "the artist of the beautiful" destroyed by an unappreciative materialistic society.[1]

Mongane Wally Serote's story, "When Rebecca Fell" (AS 170–72), which depicts a painter-sculptor as hero, is a lot more complex to understand than any of the other stories about the artist. What is certain, however, is that Serote means to use the story to draw our attention to the absolutely uncongenial environment in which the black artist is compelled to create in the apartheid enclave of South Africa. The story reveals that the very fact that the artist still manages to produce under such circumstances bears testimony to the great power of the artistic motivating force that stimulates creativity. It also underscores the zeal and dedication with which the artist creates and, consequently, the great love he must have for his creations. In this story a molded sculpture named Rebecca falls and breaks as Dumile, the sculptor, tries to mount it. The accident occurs because of the absence of proper mounting facilities. The story ends by drawing attention to the depth of the pains of this loss to the artist: "As I stood there...I caught Dumile's last look at Rebecca. Mothers know it, the look at the heap of soil that was once their son and daughter" (AS 172).

It must be evident from these examples that African short story writers create short stories about artists primarily to draw our attention to the human value of art, the beauty and purity of the idealism that usually possesses and motivates artists, the sensitivity of artists, and their love for their creations, as well as the uncongenial atmosphere in which artists operate in Africa. Being themselves artists, it is obvious why short story writers should draw our attention to these facts.

THE THEME OF RELIGION

Religion and the attitudes and practices of its adherents constitute a typical theme in African short stories. Authors treat this theme either to reinforce religious beliefs and practices or to question them. When the former is the case, authors present religion and its rituals in a manner that lends them authenticity; but when the latter is the objective, authors undermine religion and its practices by creating satires on religious bigotry and hypocrisy and by showing the inefficacy of rituals and their anti-human characteristics.

Two short story writers who have most frequently patronized the theme of religion are I.N.C. Aniebo and Bessie Head. One of Aniebo's stories on the religious theme, "Dilemma" (WTD 135–40), belongs to the category of stories that affirm the integrity of religion—in this case, the traditional African religion. The story is about the dilemma of Mgbeke, the priestess of *Ajala* (the goddess Mother Earth) who is to choose between either saving her son, Nwankwo, or allowing him to die. Mgbeke as the priestess had called upon Nwankwo to carry out a sacrifice to expiate his sins but Nwankwo had further compounded the sins by throwing a challenge to *Ajala*. The enormity of his sacrilege soon dawns on Nwankwo, who agrees to perform the expiatory sacrifice.

In spite of his remorse, however, Nwankwo overdelays making the sacrifice. The mother is left to decide either to perform the sacrifice on his behalf or "let him die and be reborn quickly, his sins washed away by his death." The mother fasts and prays for three days and nights before resolving her dilemma. She decides to let her son die and reincarnate. Three days later, Nwankwo dies suddenly and in circumstances that do not even remotely suggest foul play. Nwankwo is speedily reincarnated as a child who is born a month after his death, but this fact does not come to the knowledge of the priestess until two months later. The story is told from an objective third person perspective, a situation that endows the details of the account, including its mystery, magic, and fantasy, with an air of reality. It is as if the narrator is himself a devotee of the goddess *Ajala*.

Bessie Head's story "Heaven is not Closed" (CT 7–12) also belongs to the category of the stories that reinforce the integrity of traditional African religions. This is done through a satirical exposure of the bigotry of a Christian priest who excommunicates a devout female convert for insisting on a marriage solemnized according to traditional rites that when closely examined do not offend the tenets of Christianity. The fanatical intolerance of the priest loses him a large proportion of his congregation who are disenchanted with the new religion because the priest cannot distinguish between the immutable inner essence of a belief and its changeable external ceremonies. The converts cannot see a genuine reason why the new religion cannot tolerate or even adapt harmless traditional customs into its ritual practices.

The story is narrated as a contest over who will win the female convert whose marriage is at issue: is it the fiance who refuses to be converted to Christianity and is a staunch upholder of traditional ways or the bigoted Christian priest? Not only does tradition win the day, but this particular priest as well as other similar missionaries of the Christian faith are given a thorough thrashing. Stating his objections to the new religion, the fiance declares:

The God might be all right . . . but there was something wrong with the people who had brought the word of the Gospel to the land. Their love was enslaving black people and he could not stand it. . . . They had brought a new order of things into the land and they made the people cry for love. One never had to cry for love in the customary way of life. Respect was just there for people all the time. (9–10)

The paradoxical and hypocritical promotion of anti-human and un-christian practices by Christians is also the theme of Alex la Guma's story "The Lemon Orchard" (WN 131–36). In the story, a Christian

minister upholds and practices apartheid and collaborates in the lynch-
ing of a black schoolteacher who dares to resort to litigation to protect
his rights. Similarly, a black shepherd youth, Jan, who claims that God
has spoken to him and appointed him the redeemer who will lead the
black people to freedom from under the racist yoke, is brutally murdered by his Christian racist employer who is enraged by the boy's
professions. This is in the story by James Matthews symbolically titled
"The Second Coming" (MASF 113–23). In his own story, "The Messiah"
(EW 12–16), Lionel Abrahams presents the racist insensitivity of a
Christian congregation that alienates a would-be Jewish Christian convert. The charlatanism, cynicism, and hypocrisy of Moslem *mallams*
is the subject of both Ama Ata Aidoo's story "A Gift from Somewhere"
(NSH 75–86) and Sembene Ousmane's story "The False Prophet" (TS
1–7).

It is not as if the foreign religions of Christianity and Mohammedan-
ism and their adherents are the only ones subjected to negative portrayal in African short stories. African traditional religious worshippers
and their ritual practices also have their own fair share of criticism.
Foremost in this respect is the criticism of human sacrifice often in-
dulged in by the devotees of the traditional gods. In Head's story "Looking for a Rain God" (CT 57–60), for instance, a severe drought drives a
peasant family to sacrifice two of their children to the rain god. Not
only does the rain fail to fall, the two adults in the family responsible
for the human sacrifice are arrested and condemned to death for ritual
murder.

While the failure of the rain to fall in Bessie Head's story casts doubts
on the efficacy of the traditional gods, Aniebo's story "Godevil" (WTD
30–42) lumps traditional religion and Christianity together in one dis-
passionate atheistic equation:

The surprising thing was that he didn't feel any worse for the lapse. As a matter of fact
he was getting better steadily, relentlessly without worshipping any gods. It was as if he
was doing so in spite of them. Did it then mean . . . ? No, that could not be.
    But the facts were inescapable. When he worshipped the gods, he lost all his children
. . . and while he was the most ardent Christian, he fell ill. Now that he neither worshipped
the gods nor thought of Christianity, he got better and even had some peace of mind
into the bargain (41).

Although the atheistic mood of this character may not be shared by
the author, it nonetheless underscores the dominant attitude of unease
and criticism pervading most African short stories on the theme of
religion. Obviously, African short story writers, while not out to en-
courage atheistic thinking, deem it necessary to voice their displeasure
at the prevalence of hypocrisy, cynicism, charlatanism, bigotry, and

inhumanism in the practices of the adherents of both the traditional and modern religions in Africa.

THE THEME OF TRADITION AND CULTURE

Quite often African short stories present various aspects of the African traditional culture from the position of either affirmation or criticism or even for mere information. These aspects include the belief in mystery, ghosts, witchcraft, and rituals. They also involve the nature of the traditional marriage and family, the traditional attitudes about birth, death, and reincarnation, as well as the sociopolitical and economic organizational institutions of the society.

The stories of Aniebo are once again a good place to start because some of his pieces, especially the one titled "Four Dimensions" (WTD 141–50), are typical of the affirmative approach to tradition. "Four Dimensions" is a story that tries to fathom the unknown and in the process reinforces traditional beliefs in mystery, death, sin, punishment, and rebirth. The story recounts the moment when an *Ajala* priest who has just passed a false judgment under oath on a dead woman is instantly crushed to death on the spot by a fallen tree. The story shows that this tragedy is not a coincidence but a summary judgment by the offended goddess, *Ajala*.

Kafungulwa Mubitana's story "Song of the Rainmaker" (VOZ 1–6) is another story that reaffirms belief in tradition. In the story, we meet a rainmaker who actually succeeds in bringing down the rain. Mubitana is a writer who is much interested in the mysteries of the traditional culture. In his story "The Day of the Ghosts" (VOZ 89–94), a youth researches whether ghosts indeed exist and he receives an affirmative answer.

Quite a number of African stories also discuss the belief in witchcraft. Aniebo's story "Of Wives, Talismans and the Dead" (WTD 45–55) presents the belief in witchcraft and the reported ability of the dead to continue to live in this world after death as a reality to the African child. The story suggests that this belief lives on in the child mainly because adults do not discourage it but rather tend to nurture it. Unlike "Of Wives, Talismans and the Dead," which casts doubts on the belief in witchcraft by presenting it as a child's "reality," William Saidi's stories "The Nightmare" and "Educated People" (VOZ 14–21 and 114–18 respectively) narrate the stories of witchcraft and sorcery as if they were incontrovertible truths. Mufalo Liswaniso's "The Mystery of the Metal" (VOZ 51–56), however, is a successful attempt at demystifying the feared witchdoctor through exposing his methods as fraudulent tricks.

In Paul Zeleza's story, "Night of Darkness" (ND 5–21), we meet a new king who tries to break tradition by marrying according to love instead of by the established custom. The attempt ends tragically for the king, who soon discovers that the king-makers will stop at nothing to retain tradition, because this is the only way they can ensure their hold on power. Another negative aspect of tradition that the supposedly modern king does nothing to stop is the habit of burying people alive as "pillows" with the dead king. The symbolic title of the story reveals Zeleza's condemnatory attitude to these backward traditions.

It is not always that ritual murder or suicide is portrayed as negative in African short stories. Paradoxically, such an act is presented as praiseworthy in the instances when it is motivated by selflessness and patriotism. This is the situation in Grace Ogot's story "The Rain Came" (MASF 180–89), where a king sacrifices an only child to bring down the rain and saves his subjects from perishing from drought and hunger. The fact that this ritual sacrifice is efficacious, having produced a heavy downpour of rains, unlike in Bessie Head's story earlier discussed, is an indication of the author's sanction of the king's model act of patriotism. The reason for such a sanction is most evident in today's Africa, where most rulers sacrifice the interests of their subjects, and not their own, to assure comfort for themselves. It is also against this background that we are to read my story "The Apprentice" (ASS 16–21), where a self-sacrificing king commits a ritual suicide in order to save his subjects from being wiped out by a plague. Again the efficacy of the king's suicide is a signal of the author's sanction not of suicide per se but of the king's supreme act of patriotism, self-sacrifice, and courage.

Since both Ogot's and F. Odun Balogun's stories are more parabolic than realistic, the acts of immolation are not literal but symbolic, the intention being to promote selfless leadership.

Traditional marriage customs are often treated by African short story writers from a critical standpoint. The situation whereby girls and sometimes men are denied the right to select whom they want to marry is often depicted with its tragic consequences. We have earlier mentioned the king who could not marry according to love in Zeleza's story. Ahmed Essop's "Noorjehan" (AS 92–97) tells the story of a student who falls in love with her bachelor teacher, but is prematurely married off against her wish by her parents to a wealthy man. The teacher soon discovers his own love for her and decides to save her by marrying her, but it is already too late. Apart from giving an interesting anthropological description of the traditional marriage ceremony, Head also provides a critical depiction of male chauvinism and female voicelessness in marriage in her story "Snapshots of a Wedding" (CT 76–80). Paradoxically, women are shown in this story as actively collaborating in their own oppression by men. Head's "The Deep River" (CT 1–6) is also in part a criticism of the African traditional mode of living for its suppression of individualism and love and for its promotion of a feudal exploitative relationship.

From this survey of the theme of culture and tradition, it is apparent that while African short story writers are anxious to preserve the positive aspects of tradition, their criticism of the negative legacies of the past is just as uncompromising.

THE THEME OF URBAN LIFE

Although African urban life short stories deal with the same universal problems of existence as stories placed in other settings, stories that concentrate attention on the peculiar characteristics of city life are those generally regarded as urban stories. Furthermore, urban stories tend to emphasize the negative influence of the city on its hapless inhabitants and rarely celebrate the successes of the lucky men and women the city has made. Operating from a moralistic and ethical platform, urban short story writers seem less concerned with highlighting the good aspects of city life than with warning the unwary and the naive of the dangers lurking behind the glittering beauty and enchantment of the city.

A lot of stories often depict the allurement of the beauty of the city on its would-be victims. This beauty is not restricted to just the physical, external glitter of urban modern facilities such as electricity, neon lights, advertisement billboards, radio, television, hotels, parks, and stadia; but even more importantly, it also concerns the attraction in the offer of freedom for youths escaping parental restrictions, the promise of jobs for the rural unemployed, and the possibility of a better lifestyle it tantalizingly dangles before the eyes of the underprivileged.

Explaining why she ran to the city, for instance, Nyaguthii, a character in Ngugi's "Minutes of Glory" (SL 82–96) who comes from a wealthy home, emphasizes her premium on personal freedom (94). On the other hand, Beatrice, another girl in the same story, has been tricked to the city by a city Don Juan on the promise of a job. Beatrice has come from poor parentage and has had the misfortune of failing her primary school leaving examination. Having no influential persons from whom to obtain patronage, she cannot continue her studies nor obtain a decent job. This is how she, like Nyaguthii, ends up as a prostitute in the city, living an unhappy life.

Ngugi's "Minutes of Glory," with its formula of a failed promise to those the city had lured, is paradigmatic of most African urban stories. The unsuspecting youth lured to the city ends up living a restless life of prostitution, crime, and poverty. Cyprian Ekwensi is a writer who specializes in depicting the ugliness hiding behind the enchantment with which the city entices its unwary victims. Bisi, the heroine of "Make-Believe Night" (RC 40–49), for instance, is dazzled by the beauty of city sophisticated living, personified in Yemi, her girlfriend, and Koni-Johnson, a new male acquaintance. Bisi's attempt to be a sophisticate herself, however, ends almost tragically for her, because Koni-Johnson turns out to be a murderous criminal. Many of Ekwensi's urban characters in his two collections of urban stories (*Lokotown and Others Stories* and *Restless City and Christmas Gold*) live the reckless, dangerous, and unfulfilling life of prostitution, crime, and poverty.

One of the negative influences of urban life on its inhabitants, as the stories show, is that it encourages the unwise to live above their income so as to remain fashionable. This always has an unpleasant repercussion, as the character in Billy Nkunika's story "Shamo's Downfall" (VOZ 60–65) discovers. Shamo steals company money to maintain an artificial standard of sophisticated living meant to impress his girlfriend and he ends up in a jail. Philip J. Daka's "Mateyo, My Son" (VOZ 142–51) similarly illustrates the tendency in those who have migrated to the city to lose their identity and sever connections with their relatives in the rural area. In the story, an aged peasant mother leaves the village for the city in search of her son who has long ago severed contact with the village. The mother roams the city a long time and almost fails to locate her son because, unknown to her, the son has already changed his native name, Matayo Dinkwi, to the Europeanized Matthew Deanqui, Esq., so as to sound fashionable.

A number of short story writers often draw attention to the plight of urban industrial workers. In Ama Ata Aidoo's "Certain Winds from the South" (NSH 47–55) we read of men lured away from the dignity of rural peasant life of Northern Ghana to the indignity of menial jobs in the urban South. These men are often lost to the city, never to return to the waiting family up North. A critic has observed that Ekwensi is the first writer in West African literature to introduce "the first picture of the new industrial man and his working community"[2] (Emenyonu 75). City life takes its toll on this new industrial man as on most other characters in Ekwensi's city stories. In the story "Lokotown" (LT 1–44), some workers dissipate their hard-earned money on the easy pleasures of wine and prostitutes until they are tragically sobered up through an unpleasant experience. However, in the stories of Aniebo, the fault is shown not to be that of the urban workers but of the peculiar problems of exploitative low wages and of the difficulties of life in general. This is the picture drawn in his "The Mortar and the Pestle" and "Rats and Rabbits" (WTD 3–16). In the latter story, the abject poverty of the industrial urban worker is further aggravated by his lack of social consciousness. This is why strikes organized to compel employers to improve conditions of service always fail.

Most urban stories, therefore, are motivated by humane, moral, and ethical considerations. They serve either as forewarning for the would-be city dweller or as a helping hand to guide the already misled out of the city quagmire.

THE THEME OF COLONIAL AND POSTCOLONIAL REALITY

The colonial and postindependence experiences of Africa are accurately reflected in African short stories. Thus, reading the stories, one gets a good picture of the process by which the colonial administration was established, what it was to live under colonial rule, how independence was reached and the goals independence was meant to achieve, and what the reality of Africa has been under black governance.

Jomo Kenyatta's parable "The Gentlemen of the Jungle" (ASS 36–39) gives an admirably ironic account of the deceit and the abuse of confidence and hospitality that accompanied the process of maneuvering Africans into the position of colonial bondage. Ngugi wa Thiong'o on his part devoted the bulk of the stories in his collection, *Secret Lives*, to presenting various facets of colonialism, the struggle against colonialism, and the disillusionment that followed independence.

Ngugi's stories accurately reflect, on the one hand, the feelings of pain and bitter anger experienced by the Africans who were subjected to the degradation of living as squatters and laborers on lands that were theirs as of right but now forcibly appropriated by settlers. On the other hand, the stories also show, although with irony, the hurt and disappointment felt by the patronizing colonizers who were indignant at what they called the ingratitude of the Africans they were trying to "civilize." These settlers could not understand the reason for the war of independence being waged by the *mau mau* nationalist fighters. They asked in perturbation: "How could they do it? We've brought 'em civilization. We've stopped slavery and tribal wars. Were they not all leading savage miserable lives?" (SL 40). The stories of these misguided colonizers are told by Ngugi with a mixture of irony and genuine human sympathy. The story "Goodbye Africa" (SL 71–79) is particularly noteworthy in this respect.

African stories provide insights into the type of independence Africans had aspired to having. Ellis Komey's story "I Can Face You" (MASF 109–12) suggests in a parabolic fashion that what was needed was genuine independence that would enable Africans to act without interference or undue influence from Europe, the United States, or the Soviet Union. The necessity for African nations to seek an independent path to development aided by borrowing usable elements of Africa's past as well as useful aspects of socialist and capitalist civilizations, is also the optimistic message conveyed through symbol and parable in my earlier mentioned story, "The Apprentice" (ASS 16–21).

As most African stories show, however, independence in Africa turned out to be a disappointment. Leonard Kiberia's story "The Spider's Web" (ASS 61–70) demonstrates, for instance, that Africans merely exchanged white masters for black masters. The corruption and incompetence of the new masters are the subjects of Taban lo Liyong's story "Fixions" (F 77–81). That these masters are often no better than murderous and despotic zombies is also the message of "Fixions" as well as two other stories by lo Liyong, namely "Asu the Great" and "The Uniformed Man" (UM 37–49, 58–67).

The point being made in Ngugi's story, "A Mercedes Funeral" (SL 113–37) is that the new elites live in absurd affluence while the modest aspirations of the common man are not only not met but made the subject of public parody. As far as Aidoo's story "For Whom Things Did Not Change" (NSH 8–29) is concerned, in spite of independence the majority of people have remained precisely where they were under colonial rule. Because the new elites are generally even more bossy and foreign in their ways than the colonial masters before them, a government rest house steward finds it hard to believe his eyes when he receives as guest an educated Ghanaian who is African in his taste and unassuming in his manners.

The story "A Meeting in the Dark" (SL 55–70) by Ngugi shows the moral dead end to which the new African elites were leading their nations. In the story, the son of an elite puts a local beauty in the family way; but being so completely acculturated, he feels ashamed that he, an educated Christian should be associated with a circumcised, unbaptized and uneducated Kenyan girl. He resolves his dilemma by killing the girl.

In his *Girls at War and Other Stories*, Chinua Achebe shows the progressive steps through which the new Nigerian elites had led their people to creating a society that "had gone completely rotten and magotty at the centre" (119). In "Vengeful Creditor" we see the callousness with which the new masters exploit their less fortunate countrymen. In "The Voter" we are treated to elite political corruption and election rigging. "Girls at War" shows that even after the elites had plunged the nation into a civil strife through greed and moral decadence, the same elites still find ways of exploiting the war situation to further enrich themselves. As is shown in "Civil Peace," the war did not solve Nigeria's problems but actually aggravated them, for after the war chaos became the order of the day. "Civil Peace," which we had thought was only an exaggerated depiction of the immediate postwar insecurity in Nigeria, has in fact turned out to be a prophetic vision of Nigeria from the eighties.

African short stories are therefore extremely accurate and critical in their depiction of the sociopolitical reality of Africa beginning from the colonial era to the present. The intention of the writers is to sensitize Africans to the reality of their sociopolitical and ethical existence in the hope of provoking a positive reorientation.

THE THEME OF APARTHEID

The theme most dominant in African short stories is apartheid and this is because South African writers patronize the genre more often than writers from any other regions of Africa. As has often been explained by critics, the unsettled circumstance in which South African writers live and write compels them to prefer the "short-distance runner" genres of the short story and poetry to the more ambitious and voluminous genre of the novel. A study of South African short stories yields abundant information concerning the nature of apartheid, the system by which it is maintained, its dominant characteristics, the ironies it engenders, and the solutions that would ensure its eradication.

Practically every story about apartheid stresses its essential nature as a legalized system of racial discrimination that respects the rights of the so-called superior white race while denying any rights to the supposedly inferior black and colored races. Michael Adonis, a colored man, is fired from his job for daring to talk back to a white man in Alex la Guma's story "A Walk in the Night" (WN 1–96). The same story makes it obvious that as a supposedly inferior person, a black or colored individual must observe absolute subservience in relating to a member of the presumably superior white race. Thus, Michael dare not look the white policeman, Constable Raalt, in the face when spoken to and he must punctuate all his responses with the magic word of submission and resignation: *Baas*, a Boer word for "master", "superior", "boss". Even when a white and a black South African have established human rapport, as in the case of the two major characters in Nadine Gordimer's story "The Bridegroom" (SMFS 61–69), the relationship between the two always remains at the master-servant, superior-inferior level.

The denial of rights to nonwhites is the concern of Ezekiel Mphahlele's story "The Coffee-Cart Girl" (ASS 137–44), in which black factory workers are denied the right to strike and an arbitrary law is suddenly passed forbidding black people from selling coffee in coffee-carts in the city. Obed Musi in his "Cops Ain't What They Used to Be" (AS 180–82) highlights the denial of freedom to black people by mocking the police curfew and pass laws that are some of the major instruments of control over nonwhites. Jacky Heyns also mocks apartheid in "Our Last Fling" (AS 183–86) by seeming to support the facile argument that blacks are not allowed to share power with whites because blacks are irresponsible. And to play up the silly claim of black irresponsibility, Heyns's characters claim that they do not want apartheid to end since it means the beginning of sharing responsibilities.

As shown from story to story, state violence is the most important instrument employed by the government and its agents, notably the police, to maintain the injustice of apartheid. Alex la Guma's "Lemon Orchard" (WN 131–36) and James Matthews's "The Second Coming" (MASF 113–23) display examples of physical violence when nonconformists are lynched to death. La Guma's "A Walk in the Night" is also an example of how the South African police constitutes itself into a roving terror to whip nonwhites into eternal submission. The trick is to get them to submit young, but when a character refuses to be processed into submission, he is labeled "a social problem" and sent to a juvenile home from where he graduates into crime and prison. This is the fate of Mafika Gwala's protagonist in "Reflections in a Cell" (ASS 150–59). Physical terror is combined with mental and psychological torture in the case of the character of Dambudzo Marechera's story "Protista" (ASS 130–36). The character is convinced that the special and harrowing conditions of his exile are specially designed to make him lose his mind: "I think the menfish are out to undermine my reason" (136).

Ahmed Essop's story "Betrayal" (ASS 124–29) shows that in addition to physical and mental violence, the apartheid state also employs the divide-and-rule tactics to keep opposition in check. The "law," which is invariably synonymous with the police, patiently waits around the corner until the various anti-apartheid groups clash over what constitutes the correct tactics to fight apartheid, and then jumps in for the kill and makes mincemeat of its divided enemies.

The economic weapon is, however, another powerful state weapon for sustaining apartheid. The nonwhites are kept perpetually engaged in slave labor, as in Matshoba's "To Kill A Man's Pride" (AS 103–27), or kept eternally hungry and deprived, as the characters in Richard Rive's story, "Rain" (Q 142–50). Under these conditions, the victims of apartheid are for the most part compelled to devote their time thinking of satisfying basic daily human necessities rather than planning how to solve the larger question of apartheid.

In fact, in their powerlessness, the victims of apartheid more often than not take out their frustrations on one another rather than confront their common enemy. Several stories are devoted to expressing this paradoxical reality of apartheid. A legalized version of this paradox is dramatized in la Guma's "The Gladiators" while his story "Blankets" shows the more common street variant (WN 114–25). In the former, two nonwhites mercilessly pummel each other in a boxing arena urged on by a bloodthirsty audience yelping like ferocious beasts. In the latter, a gangster sticks a knife into another gangster's back and kills him. In Alan Paton's "The Waste Land" (DGH 79–84) a son leads a gang to waylay and rob his own father, while in Casey Motsisi's "On the Beat" (MASF 124–28) a man invites his friend to a party purposely to rob him. As Bereng Setuke's "Dumani" (AS 58–68) and other stories show, train hooligans visit purposeless violence on the commuters in black, but not European, trains.

Several stories also show that the dialectical statement that violence breeds violence is true not only in the sense presented above whereby the victims of state violence visit violence on one another; but also in the sense that the victims of apartheid fight back with violence to destroy apartheid and their oppressors. Daniel Kunene in his story "The Spring of Life" (AC 54–86) shows the gradual and natural process by which a person becomes a freedom fighter in South Africa. Denied rights and freedom and deprived of dignity, pride, and basic necessities, a South African nonwhite soon discovers that he has no option left but to become a freedom fighter. When, according to the title of Miriam Tlali's story, an individual has reached this "Point of No Return" (AS 137–49), even the tears of the loved ones are powerless to hold the hero back from going to the forest to join the camp of freedom fighters. Similarly, the deprivations suffered by the relatives of those the police arrest cease to be sufficient deterrent on relatives to withhold support from the fighters. This is what is shown in Mothobi Mutloatse's story, "The Truth, Mama" (AS 150–55).

Several stories suggest ways to end apartheid. The necessity for the whites and nonwhites of South Africa to share the nation's wealth on the basis of humanity, mutual respect, and love is the suggestion in la Guma's story "A Matter of Taste" (WN 125–30). There is a call for the unity of all nonwhites in Black Stan Motjuwadi's story "What is not White is Darkie" (AS 187–89) in a concerted effort to defeat apartheid. The unity of all anti-apartheid groups irrespective of race is the implication of the earlier mentioned story, "Betrayal," by Essop. The need for white people to join the anti-apartheid movement constitutes the main burden of the plot in James Matthews's story "Azikwelwa" (Q 16–22).

The need to put an end to apartheid is made evident in Casey Motsisi's story "Riot" (PASS 101–11), which shows that apartheid destroys the best samples of humanity in its enclave. In the story, it is the humane policeman who gets killed in the riot. A number of stories also demonstrate that in fact the whites have more to gain by dismantling apartheid than by sustaining it. Mango Tshabangu's poetic prose "Thoughts in a Train" (AS 156–58) shows that once apartheid is ended the whites will finally get rid of the oppressive fear that dominates them and makes them imprison themselves in "stone walls and electrified fences" (157).

The implication of the earlier discussed Heyns' story, "Our Last Fling," is that the minority white will no longer be overburdened with shouldering the whole responsibility of administering South Africa because the majority nonwhites will be there to share the responsibility with them. Finally, the story "To Kill a Man's Pride" by Matshoba, referred to earlier, makes a point of questioning the humanity (and therefore the superiority) of any set of people who would subject other human beings to the degradation of apartheid (AS 116). The obvious implication of this story, therefore, is that the whites in South Africa will only recover their lost humanity by dismantling apartheid.

THE IRONIES OF LIFE

Quite often African writers make the common ironies of daily life the subject of their short stories. Their intention of doing this is to delight our sense of wonder by recounting the ironic twists in the events we often witness along our paths in life. Other times, the purpose of these writers is to challenge our complacency and make us question our former attitudes to and assumptions about life.

To the latter aim belong some of the stories by Kole Omotoso published in the collection *Miracles and Other Stories*. Most of the pieces in this collection reveal a surprising reality in the attitude of Nigerians to children. The Nigerian society prides itself in its reputed respect for and treatment of the elderly and the child, but Omotoso's stories show that Nigerians are far from according the child due respect and humane treatment. In one story, for instance, a child is sacrificed to make money, in another he is crushed to death by a careless rich car owner. Even in less tragic examples, the fate of the Nigerian child is not enviable. He either lives in the poverty of urban life sharing a room with his prostitute mother or he is cheated by adults who trick him into gambling. Omotoso is obviously anxious for us to know that there is an ironic gap between our professed love for the child and our actual treatment of him. He would no doubt be pleased if we bridged this gap.

Both Achebe in "Civil Peace" (GAW) and Aniebo in "A Hero's Welcome" (WTD) jolt our belief in the usual assumption that life is safer in peace time than during war. Both stories however show that quite the opposite could well be the case. In the Achebe story, life became far more precarious for the citizens after the Nigerian civil war than during the war, while in Aniebo's story, a soldier who successfully escaped death in combat during the war comes home to die in a brawl with his father.

Cyprian Ekwensi is another writer who loves to build his stories on the intriguing ironies of life. It is obvious that no one should believe that he or she is indispensable in any position in life, but we do quite often forget this basic fact of life. This was the mistake made by a consultant doctor in an Ekwensi's story ironically titled "The Indispensable" (RC 68–72). The doctor is made to believe and he becomes convinced that his surgical expertise is indispensable to his unit. Consequently, out of a generous disposition he allows himself to be overworked. But as soon as he collapses and dies from exhaustion, his unit quickly finds a replacement.

A number of African short story writers often use the experience of those who steal to portray the unexpected ironies that life can at times throw up. In both Grace Ogot's "Green Leaves" and David Owoyele's "The Will of Allah" (ASS 22–28; 40–48) a thief who is trying to steal from a thief is killed. In Ogot's story, the thief is trying to steal from a thief believed to be dead, while in Owoyele's story two thieves trick each other into dipping hands into a gourd supposedly containing valuable treasures. They are bitten in turn by the cobra inside the gourd and they both die. In Zeleza's story "At the Crossroads" (ND 126–32) the major character is a policeman who discovers to his amazement that the murderer he pursues in the dark and apprehends is his own son.

The theme of love and family provides the basis for the ironies of some African short stories. An acculturated character in Eldred Durosimi Jones's story titled "A Man Can Try" (MASF 104–08) abandons a loving black wife for an unloving white woman. In Ekwensi's "Coin Diver" (LT 79–86; MVA 117–23), a much sought-after city belle leaves all suitors to marry a shy, poor lover. The story "Opaque Shadows" (MMAS 132–43) by Solomon Deressa depicts an Ethiopian man succumbing to the assiduous seduction by an American tourist lady. The hero of Mafika Pascal Owala's story "Side Step" (AS 98–102) formerly rejects the advances of a precocious school girl, but years later, when the girl turns into a pretty young lady, she rejects the desperate advances of the hero. Finally, we have Abioseh Nicol's famous story "The Truly Married Woman" (MAS 28–39), where the heroine obediently serves her husband with zeal and care for several years of marriage and children. She even serves his morning tea in bed. However, the morning after they solemnize their old marriage in the Christian church, the heroine demands that the husband should minister to her needs and serve her tea in bed since she is now a "truly married woman."

CONCLUSION

African short stories, as this chapter has shown, treat varied subjects ranging from art, religion, tradition, and culture to urban life, politics, apartheid, and life ironies. The ways these themes are treated reveal both the historically conditioned peculiarities of the African experience as well as the universally shared characteristics of the African personality. The African short story is thus as valid as any other genre of African literature in shedding light on the human condition in Africa. Therefore, to neglect its study as has been done so far by the critics of African literature is to ignore its potential as a major instrument of literary and critical exploration of the African reality.

NOTES

1. The allusion here is to the American short story "The Artist of The Beautiful" by Nathaniel Hawthorne (Pearson 1139–56).

2. Adrian Roscoe is quoted by Ernest Emenyonu in *Cyprian Ekwensi* (75).

3

Linguistic Characteristics of African Short Stories

Next to poetry, the short story is the most exacting of verbal art forms. The genre demands from its practitioners the most scrupulous discipline in the use of words. It is not, according to Anatole Broyard, that the short story writer must use "uncommon words" but that he must use "common words uncommonly well" (quoted in Burnett 46). To achieve this goal, the writer, says Hallie Burnett, must "give thought to each word and weigh each one spoken or written for its true sense, its effectiveness, and its color" because "each word a fiction writer uses must have meaning, weight, feeling, and particularity" (46–47, 72). In fact, from Edgar Allan Poe upwards every master in the genre has known that a single inappropriate or superfluous word can ruin a good short story.

When African short stories are measured against these very tough standards, it is evident that many of our writers have diligently obeyed the laws of this demanding literary form. From the angle of language usage, not too many African short stories in English can be faulted. In fact, a lot of stories that might otherwise have failed due to the shallowness of their themes or the poor handling of plot are redeemed by the high competence in language usage. For example, even though Cyprian Ekwensi's stories tend to be thematically thin and melodramatic in resolution, the level at which language is handled is generally high in spite of Anna Rutherford's just claim that Ekwensi's language is cliche-ridden (Petersen and Rutherford 65). In his best stories this fault is compensated for by Ekwensi's "sophisticated sense of detail" (Komey and Mphahlele 11), his adroit use of pidgin (Chukwuma, "Prose of Neglect" 23), and the appropriateness of his diction and faultless syntax. Similarly, the only redeeming quality in Bereng Setuke's journalistic story "Dumani" (AS 58–68) is its language, which manifests an authentic knowledge of the speech of its characters and a competent use of verbal irony, metaphor, and rhythmic repetition. Although Mtutuzeli Matshoba's "To Kill A Man's Pride" is like a journalist's sociological report, its high points are when language is used poetically as on (AS) page 116. There are other stories that fall into this category, but I should stress that I am certainly not claiming linguistic competence for all of African short stories, since certainly there are failures in this regard. What I am claiming is that African stories are generally well written from the standpoint of language usage, which, when all is said and done, is the most crucial aspect of the short story as a genre.

One of the factors responsible for the success of the language of African short stories is their scrupulous terseness, compactness. Few writers indeed produce *the long short story* that shares a common boundary with the novella; most write *the short story*, and the majority of the highly successful stories often fall under ten pages; a large body of stories qualify as *the short short story*, spreading between two and five pages. The writers achieve this terseness through a variety of means. They employ accurate imaginative diction and condensed syntax. Most writers go straight into the action of their stories without wasting words on preliminary introduction. Contracted forms and elliptical syntax are often used and the writers sometimes take poetic license to disregard certain rules of grammar. Thus, it is common to have incomplete sentences, one-word sentences, and even paragraphs that are shorter than a line. The result is that with a few deft strokes the best writers succeed in introducing their themes and characters, accurately establishing the particular setting, and subtlely evoking the proper mood. The best stories of Chinua Achebe, Ngugi wa Thiong'o, Alex la Guma, Alan Paton, Taban lo Liyong, Sarif R. Easmon, Ama Ata Aidoo, David Owoyele, Leonard Kibera, Mango Tshabangu, Abioseh Nicol, Obed Musi, and Jacky Heyns, some of which qualify as masterpieces, are written in this manner.

Sometimes the writer departs intentionally from the demand of conciseness to cultivate the deliberate grandeur of epic narratives. Such is the case with Easmon's "The Feud" (TF 1–39) and Daniel Kunene's "The Spring of Life" (AC 87–103). Other times, the tedious length might be intended to achieve a set artistic objective, as in the case of Paul Zeleza's "The Journey Home" (ND 94–108) whose humorous ramblings, digressions, and circumlocutions are meant to comically reflect the character's confused mind. It is for this reason that it might paradoxically be true that on occasions a really short story might be too long. An example is Zeleza's "At The Crossroads" (ND 126–32), which has been overwritten—a point that becomes clearer if compared with his other story, "The Wrath of Fate" (ND 170–77), and with Paton's "The Waste Land" (DGH 79–84)—two stories that end at the most appropriate place. Moreover, "At The Crossroads" shares a common theme with "The Waste Land." Similarly, the nature of syntax may be dictated by the tempo of action. Although "The Feud" is a long story, the tempo of narration is fast because Easmon wants the fast dramatic action of his epic plot to be matched by a fast tempo of narration. Consequently, he predominantly uses short, brief sentences. Ngugi's sentences in "A Mercedes Funeral," on the other hand, are long and winding in order to make the consequent slow tempo of narration reflect the leisurely atmosphere of the setting of the narration, which is a beer parlor (SL 113–37).

In some respects, the short story resembles drama with its emphasis on action and dialogue. The short story usually concentrates on a single or a few actions and it often likes to make the plot permanently memorable by dramatizing it in vivid action and effective dialogue. Even though African short story writers also compose introspective works, the vast majority of their stories are dramatic and some are strikingly so. Paton seems to be the most outstanding in this respect and his "Debbie, Go Home" and "The Waste Land" (DGH 9–23; 79–84) are hardly distinguishable from radio drama. Other masters such as Achebe in "Civil Peace" (GAW 82–89) are no less successful in their skillful dramatization, nor can we ignore the artful balancing of description, action, and dialogue in writers like William Saidi ("Haruba," VOZ 66–74), Ezekiel Mphahlele ("The Coffee-Cart Girl," ASS 137–44), Ahmed Essop ("The Betrayal," ASS 124–29), Abdulrazak Gurnah ("Bossy," ASS 49–60), and others. Some writers, particularly Ama Ata Aidoo, experiment with the language of dialogue. In at least four of the stories in her collection, *No Sweetness Here*, Aidoo records only one side of the conversation but in such a way that the responses from the second speaker are known to the reader without being stated. This seems an attempt, and it is quite a successful one, to combine the solemnity and seriousness of introspection (since her themes are usually weighty and tragic) with the demand for memorable dramatic action and dialogue.

Another factor responsible for the linguistic success of African short stories is the writers' imaginative approaches to the use of language. Since these writers are bent on capturing African reality, and English, the medium of expression in our case, is overburdened with the reality of a different culture, they had of necessity to do violence to standard English—to quote Ellis Ayitey Komey and Mphahlele (MASF 12)—in order to create an authentic image of Africa. Consequently, the English of the African short story is certainly not the same as that in British short stories or the other type in American stories. African short stories in English accurately reflect the uniqueness of the English language as it is spoken and written in English-speaking Africa at the various levels of communication within society. This is most evident in the language individualization of characters in the stories. Again, not all the writers succeed in accurately capturing in their stories the nuances of English used in Africa, but all the great masters do, and this more than thematic preoccupation is what defines the Africanness of the African short story in English. Furthermore, this, more than the competence in handling the stylistic and technical devices of the short story, is what constitutes the essence of the African short story writer. When this language yard-stick is applied, we will sadly discover that we do have many competent short story writers in Africa but not many competent African short story writers. This is what makes a collection like *No Sweetness Here* a much more interesting work than the equally competently written collection, *The Feud*.[1] Unlike in the latter, the narrators and characters in the former speak precisely the way Africans (in this case Ghanaians) speak in respect to the types of words they use, the pattern and tone of their speech, the kinds of figures of speech they employ, the nature of their conversations, and their mannerisms. Aidoo is so knowledge-able about these things that in one instance ("Something to Talk about on the Way to the Funeral") she uses gossip as a narrative technique.

The various attempts to make language authentically reflect African reality are evident in the increasing use of translated and untranslated indigenous African languages, urban colloqualism, and slang, especially in Southern Africa's short stories. While Mafika Gwala, for instance, would not translate the African language he uses in "Reflections In A Cell" (ASS 150–59), Mbulelo V. Mzamane translates incorporated Af-ricanisms in "The Soweto Bride" (SCSA 117–32), even though he does not in "A Present For My Wife" (AS 22–34). Mongane W. Serote's, "Let's Wander Together" (EW 160–63) and Moteane Melamu's "Bad Times, Sad Times" (AS 41–53) demonstrate a good use of colloqualism. Musi ("Cops Ain't What They Used To Be," AS 180–82), Heyns ("Our Last Fling," AS 183–86), and Black Stan Motjuwadi ("What Is Not White Is Darkie," AS 187–89) are deft users of slang. Pidgin and proverb are frequently used in West African short stories and the stories of Achebe, I.N.C. Aniebo, and Ekwensi are typical in this respect. East African short story writers are not as aggressive in this matter as their counterparts from Southern and West Africa. Ngugi and Grace Ogot, however, do use translated and untranslated Africanisms, although not frequently. For instance, Ogot's use of indigenous exclamatory words in "The Green Leaves" (ASS 40–48) is artistic and Ngugi accurately captures the speech mannerisms of his narrator in "A Mercedes Funeral" (SL 113–37).

On the average, the language of African short stories is consciously rhythmic; indeed the language of some stories is so carefully arranged that the resultant stories are regular prose-poems. Two spectacular examples of short story prose-poems are Achebe's "The Madman" (GAW 1–10) and Mango Tshabangu's "Thoughts in a Train" (AS 156–58). To a lesser extent, the stories of Kafungulwa Mubitana (VOZ 1–6, 89–94, 122–30) are poetic. What make these stories and those similar to them rhythmically poetic are the extreme terseness of their language and the use of the devices of repetition, song, sound devices, figures of speech, imagery, and symbolism. Unfortunately, lack of space does not permit the elaborate discussion of the type I have carried out in Chapter 8 regarding the poetic elements in Achebe's story, "The Madman." I shall therefore limit myself to pointing out examples of stories that exhibit the enumerated poetic devices.

The terse nature of the language of African short stories has already been discussed. It remains only to add that in short story prose-poems, terseness closely approaches the level in poetry. Repetition, often with variations, of the same or similar single words, phrases, and sentences is evident in Kibera's "The Spider's Web" (ASS 61–70), Gurnah's "Bossy" (ASS 49–60) Ngugi's "Minutes of Glory" (SL 82–96), Nadine Gordimer's "The Bridegroom" (SMFS 61–69), Mzamane's "A Present For My Wife" (AS 22–34), James Matthews's "Azikwelwa" (Q 16–22), Baleni Khumalo's "I Did Not Know" (VOZ 57–59), and Mubitana's "Song of the Rainmaker," "The Day of the Ghosts," and "The Spearman of Malama" (VOZ 1–6, 89–94, 122–30), as examples.

Songs and refrains are frequently employed in Mubitana's stories mentioned above and in Charles Rukuni's "Who Started the War?" (AS 173–79). Ogot uses dirge and sound devices such as onomatopoeia and alliteration in "The Green Leaves" (ASS 40–48). Figures of speech such as simile, metaphor, hyperbole, and metonymy occur in Kibera's "The Spider's Web" (ASS 61–70), Gordimer's "Bridegroom" (SMFS 61–69), Bessie Head's "Snapshots of a Wedding" (CT 76–80), Heyns's "Our Last Fling" (AS 183–86), and Owoyele's "The Will of Allah" (ASS 40–48). Ogot's images, often drawn from nature, are visual and strikingly beautiful even out of context: "And bending across the path as if saying prayers to welcome the dawn, were long grasses which were completely overpowered by the thick dew" ("The Green Leaves," ASS 45). "The red rays of the setting sun embraced Oganda and she looked like a burning candle in the wilderness" ("The Rain Came," PASS 22). The equally nature-based images of Alex la Guma are similarly visual and captivating: "The sun hung well towards the west now so that the thin clouds above the ragged horizon were rimmed with bright yellow like the split yolk of an egg" (WN 125). "The sun was almost down and the clouds hung like bloodstained rags along the horizon" (WN 128).

In most cases the images are symbolic. For instance, the picture of the young girl, Oganda, who looks like a burning candle in Ogot's story is a symbolic reminder of her role as a sacrificial lamb. Kibera's story "The Spider's Web" is among the best written of African symbolic stories. The story has a systematic, well-constructed structure anchored on objects such as a young tree, spider's web, queen bee, cap, knife, coffin, books, bow and arrow. The spider's web, for instance, goes beyond its physical reality on the ceiling to encompass other metaphoric webs. The latter include the imperceptible growth of the exploitation of blacks by blacks to the extent that colonial exploitation by whites became even preferable. It also stands for the gradual erosion of the expectations and promises of independence that in its turn weaves a web of discontent, revenge, murder, and suicide in the minds of the exploited, represented here by Ngotho. The emasculation of the new elites like Mr. Njogu, Ngotho's master, is symbolized by the replacement of bow and arrow by books and medicine tablets in the master's bedroom. There is a web of blood in the knife that stabs the base of the tree that stands for both the queen bee, Mrs. Njogu, and her husband, the bee. Ngotho often vents his anger on this tree planted by Mr. Njogu because at first he could not directly confront either Mr. Njogu or his wife. The elite's refusal to confront reality is symbolized in the image of the man who prefers blurred vision: "Mr. Njogu didn't like what he saw. He threw his glasses away and preferred to see things blurred" (ASS 70). The hopelessness of the situation is suggested to Mr. Ngotho by the fact that even the future elite will be like the present in their refusal to face reality. This is symbolized by the cap that obscures vision: "But as he looked at their pregnant wives he could foresee nothing but a new generation of innocent snobs, who would be chauffeured off to school in neat caps hooded over their eyes so as to obstruct vision" (ASS 68).

The existence of complex symbols necessarily makes some African stories difficult to understand, especially by the unsophisticated reader. The difficulty is further compounded by the existence of ambiguity, and literary and other allusions. The ending of Kibera's symbolic story "The Spider's Web" is left hanging, but the details suggest suicide. This will certainly create doubts in the mind of the ordinary reader as to what actually happened at the end of the story. Similarly, only the well-read who are familiar with T. S. Eliot's waste land symbolism will fully grasp the meaning of Alan Paton's story "The Waste Land" (DGH 79–84).

Unlike his European counterparts, the African writer does not shy away from allowing the prose of his story to acquire the rhythm of poetry.[2] This is precisely because the African short story is a continuation of the traditional tale that was, and is still, fond of employing the devices of oral poetry such as repetition, song, refrain, alliteration, and onomatopoeia. The recent claims that the short story is not an outgrowth of oral literature, that the two "represent closed artistic systems," that they are "mutually exclusive forms that cannot shade or develop into each other" (Petersen and Rutherford 10, 62) must, of course, be ignored. This is not simply because many critics have affirmed the contrary, but because the evidence is overwhelmingly in favor of the existence of a past and still growing link between the oral tale and the short story.[3] However, even though what the two genres share in common far outweighs what separates them, it would be equally unwise to totally merge as it would to completely divorce them. In any case, the most significant trend in all the genres of African literature in recent times is the attempt of our writers to enrich written literature with forms and techniques borrowed from oral literature.

In the area of the short story, the attempt began with not just an anthropological but a creative gathering and retelling of oral tales. Two good examples are Taban lo Liyong's *Eating Chiefs* and Martha Mvungi's *Three Solid Stones*. Also, writers like Susheela Curtis in "About a Girl Who Met a Dimo" and Bob Leshoai in "Tselane and the Giant" (SCSA 40–41, 58–67) have respectively translated Sesotho and Setswana tales into English. The homecoming attempt is now at its sophisticated level of creating modern tales as well as deftly incorporating the stylistic elements of folktale into the short story. These attempts have already produced excellent results, the most significant being the short stories and modern tales by lo Liyong (*Fixions*), Dambudzo Marechera ("Protista," ASS 130–36), and Jomo Kenyatta ("The Gentlemen of the Jungle," ASS 36–39).[4]

Many short stories require the reader to suspend disbelief, because their plots are partly or wholly fantastic in the manner of traditional folktale. Of course, the folktale may not be the exclusive source of the fantastic plot; our writers are equally familiar with European gothic stories, science fiction, and Western surrealistic prose, among other possible sources. Nonetheless, it is improbable to conceive that the African folktale has no influence on African short stories soaked in mystery, witchcraft, dream, and superstition, such as Ekwensi's "The Great Beyond" (RC 34–39), Saidi's "The Nightmare" (VOZ 14–21), and Abioseh Nicol's "The Judge's Son" (MASF 162–71). There are short stories that use folktale narrative formulas unchanged or slightly altered. The formula for beginning a tale is echoed in Gurnah's "Bossy," which began in this manner: "A long time ago that was, sitting on the barnacled pier, swinging our legs through the air" (ASS 49). This beginning formula is similarly retained by Leshoai in the folktale he inserted into his story "The Moon Shall Be My Witness," incidentally at a place very close to the beginning of his story: "There were once two friends who lived in Mahlomola, by the names of Ou Breench and Skeelie" (AS 129). It is not impossible that he has in fact fabricated this inserted folktale himself, although the greater probability is that he has taken it from the existing folktales of his people.

Except for a few linguistically dense short stories such as lo Liyong's "Sages and Wages" (F 11–20), Solomon Deressa's "Opague Shadows" (MMAS 132–43) and Marechera's "Protista" (ASS 130–36), the language of African short stories takes after the simplicity of the folktale. Similarly, hardly is there an African short story that is written for the sole purpose of providing only entertainment. Again, following the example of the tale, the short story in Africa is always didactic, even though unlike the tale, the didacticism is more implicit than explicit.

It has been correctly observed that the language of African short stories is primarily realistic (Gray 11, and Scanlon 2). Thus, except in the cases of the stories with fabulous plots, the objective of the authors of African short stories is to create the illusion of reality. Hence, language is specifically oriented toward creating authentic characters who speak particularized idioms. Similarly, setting and the several materials and details in the story are presented in realistic language. Indeed, the tendency to create realistic stories has led some writers into producing naturalistic fiction and sociological, journalistic documentations that do not seriously qualify as short stories. This tendency is noticeable in many stories by Gordimer and Head. It is also prominent in individual stories by other writers. Some examples are Kole Omotoso's "Issac" (M 35–42), Simon D. Katema's "The Baby" (VOZ 134–41), Mufalo Liswaniso's "The Mystery of the Metal" (VOZ 51–56), Bereng Setuke's "Dumani" (AS 58–68), Mtutuzeli Matshoba's "To Kill A Man's Pride" (AS 103–27), and Sipho Sepamla's "King Taylor" (AS 80–91).

What has not been adequately discussed, however, is the attempt by some African writers to transcend realism through modernist linguistic experimentation. The tendency to adopt folklore's fabulous plot, already discussed, is one obvious example at transcending realism. Aidoo's experiments with narrator, also discussed above, should similarly be seen as an attempt to improve upon the methods of realism. The capturing of two concurrent realities—the official interrogation on one hand and the thoughts of the hero on the other—leading to an unusual textual arrangement at the beginning and end of Kunene's "The Spring of Life" (AC 54–86) is also an obvious attempt at improving the traditional mode of registering reality in realistic stories. Marechera's "Protista" (ASS 130–36) very strongly resembles existentialist and surrealist fiction of the West. In "The Journey Home" (ND 94–108), Zeleza is obviously trying to make his form reflect his content. He presents a confused, forgetful character and so he makes his style a verbous, digressive, comic rigmarole. The cynically ironic tone of narration in Gurnah's "Bossy" (ASS 49–60) goes beyond the propriety of realism. So does the dense symbolic language of Kibera's "The Spider's Web."

Also the studied casualness of the style of Serote's "Let's Wander Together" (EW 160–63) and this story's plotlessness and narration that is sustained almost wholly by colloqualism and slang are signs of its modernism. And Deressa's "Opaque Shadows" (MMAS 132–43), with its existentialist characters and dense language, certainly has gone a step beyond realism.

However, the most consistently modernist of our short story writers is Taban lo Liyong, who is in fact a postmodernist artist. I have analyzed his absurdist language and stylistic techniques in detail in Chapter 12. It remains only to state here without going into details that his collection, *The Uniformed Man*, will make a lot of more sense if read as a parody of modernist techniques. For instance, he uses the story, "Project X" (UM 36–46), to parody the modernist minimal story. His excessive use of digressions and allusions is a parody of these techniques as used by modernist writers. His overfamiliarity with, and almost insulting attitude toward, the reader; the almost pornographic breaking of taboos with regard to sex; and the overassertion of his overconfident ego in the stories in the collection must be seen in the same parodic light.

Undoubtedly, the single most prominent aspect of the language of African short stories is irony; and because of its importance, its structure and function within African stories will be discussed in the next chapter.

NOTES

1. In his review article, Jack B. Moore correctly sees this shortcoming as one of the more serious faults in Easmon's collection (152–54).

2. The novelist, Manuel Komroff, is quoted as having said that he always took care to prevent his prose resembling poetry (Burnett 46).

3. See the following critics among the many who have affirmed the common heritage of the oral tale and the short story: Chinua Achebe (Achebe and Innes IX), Helen O. Chukwuma ("Prose of Neglect" 20), Aileen Julien (83–93), Charles R. Larson (*Modern African Stories* 7), Philip A. Noss (3,13,15,17–18), and Carolyn A. Parker (55,57).

4. For an excellent discussion of Taban lo Liyong's modernist-folklorist narrative style, for instance, see Elizabeth Knight. It must be pointed out, however, that Knight underrates the achievements of lo Liyong in respect of certain stories in the second collection, *The Uniformed Man*, mainly because she interprets those stories literally rather than as parodic satires on modernism–postmodernism.

4

The Structure of Irony in African Short Stories

INTRODUCTION

Critics and writers alike have frequently commented on the fondness for irony on the part of African short story writers. "Irony," asserts Helen Chukwuma, "is a prevalent feature of the African short story" ("Prose of Neglect" 26). Kathleen Fatton on her part discusses in her 1983 African Literature Association (ALA) conference paper how Alex la Guma uses an ironic and metaphoric structure to create a "fiercely optimistic political vision" in *A Walk in the Night*. G. D. Killam, who in his *The Writings of Chinua Achebe* recognizes "grades of irony" in Achebe's stories, is among several critics who have in part attributed the artistic success of *Girls at War and Other Stories* to Achebe's skillful use of irony (112, 107–8).[1] Nadine Gordimer could easily have been speaking both for herself and her fellow writers in the unnumbered page two of the introduction to her collection *Some Monday For Sure* when she identified her style as basically ironic: "My approach in these stories, as in very many others, is that of irony. In fact, I would say that in general, in my stories, my approach as a short story writer is the ironical one, and that it represents the writer's unconscious selection of the approach best suited to his material."

Thus, given African short story writers' fondness for irony, which is the love for creating in their stories a sense of incongruity between, on the one hand, beliefs, actions, and statements, and on the other, actual reality contradicting these beliefs, actions, and statements; that is, given African writers' love for creating "a reality different from the masking appearance,"[2] it is necessary to closely examine the pattern of usage as well as the functions of this device in African stories.

TYPES OF IRONY

Analysis reveals two major types of irony in African short stories: structural and verbal (see diagram of "The Structure of Irony in African Short Stories"); and, invariably, the former provides the occasion, the situation, for the latter. Structural irony results from the use of "a structural feature which serves to sustain the duplicity of meaning" (Abrams 81) in a work of fiction, while verbal irony, also called rhetorical irony, "is a figure of speech in which the actual intent is expressed in words which carry the opposite meaning" (Holman 236). In creating structural irony, African short story writers mostly employ four interrelated structural features, either singly or in combinations of two or more. First, there is the use of naive narrators and second, naive protagonists. Sometimes, the two are merged into the naive protagonist-narrator. Third, there is the narrator or protagonist who is not naive but nonetheless manifests "a failure of insight, viewing and appraising his own motives, and the motives and actions of other characters, through the distorting perspective of his prejudices and private interests" (Abrams 81–82). In the fourth type, none of the three features already mentioned is dominant, although they may be present in some degree; rather, what emerges is a string of ironic situations sufficiently prominent to give the plot structure an ironic outlook.

Two statements already made should now be recalled in order to clarify the issue of situational irony, defined as "when a set of circumstances turns out to be the reverse of those anticipated or considered appropriate" (Beckson and Ganz 120). The first of the two statements in question says that structural irony invariably provides the occasion or situation for verbal irony. The second states that in the fourth type of structural irony what dominates is a string of ironic situations that is so prominent as to impose an ironic structure on a given story. It should be evident from these statements that situational irony to a great extent is accounted for by structural and verbal irony between them and that situational irony functions independently only when ironic situations are not organized into a systematized unit. It is for this reason that dictionaries of literary terms rarely identify the three categories together.[3] An initial attempt to separate the three in my analysis of the stories led to repetition; hence, I have discussed only

THE STRUCTURE OF IRONY IN AFRICAN SHORT STORIES

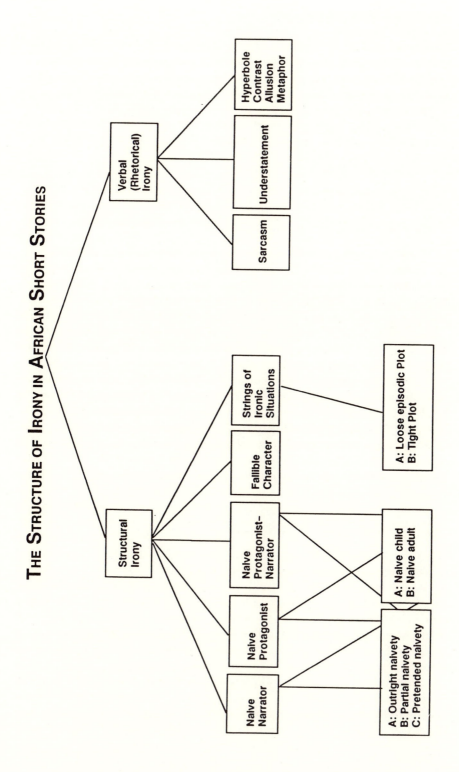

structural and verbal ironies, the more so that the situational ironies will manifest themselves in the course of analyzing these two types.

It should be noted, however, that when a writer rarely employs structural irony, situational irony tends to become more prominent in his or her works. This, for instance, is the case in Chinua Achebe's stories; and hence, when the structure of irony in his stories is analyzed in Chapter 7, situational irony is dominant, followed by verbal irony, with structural irony featured minimally.

STRUCTURAL IRONY

The Naive Narrator

The first category of structural irony is also graduated into three types. There are the outright naive narrators like the protagonist-narrators in Kole Omotoso's "First Lash" (M 1–25) and Paul Zeleza's "The Journey Home" (ND 94–108). The former is a primary school pupil while the latter is a family man who is congenitally stupid and forgetful. Naive narrators of this class are few in African stories but the consistent irony this structural feature engenders is thoroughly enjoyable, being the source of light humor. In "First Lash," for instance, events are faithfully narrated from a child's naive point of view. Duro, the child protagonist-narrator, is a Nigerian school pupil who on one occasion went about declaring his love for Moni, a fellow pupil, by faithfully copying out a foreign letter that spoke of love in the background of snowstorm, cold, icelings, and castle. Duro innocently admits that he "didn't understand the letter," but he nonetheless surreptitiously hand-delivers the letter to the girl, using the following as his return address:

The House of Love,
Street of Affection,
Lovely Dated.

The second group of naive narrators comprises people who are not as totally naive as those in the first. They are mostly young men whose partial naivety is a result of their age, limited exposure, and inexperience. Such are the narrators we find in Mbulelo Mzamane's "The Soweto Bride" (SCSA 117–32) and Taban lo Liyong's "The Education of Taban lo Liyong" (UM 16–35). The irony their naivety sustains is equally interesting as is evident in lo Liyong's story, which can easily be misunderstood except that one perceives the irony at the foundation of its structure.

The deliberate excessiveness in the use of allusions, the uncamouflaged ostentatiousness of these allusions, the disrespectful flaunting of erudition, the shocking candor of the unrepentant protagonist-narrator, and all the other excesses of style have obvious ironic intention. They are purposefully organized by lo Liyong as a parody of the modernist preference for first-person narrator, narrative candor, learned allusions, erudition, and other such modernist devices. There is also subtle irony in the manner in which lo Liyong presents himself as an undergraduate narrator in the story. Taban the undergraduate protagonist-narrator was hardly aware, as the older Taban, author of this story, is, that his vicious attacks on his classmates, teacher, renowned philosophers, scientists, politicians, other personalities, and various institutions, plus his spirited defense of his rights and his advocation of a radical philosophy of education, were all—in spite of the individual merit of these positions—the psychological reaction of a proud naive undergraduate who believed himself disgraced in class for failing to answer a simple question from his professor. He felt the psychological urge to rectify the situation by trying to show that he was intellectually superior to everyone in that class, including his professor. This is the subtle irony that provides amusement to the informed reader at the expense of the naive protagonist-narrator.

The third type of naive narrators consists of those who demonstrate such sophisticated insight in the telling of their stories that we suspect that they have simply donned the garb of naivety in order to mitigate through ironic humor our emotional response to the usually tragic nature of their subject matter. For instance, Obed Musi's "Cops Ain't What They Used To Be" (AS 180–82), Jacky Heyns's "Our Last Fling" (AS 183–86), la Guma's "A Matter of Taste" (WN 125–30), and Mongane Wally Serote's "Let's Wander Together" (EW 160–63) would all have been too oppressive but for the pretended naivety that has not only removed bitterness and bluntness from their criticism of apartheid but has in fact turned the reading about this ugly reality into a pleasurable exercise. In Heyns's story, for example, apartheid is presented as a burden on the whites and a source of pleasure for nonwhites, a pleasure the latter are not anxious to terminate by bringing an end to apartheid. On his part, la Guma studiously avoids even the remotest allusion to the permanent racial disharmony created by apartheid, even though this is his central concern. Instead, he presents a moment of harmony, community, sharing, and perfect relationship between two black workers and a vagrant white. What makes the story such a rare gem is the mild, lovely sarcasm that hyperbolizes a scanty and roughly prepared coffee, shared by three persons in a dirty bush environment, into a sumptuous dinner enjoyed in a luxurious atmosphere. Thus, the pretended naivety would have it that apartheid is either nonexistent or that it is a pleasant experience, but the obvious intention is to heighten our abhorrence for this obnoxious reality by the force of ironic contrast.

The Naive Protagonist

While children as naive narrators are understandably few in African short stories, writers often prefer them as the second feature of structural irony—the naive protagonist. It is a far more demanding task to sustain a credible point of view in the case of a child protagonist telling his own story than when the narration is entrusted to an adult. This is because the writer, as an adult, better understands the psychology of the adult than that of the child. When a writer is up to the task, however, the child as a protagonist-narrator is preferrable since irony becomes more potent using the style of defamiliarization evident in the child protagonist-narrator. The child in his innocence, simplicity, and inexperience perceives the world in ways that are already strange and unfamiliar to adults. Our short story writers, however, prefer the easier alternative of child protagonist to the more difficult child narrator. It must be stated immediately, however, that this alternative is simpler not in absolute but comparative terms. The success of the narrative with the child protagonist still depends on the use to an extent of the technique of defamiliarization. The child's point of view must be reflected by and large, otherwise the irony will be considerably weakened.

Some writers succeed admirably in creating effective irony using the child protagonist. The image of hypocritical, unchristian Christians is strikingly and ironically conveyed by Lionel Abrahams in "The Messiah" (EW 12–16) by faithfully rendering the point of view of the boy, Felix, a fervently religious Christian Jew who naively dreams of becoming the Messiah who the Jews are still expecting and who the Christians believe will return. As the Messiah, Felix will eradicate the hatred between Jews and Christians and establish universal love, peace, and harmony.

The same biblical motif is ironically evoked by James Matthews in "The Second Coming" (MAS 113–23) where Jan, a black shepherd youth, believes he heard a divine voice appointing him the chosen one, the redeemer who will lead his people to freedom out of the oppression of apartheid. Jan's employer, Mr. Dirk van Zyl, who considers himself God's vassal, is outraged that his black employees have the "audacity to believe that the voice of God has made itself heard to Jan, the shepherd, the hotnot," and not to him, "His dutiful servant" (121). Mr. Zyl with pious rage whips Jan to death after first tying him up "so that he hung between two trees, the thorns pressing into his arms, his feet hanging free off the ground" (122). With the obvious reference to Christ's crucifixion, it is clear that Mr. Zyl has ironically helped Jan to fulfill his mission as a redeemer. Jan's "crucifixion" will keep fueling the desire for freedom among the cowed blacks. Furthermore, Jan's murder in a realistic manner also reminds us of the usual fate of black activists in South

Africa. Thus, apartheid is effectively portrayed in its hypocritical and murderous aspects, thanks to the irony reinforced with symbolism, both of which are associated with the naivety of the teenager, Jan. I.N.C. Aniebo creates similar ironic effects in "Of Wives, Talismans and the Dead" (WTD 45–55) while telling the story of the child, Ibe. Taban lo Liyong's ironic story, "Herolette" (UM 5–15), is even more successful because of the additional touch of modernist experimentation.

Apart from the child, African short story writers often exploit the irony inherent in other types of naive protagonists. A frequent example is the naive provincial who visits town, as in Philip J. Daka's "Mateyo, My Son" (VOZ 142–51). The irony in this technique is further heightened in the case of Ama Ata Aidoo's Story, "In the Cutting of a Drink" (NSH 30–37), where the naive protagonist is also the narrator. Superstitious villagers occasion the irony in Achebe's "Dead Men's Path" (GAW 75–81), while it is the morally fastidious prostitute in Ngugi's "Minutes of Glory" (SL 82–96) and the naive teenager schoolboy who overexaggerates his guilt to the point of committing murder in order to preserve his good Christian name in "A Meeting In the Dark" (SL 55–70). The Rest House cook in Aidoo's "For Whom Things Did Not Change" (NSH 8–29) believes that something must be wrong with the new guest, the black medical doctor who, to use Aluko's coinage, does not behave as "the black white man" as all his previous guests have done. Adelaide Casely-Hayford's naive undertaker in "Mista Courifer" (MAS 50–59) is ironically amusing because he is so socially, culturally, and politically backward that he lives, and insists that his son must live, like "the black white man." The superstitious Christian in his double allegiance to traditional religion and the Christian faith is the source of irony as the protagonist in Achebe's "Chike's School Days" and "The Sacrificial Egg" (GAW 35–47). A hypocritical and eccentric politician, who naively believes his party can forge racial harmony, goes to a black rally to condemn black political agenda and is surprised that he is booed (Alan Paton: "The Hero of Currie Road," EW 124–33). Abioseh Nicol's story "The Truly Married Woman" (MASF 28–29) is deservedly famous for its subtle exploitation of the irony occasioned by the pretentiousness of his naive protagonists.

In the stories "The Uniformed Man," (UM 58–69), "He and Him" (F 32–38), and "Fixions" (F 78–81), lo Liyong in his characteristic modernist fashion exaggerates the naivety of his protagonists to the point of absurdity. Instead of human beings, we have zombies whose systematic self-destructive actions are the source of the narrative irony. For instance, the story "A Prescription for Idleness" (UM 1–4), which is a modern fable, entertains us with a zombie animal, Earl Hasty Hare, who is contesting with Count Cuckle Cock for the hand of the beautiful

Miss Gazelle. In order not to seem inferior to the count who could stand on one leg, "his Highness Earl Hasty Hare ran to the nearest butcher's shop [and] had three legs amputated" (4). The Earl fainted, fell sick, and was hospitalized; and meanwhile Count Cuckle Cock married Miss Gazelle. As usual lo Liyong's story does more than one thing at the same time. You would notice the extension of irony to the use of the poetic device of alliteration in the names of the characters.

Failure of Insight

For the third feature of structural irony, we have the character who may be either a protagonist or a narrator but who sometimes combines both roles as a protagonist-narrator. He is different from the two categories discussed above because he is not naive. He is, however, so biased in some respect that he manifests a failure of insight that the writer exploits to create an ironic narrative. Invariably the characters act on the basis of firmly held but wrong principles which prevent them from fully apprehending true reality. Most stories about apartheid, for instance, present their white characters as religiously believing in their racial superiority, but the irony is that these stories systematically reveal that only a morally inferior being can believe in and practice apartheid. The protagonist-narrator in Mutuzeli Matshoba's "To Kill A Man's Pride" (AS 103–22) is, for instance, "disgusted to think that it was humans who let other humans" live like they do in Soweto hostels, reputed to be comparable to Nazi concentration camps (103–16). The character is convinced that "no *normal* human being could consciously tolerate other people living that way" (118; emphasis added). Daniel Kunene, on the other hand, does not permit his characters to speak in this explicit manner; rather, he makes the same statement in an implicit fashion. Throughout his story "The Spring of Life" (AC 54–86), he systematically contrasts white and black human relationships, and it becomes obvious that the whites who practice apartheid are morally inferior to the oppressed blacks.

In Ahmed Essop's story "The Betrayal" (ASS 124–29), we meet a South African Indian politician who is fighting to destroy apartheid. He is, however, so blinded with selfishness that he cannot see the obvious contradiction in the political philosophy he has adopted in order to become acceptable to all as the political leader: "It has always been a thesis of mine that there is no essential conflict of principles between Gandhi and the Western political philosophers, that violent revolt and a passive revolt are aspects of the dynamics of man's search for freedom" (125–26). When his position as "the leader" is finally threatened, he initiates a desperate chain of reactions that ironically destroys both the opposition party and his own party and in addition sets the hands of the clock backwards in the common fight to eradicate apartheid.

Achebe's protagonist in "Girls at War" (GAW 103–23) is so proud of himself as a principled, moral, and patriotic Biafran that he pours scorn on all those he considers responsible for the moral rottenness of the society. Yet detail after detail the story subtly but remorselessly reveals that Reginald Nwankwo belongs to the intellectual elite whose moral bankruptcy and failure of leadership are actually responsible for the rotten state of the society. Another such intellectual is Cletus, the protagonist in Achebe's "Sugar Baby" (GAW 90–102). In a similar vein William Saidi presents a couple in his "Educated People" (VOZ 114–18) who boast of being educated, principled, and practical people. In reality the story reveals them as people who are superstitious, tactless, and unwise, and are regarded by their neighbors as "conceited bastards" (115). It is their firm belief, for instance, that "practical people did not leave conversations unfinished, even if they turned out to be disappointing or bitter" (116).

We also have other characters who are similarly misguided by the ill-conceived principles they live by. Sule, one of the two protagonists in David Owoyele's beautifully crafted story "The Will of Allah" (ASS 22–28), is "a deeply religious man" whose "fear of Allah was quite genuine" (23). He is convinced, however, that "Allah left the question of a means of livelihood for each man to decide for himself. Allah, he was sure, gives some people more than they need so that others with too little could help themselves to some of it. It would certainly not be the intention of Allah that some stomachs remain empty while others are overstuffed" (23–24). It is on the basis of this philosophical conviction that Sule unapologetically chooses stealing as a profession, and he calmly explains the righteousness of his profession to the "ignorant" judge who presumes to lecture him during the course of a trial (22–23). The irony that gives structure to Mbulelo V. Mzamane's story, "A Present For My Wife" (AS 23–34), is similar to that in Owoyele's story. In Mzamane's story there are two couples who are neighbors. The two women religiously object to stealing, yet insist on living above the income of their husbands. One of the men meets the excessive demands of his wife by stealing. The other, who is the narrator, prides himself in his uprightness and condemns stealing. As the story progresses, however, we discover that this "honest" man does not steal only because he is not clever and courageous enough to do so. In fact, he consistently pilfers money from his wife's purse and endlessly encourages his neighbor to steal for their mutual benefit. But up to the end he considers himself a morally superior being. The structure of irony on which rides the plot of lo Liyong's "A Traveller's Tale" (F 48–51) derives from the hypocrisy of an Italo-American woman who is so sex-starved "she wanted to be raped. She looked forward to it" (49). However, when her wishes are fulfilled in the most bizarre fashion in a public place and, incidentally, with her full cooperation and participation, she turns around and mumbles self-righteously: "Why did he want to rape me?, me a mother of four?, and among all these people?" (51). And she is quite sincere in her complaints and totally unaware of her hypocrisy.

Strings of Ironic Situations

The fourth feature of structural irony, as earlier stated, does not rely on the naive narrator or the naive protagonist or the fallible character who manifests a failure of insight; rather, we have a succession of ironies within a story, ironies that are so frequent and prominent that they succeed in imposing an ironic structure on the plot. The stories in this group fall into two broad divisions, namely, those that have a loose episodic plot and those that may have a central, unified plot but depend more on the series of ironic situations than on their central plot to achieve an ironic structure.

To the first division belongs Casey Motsisi's "Sketches of South African Life" (MASF 124–28). The first sketch presents two bugs in a conversation concerning what they would do were they to evolve into men. It transpired that one of them would be power-hungry, dictatorial, selfish, and intolerant. The other bug got bored with the conversation and, stifling a yawn, said: "Stop talking like a human being and let's sleep" (125). The second sketch portrays the state of degradation and abject want to which apartheid had so reduced black South Africans that a friend would invite another friend to a party in order to waylay and rob him. The third sketch shows the case of a black South African journalist who walked into a police station and begged to be arrested for drunkenness. This was because the charge for drunkenness was much less than the fine his editor would have imposed on him had he gone to work late and, to top it, in a drunken state. These sketches are, of course, linked, since they present the human condition as it exists under the abnormal situation of apartheid.

We can similarly establish a common unifying irony in Abdulrazak Gurnah's "Bossy" (ASS 49–60) but what is more striking is the string of ironies that suggests this central irony. This extremely well-written story has a tragic vision: human society is suffocating and inimical to life but nature, where we seek escape, is actually unreliable, deceptive, and treacherous. However, this central irony is only implicitly suggested by the several explicit ironies concerning the communication of things other than was intended (the negative effect of Kanm's friendly letter on Haji), and the escapes into both madness (Yunis nicknamed Wire) and prostitution (Rashidi's sister). This irony is further illustrated by the gulf between the proclaimed beautiful intentions of explorers, missionaries, civilizers, and politicians and the actual ugly realities of racism, slavery, religious and civil wars, colonization, exploitation, on the one hand, and the implacable viciousness of nature symbolized by the storms of shark-infested seas and oceans, on the other hand.

Among the stories in the second division of the fourth feature of structural irony, the most prominent is Leonard Kibera's "The Spider's Web" (ASS 61–70). Here, as earlier stated, there is a prominent central irony that gives birth to several other minor ironies, unlike in the case of the first group where the central irony is the child of the prominent minor ironies. The central irony in "The Spider's Web," an artistically accomplished story with a circular plot structure and a dense, well-handled symbolic pattern, is that black rule in Kenya is worse than colonization, as far as the common man is concerned. There are several minor ironies that emerge from the details of this central fact. For instance, Lois became an heroine during the colonial days for standing up for her rights by returning a slap she had unjustly received from a white woman school inspector. Ironically, it is the same hand she later used to slap Ngotho, an old man, in an act of oppression that typified her customary action as the new boss who had replaced Ngotho's white mistress after the granting of independence. There is a transformation from the defender of the oppressed to the oppressor of the defenseless. Similarly, Ngotho observed with dismay that the hen-pecked white husband of his former white mistress during the colonial days was even more of a man than the emasculated husband of Lois who as a black man was traditionally regarded as the archetype of masculinity. Ngotho was alarmed because Lois's husband, Mr. Njogu, was a representative of the new black elite in Kenya. Another ironic detail concerns the erection of a hotel by some businessmen on the spot on which had stood the sacred fig tree, symbol of the old god. Under these circumstances, it was not a surprise that going to church, rather than ensure Ngotho's peace of mind, destroyed it; that the room where Ngotho had lived for several years suddenly began to feel like a suffocating coffin; that the morning of the tragic day Ngotho took his life was "a beautiful Sunday morning" (62); and that the greatest mourners at his funeral were the very people who had driven him into suicide—Mr. and Mrs. Njogu.

A similar pattern of irony is also observable in Ngugi wa Thiong'o's "A Mercedes Funeral" (SL 113–37) in which the central irony relates to Wahinya, a poor man who wanted to die inside a Mercedes car. Wahinya's death occurs in an election year when politicians are seeking all sorts of ways, however, bizarre, to gain popularity. They see Wahinya's burial as a unique opportunity and start competing for the exclusive right to organize it. In the process, Wahinya, a symbolic representative of the common man whose dreams and aspirations are usually bitterly disappointed under Kenya's political set-up, this Wahinya who was unknown in life and died in abject poverty, becomes suddenly transformed into a celebrity, one who in death is much larger than in life. The fuss by the politicians to secure the exclusive right to bury Wahinya suddenly exposes several ironic details of Kenyan life. There are the politicians who are so culturally backward that they change their African names to European ones in order to be fashionable (114–15); there are educated elites who lack the correct perspective on African history while an illiterate like Wahinya has the right knowledge about the African past (123); there are politicians whose publicly declared intention for going into politics was to help themselves to public funds (115); there are imported expatriate experts who earn more than their African bosses (129); and finally, there also are churches that bury only the rich even while their priests solemnly intone the words of the Bible: "Blessed are the meek and poor." (133). In the end, Wahinya's dream of dying inside a Mercedes nearly comes true, for ironically the coffins brought by the politicians for his burial include one that "was not a coffin at all, but really an immaculate model of a black Mercedes Benz 660S complete with doors and glasses and maroon curtains and blinds" (135).

VERBAL IRONY

African short story writers often exploit the situations created by the various types of structural irony to further enliven their narrative with verbal irony. The entertainment and satirical objectives of the author receive greater emphasis through verbal irony, which is often more easily recognizable than the more subtle structural irony. The degree to which verbal irony can enhance the artistic quality of a story is evident, for instance, in the transformation experienced by the title of a Jomo Kenyatta's story from a 1972 to a 1985 anthology. With the injection of a dose of irony, the fable is transformed from the anthropological flatness of "The Man Who Shared His Hut" to the satiric artistry of "The Gentlemen of the Jungle." The ironic touch produces a devastating satire, for those referred to as "gentlemen" are actually a group of men who exemplify the most despicable type of immorality, treachery, abuse of confidence and hospitality, shameless imposition, and exploitation.[4]

African short story writers create verbal irony using mainly the devices of sarcasm and understatement. Other devices such as hyperbole, contrast, allusion, and metaphor are also employed, although infrequently. Only the first two, therefore, shall be treated in detail, while the latter group shall be mentioned in passing.

Sarcasm, understatement, and others are, of course, independent devices in their own rights. They become instruments of irony when they function within a verbal statement primarily to reinforce the sense of irony defined in the first page of this chapter as the "incongruity between belief and reality, or between an expectation and its fulfillment, or between the appearance of a situation and the reality that underlies it." In any case, sarcasm is essentially ironic because it praises what in reality it condemns or, more rarely, condemns what in fact it praises. Understatement similarly reinforces the ironic incongruity existing between the literal meaning of a verbal comment and its actual import when for the sake of an artistic effect (in this instance, irony) it represents a situation as considerably less than it actually is.

Sarcasm

The most favored device is sarcasm wherein the speaker in the guise of apparent praise condemns the object of his speech. The technique is often observable, as in the case of Jomo Kenyatta's fable, in story titles. Bessie Head's "The Village Saint" (CT 13–18) does not tell the story of a saint but of a hypocrite, just as Cyprian Ekwensi's "The Indispensable" (RC 68–72) is a story of how nobody is indispensable. Sarcasm is also at the root of the names writers select for their characters. Kunene calls a particularly disgusting officer in a South African pass office "Mr. Blessing" when indeed he is the bane of every black man who comes to obtain a pass (AC 56). Heyns pretends sympathy for his apartheid oppressor in South Africa and sarcastically refers to him as "the poor white man" (AS 184), while Musi in the same sarcastic vein praises Bloemfontein, where blacks live under strict curfew laws as "that centre of culture and agriculture" (AS 181). The satiric irony of the rhyme is also intended to reinforce the sarcasm. Obviously, a center of culture should not repress as does Bloemfontein. Zeleza describes the appearance of "the pillows" who were to be ritually buried alive with their chief in a sarcastic manner: "Their faces were stony, registering neither fear nor remorse, a clear manifestation that they were the chosen ones of the ancestral spirits" (ND 9). Solomon Deressa's opening paragraph in "Opaque Shadows" is devastating in the sarcasm with which he treats the religious pretensions of the Church of Ethiopia:

The building in which it [the Cafe] is housed is said to belong to His Holiness Our Father, though no one seems to be sure which one of the Holinesses is meant since we have fourteen of them, each of the Imperial provinces being democratically entitled to its very own Holiness. The glum elderly proprietress won't say whom she pays rent to, out of concern for her immortal soul. So the story goes, if you can trust Abyssinian fabulators (MMAS 132).

Sarcasm does not always come in the form of registering blame through praise. It sometimes comes, though rarely, in the guise of apportioning blame when praise is intended. Such is the example in the conversation between Piet, the cook, and his master in Nadine Gordimer's "The Bridegroom":

"Oh Piet! Kerel! What did you do to the koeksusters, hey?" he called out joyously. . . . "Whatsa matter with the koeksusters, man?" . . . "You must tell me. I don't know what's matter." "Here, bring me some more, man." . . . "You must always make them like that, see?" (SMFS 65–66)

It must however be noted that sarcasm is not always as successfully employed by African short story writers. Sometimes, a writer who artfully uses it on one occasion can ruin its aesthetic effect on another occasion. Such, for example, is the case with Bessie Head. In "The Collector of Treasures" she narrates about a postindependence misbehaving husband who abandons his wife and children and she aptly ends with the sarcastic remark: "Independence produced marvels indeed" (CT 92). In the "Snapshots of a Wedding," however, she spoils what might have been a good use of sarcasm when she unnecessarily starts explaining the meaning of a sarcastic statement: " 'This is going to be a modern wedding.' He meant that. . . . " (CT 76). It seems Head underrates the ability of her reader to understand the subtle nuances of irony, something that no reader, naive or sophisticated, likes.

Understatement

Understatement is effectively used to create verbal irony by a number of short story writers. Moteane Melamu is a good example. In the refreshing story "Bad Times, Sad Times" told in the hyperbolic language of a naive, loquacious narrator who knows no inhibitions, we read: "A resounding backhand almost decapitates me. That's merely to establish a point or two about who's boss. I know this is only a preliminary—the shape of things to come if I persist in my stubbornness" (AS 48). There is also this beautiful understatement that seeks to lighten the tragic significance of its apartheid burden in "Thoughts In a Train" by Mango Tashabangu: "He was a good man, Bayekile. It is not his fault that he did not live to face a stray bullet" (AS 156). David Owoyele also employs it in the following dialogue between Sule and Dogo, two characters in "The Will of Allah" on a criminal mission in the dead of the night:

"Didn't know you had a sweetheart there," said Dogo. "I'm not going to any woman," said Sule. "I am going to collect stray odds and ends—if it is the will of Allah." "To steal, you mean?" suggested Dogo. "Yes," conceded Sule (ASS 24).

Both Heyns and Musi are great masters of the understatement. In "Our Last Fling," Heyns describes a character, Vyf, who has lost five fingers: "He never explains the fate of the missing five but it is said they were found trespassing while still attached to him—and summarily severed" (AS 183). In the case of Musi's "Cops Ain't What They Used to Be," we read about a group of black boys who are challenged at night by South-African police who demand their pass: "None of us was any keener to produce a reference book because of such minor but disastrous defects in them like their not having been signed by our employers, Nick owing tax for donkey's years, etc. All of us were generally not pleased by this set up" (AS 181).

Musi also demonstrates at the end of the same story his ability to use literary allusions ironically. Witness his references to the poetry of Thomas Gray and John Donne (AS 182). Owoyele, among others, uses the ironic metaphor. For instance, he refers ironically to the "legal chin" of the judge who is trying Sule, the thief by philosophical conviction, and who speaks of being "on duty" when stealing ("The Will of Allah," ASS 23,24). One of the most striking instances of the use of ironic contrast is the occasion when a writer selects to tell the story about an ugly tragic reality in a beautifully lyrical language. Two excellent examples are Achebe's "The Madman" (GAW 1–10) and Tshabangu's "Thoughts In A Train" (AS 156–58).

CONCLUSION: THE USES OF IRONY

Irony performs a number of functions in African short stories. In the first place, the African short story in its fondness for irony is expressive of modern temper and modern sensibility, which is predominantly ironic. It is not surprising that Hallie Burnett, after studying American and European short stories for several years, discovered that "the middle-rise story is now predominant, with irony more often than not the final word on the dramatic action" (64). The modern age is far from the age of innocence and cannot accept, therefore, the unidimensional perception of reality as either simply good or bad. Since T. S. Eliot, there has been a demand for "internal equilibrium" in perception, a demand that implies "the recognition," in dealing with any one kind of experience, "of other kinds of experience which are possible" (Abrams 83). In frequently resorting to the use of irony, therefore, the African short story is trying to present a balanced view of reality in its multidimensional complexity.

In the second place, African short story writers use irony as a satiric device to enhance the communication of thematic intentions. The naivety, ignorance, hypocrisy, and willfulness that blind people to a correct interpretation of reality are exposed and subjected to the ridicule of sarcasm, understatement, hyperbole, and the other weapons of ironic humor. The aberrations as apartheid, postindependence black-black exploitation, and neocolonialism promoted by a misinformed vision of reality, will, hopefully, he cured by the application of irony. Thus, irony is meant to have a curative effect, restoring the true perception of reality and regulating human conducts.

In the third place, irony serves a psychological need for the writers themselves. Aidoo gives a hint of this psychological function of irony when her narrator stops at a point in the telling of the story "Two Sisters" to remark: "They burst out laughing again. And yet they are sad. But laughter is always best" (NSH 91). Kofi Aidoo on his part takes off from there to explain why "laughter is always best." He says: "Laughter is a glorious, sacred thing—a gift from God. In this old life of ours that can be so hard and bitter, laughter is often our only defense against life. And also our only defense against death, enabling us to look at it straight in the face and even, sometimes, play the fool with it" (Epigraph to *Saworbeng*).

The use of irony to perform a psychological function is most evident in the case of South African short story writers. Lewis Nkosi in his introduction to *The Will To Die* emphasizes this point in his comments on Nat Nakasa and Can Themba. They adopted irony as a survival game that they played with the authority and with which they reassured "very dumb citizens whose sense of security was threatened by any 'native' who seemed imaginative enough and talented enough" (vii–viii). As a psychological mode of coping with harsh reality, as a means of giving meaning to life, irony, however, has its limitations. These limitations are pointed out also by Lewis Nkosi, who because of his geopolitical placement on the continent of Africa should know better about the elasticity of irony in containing human pain and suffering. He says: "Nevertheless, irony is a personal stance; in South Africa it is defensive. Irony cannot defeat a brutal and oppressive regime; it can only assist for a while in concealing the pain and the wounds until the anguish is too deep and unbearable to be contained within a perpetual self-contemplating irony" (ix).

Finally, in mitigating the harshness of reality through the injection of humor, irony fulfills an aesthetic function. Without undermining their satiric intention, African short story writers succeed through a variety of ironic modes in making the reading about the pains of existence pleasurable rather than oppressive, as it otherwise might have been.

NOTES

1. Notable among the other critics are Charles R. Larson (*More Modern African Stories* 10), Ian Munro ("Chinua Achebe," Petersen and Rutherford 86–87) and Charles Nnolim ("Short Story as Genre" 19–24).

2. This definition of irony is derived from Karl Beckson and Arthur Ganz (119) and Hugh C. Holman (279).

3. Neither M. H. Abrams nor H. C. Holman, for instance, identifies situational irony separately.

4. Jomo Kenyatta's story bore the title "The Man Who Shared His Hut" in Barbara Nolen's 1972 anthology *More Voices of Africa*. The new title "The Gentlemen of the Jungle" is in Chinua Achebe's and C. L. Innes's 1985 anthology *African Short Stories*.

PART II

TWO REPRESENTATIVE WRITERS, TWO ARTISTIC TRENDS

5

Tradition and Modernity in the African Short Story: Achebe and lo Liyong

The short stories of Chinua Achebe and Taban lo Liyong have been singled out for examination in this study because they are representative of the major thematic concerns and artistic trends in the African short story. The range of subject matter of these authors covers various aspects of the African dilemma. They present Africa's colonial past and its modern neocolonial reality together with the attendant degradation of racial discrimination, economic exploitation, and cultural assimilation. They depict the failure of leadership on the part of the elites of traditional and modern Africa and the moral corruption, selfishness, ignorance, and inefficiency that are at the root of this failure. In their works, the African predicament is discussed through the presentation of individual African and non-African characters whose lives at the same time become interesting studies in the nature of man as a universal being. Thus, like other African short story writers, Achebe and lo Liyong are concerned not only with Africans but also with man in general.

As earlier stated in Chapter 3, most of African short stories are written in the realistic mode, and Achebe's stories are undoubtedly among the best examples in this style. A few short story writers adopt the modernist experimental approach, and lo Liyong is certainly the most exciting of African avant-garde short story writers. Both Achebe and lo Liyong also demonstrate the artistic return to origins that has led many

African short story writers to borrow artistic techniques from African folklore. This indebtedness to folklore is evident not only in the folktales they creatively retell for children but also in their realistic and modernist works, as well as in their attraction to Amos Tutuola, their forerunner in the integration of folklore and written literature.[1] Chapter 9 details the return to origins phenomenon in African literature, but meanwhile it should be obvious that in examining the short stories of Achebe and lo Liyong, I am also analyzing the best examples of the African experience in this genre. These examples, as shall be seen, compare favorably with the best short stories anywhere in the world.

Achebe and lo Liyong are similar in several respects, although their similarities are more in the area of themes than in the artistic modes they adopt. They are both well-intentioned but uncompromising social critics. Achebe, for instance, condemns maladministration and abuse of social institutions such as the Nigerian school system ("Vengeful Creditor"), religion ("In a Village Church"), the traditional marriage system ("Marriage is a Private Affair"), and traditional divinatory and medical establishments ("Chike's School Days"). On his part, lo Liyong argues that society itself is a monster that establishes coercive harmful institutions such as the army ("The Uniformed Man"), formal education ("The Education of Taban lo Liyong"), and traditional African marriage customs that deprive a girl of her right to marry by choice ("It is Swallowing"). They both expose the charlatan tradition medicine man in such stories as "The Madman" and "Akueke" by Achebe and "Odobo pa Apwoyo Gin Ki Lyech" and "It is Swallowing" by lo Liyong.

Both Achebe and lo Liyong are highly critical of African political, administrative, and intellectual elites with whom they associate the misfortunes of Africa. Achebe believes that the failure of moral leadership on the part of these elites due to their selfishness, hypocrisy, short-sightedness, and ignorance was responsible for slavery and the European colonization of the traditional African society and the subsequent permanent sociopolitical and economic crisis of modern Africa. Several stories are discussed in Chapter 6 to support this view. It is likewise evident in "Fixions" and "Asu the Great," for instance, that lo Liyong is also convinced that the neocolonial situation of modern Africa is primarily the responsibility of African leaders who out of greed and ignorance collaborate with the enemies of Africa.

The two writers also have similar views concerning humanity. Humans, they believe, are endowed with the capacity for both good and evil, with either of these tendencies becoming dominant under certain socioeconomic conditions. The neocolonial situation of modern Africa has largely promoted the growth of the negative factor in Africans, who have consequently become selfish, hypocritical, and vain. The African ruling elites, for instance, having refused to control these human weaknesses and place communal interest above personal aggrandisement, have turned Africa into a land of continuous political chaos, economic underdevelopment, exploitation, and poverty. Although the two writers have no illusions concerning human nature, none of them has yet lost faith in mankind. Taban lo Liyong believes that humans at their best are freedom-loving beings who would never accept curtailment of freedom. Even when physically incarcerated, humans can still liberate themselves mentally. This is part of the message of "A Prescription for Idleness" and "The Education of Taban lo Liyong." Humans are also courageous beings who would advance the frontiers of knowledge even at great personal risk ("The Old Man of Usumbura"). Achebe believes that if one is determined enough, there is sufficient inner power, wisdom, and personal resources to overcome apparently insurmountable odds ("Akueke" and "Civil Peace"). The common man in particular is revealed in these last two stories, as well as in "Girls at War" to be endowed with virtues and heroic qualities that society's elites lack.

There are areas of thematic differences between Achebe and lo Liyong, however, and these relate primarily to the geographical setting and historical periods from which they draw their subjects, as well as the ideological and political temperaments that define the moods permeating the presentation of their themes. Lo Liyong focuses his attention on modern times, mainly the postindependence era; even his folk tales are updated to the contemporary period. The range of Achebe's materials covers the last years of the precolonial period, the early days of colonization, and the postindependence modern. While Achebe places his story in one particular geographical location—the Ibo society of Nigeria in its traditional and modern setting, lo Liyong sets his stories primarily in Uganda but also in the United States and some, like "Project X" and "He and Him," in unspecified, universal locations.

The stories of both writers are based on the African experience and relate first and foremost to Africa, but they also have universal application, particularly when examined as studies either of human nature in general or of specific individuals. Thus, Achebe can be said to have achieved universal thematic relevance in his stories by narrowing his vision to encompass only his Ibo community, while lo Liyong attains the same goal by a broadening of vision to embrace regions outside of Africa.

There is always a tragic pall attending even the most humorous of Achebe's stories. Such is the case, for example, with "Civil Peace" and "The Voter." In the case of lo Liyong, there is always the harmless, humorous cynicism that has become a pose with the modernists and with which they deal with unpleasant realities. This is true even in his most tragic stories such as "It is Swallowing," "Asu the Great," and "The Uniformed Man."

Fortunately, however, beneath lo Liyong's cynical pose is the optimism of his radical ideology that makes him admire revolutionary personalities like Jesus Christ, Lord Byron, Kwame Nkrumah, and others.[2] As his essays abundantly reveal, lo Liyong has a nihilistic temper that demands a radical change in the status quo. Achebe, on the other hand, is essentially a liberal nationalist who in his most recent work, *Anthills of the Savannah*, condemns violent revolution and advocates reform.[3] These ideological differences are naturally reflected in their narrative points of view and characterization. Except for the heroines of Achebe's "Akueke" and "Girls at War," lo Liyong's typical protagonist, especially in *The Uniformed Man*, is generally more dynamic and positively self-assertive than Achebe's. The protagonists of "Herolette," "The Education of Taban lo Liyong," "Asu the Great," and "It is Swallowing" are typical examples.

The major difference between Achebe and lo Liyong, however, is in the area of artistic styles. Achebe is the undisputed master of the realistic story conveyed through irony and a lucid, simple, proverbial language that at times reaches the height of poetry. Taban lo Liyong, on the other hand, is the most accomplished master of the experimental story in Africa. He is a gifted stylist who through daring experimentations has achieved a unique Tabanian technique of synthesis whose beauty recalls, if not equals, the perfection of Tutuola's mythical hero, "the complete gentleman." Like the famed hero, lo Liyong's modernist synthesism has borrowed parts from the technical storehouse of style of African orature, European realism, and Western modernist and postmodernist experimentations. Unlike "the complete gentleman," however, his synthesism is in no danger of dismemberment, for its parts have been borrowed for good and integrated permanently by an accomplished aesthetician.

Achebe is a detached, highly disciplined narrator who uses third-person narrator in all but four of fourteen stories ("Uncle Ben's Choice," "Sugar Baby," "Polar Undergraduate" and "In a Village Church"). In fact, two of the four stories using the first-person narrator were subsequently excluded from the second and the latest edition (1977) of the collection.[4] The third-person narrator also dominates lo Liyong's first collection, *Fixions*. However, in line with the assertive ego of most modernist avant-garde writers—an ego that is the result of both a sound knowledge of the way the literary art operates and a confident dexterity in its manipulation—lo Liyong not only predominantly uses the first-person narrator in his second collection, but makes the majority of the stories autobiographical. There are seven stories in *The Uniformed Man* and of these, the following are autobiographical and in the first person: "Herolette," "The Education of Taban lo Liyong" and "The Uniformed

Man." The fourth, "Asu the Great," combines, especially in the middle, both the first and the third-person narratives.

Some similarities exist in the artistic approaches of Achebe and lo Liyong. For instance, both are interested in oral literature and have assimilated its techniques in composing especially their children's stories. But even here there are differences. While lo Liyong stylizes his folktales, as is evident in "The Old Man of Usumbura", Achebe remains faithful to the traditional mode of the genre. As I have shown elsewhere, however, this does not mean that there is no distinctive Achebean stamp to the folktales he retells.[5]

Forest L. Ingram provides an excellent study of the story cycle in *Representative Short Story Cycles of the Twentieth Century*, where he defines a "composed cycle" as "one which the author had conceived as a whole from the time he wrote the first story." An "arranged cycle" consists of "stories which an author or editor-author has brought together to illuminate or comment upon one another by juxtaposition and association." The "completed cycle" contains "sets of linked stories which are neither strictly composed nor merely arranged. They may have begun as independent dissociated stories. But soon their author became conscious of unifying strands which he may have, even subconsciously, woven into the action of the stories. Consciously, then, he completed the unifying task which he may have subconsciously begun." He further explains that "the process of completion may consist merely in adding stories which collect, develop, intensify, and extend the thematic patterns of the earlier stories in the series . . . or it may include extensive revisions of earlier stories in the cycle . . . or, finally, it may also entail regrouping and rearranging" (17–18).

Although *Girls at War and Other Stories* is definitely neither a "composed" or "completed" cycle since the various stories comprising it do not show any strong thematic and structural links, the collection can certainly be profitably examined as a loose cycle of "arranged" recurrent themes and symbols. Some of the themes that can be traced as cyclic structures through associations by symbols, characters, and setting are failure in moral leadership, cultural alienation, frustration, and the themes associated with general human nature such as selfishness and hypocrisy, courage and heroism. That I have not treated Achebe's *Girls at War* as a cycle is because it is not as neat or close a cycle as is lo Liyong's *The Uniformed Man*. The latter collection may not have been a "composed cycle" as my study suggests; it may not even be an "arranged" or "completed" cycle, and the idea of a unified cycle may not even have crossed the mind of lo Liyong beyond the collection of disparate individual stories that he just happened to have put together. Even if this were the case—which I very much doubt—my analysis of the collection as a cycle would not for that reason lose its validity. On the contrary, it would only have succeeded in revealing the subconscious design that none can deny actually exists in lo Liyong's collection. In fact, I believe that further research will identify other cycles that may have escaped my attention in this study.

Thus, if we are to name the defining characteristic of the traditional African short story of which Achebe's stories are a good example, that characteristic would be its realism. Characters in the traditional short story are real and believable and are often identifiable with specific historical settings. The actions of the characters are convincing and are narrated reliably within a logical plot. The language the characters use duplicates the way actual people speak. Readers for these reasons quite easily identify with the characters and situations in the traditional short story. Moderation and verisimilitude are the watchwords of the traditional story, even when it engages in artistic experimentations.

The experimental short story typified by lo Liyong's stories is the direct opposite of the traditional short story. The courage and dynamism characteristic of the adventurer are the hallmarks of the writer of the experimental story looking for new ways to explore reality. Consequently, the experimental short story dispenses with verisimilitude and embraces fantasy. Neither character nor situation need be believable. It is sufficient that parabolic and implied meaning can be gleaned from fabulous and seemingly illogical events and plots. Language in the experimental story often takes poetic license with diction and syntax. The more experimental a short story becomes the bolder are its departures from the norms of the traditional realistic story; and the more outrageous and shocking are its methods of depicting life. This, for instance, is the reason Achebe's and lo Liyong's stories attract diametrically opposed readers' and critics' reactions even though, as seen above, their thematic preoccupations are similar. Unlike Achebe's stories, which have been generally well received, lo Liyong's stories have attracted adverse and controversial comments, as we shall see in subsequent chapters.

However, the impression must not be created as if the traditional short story is mundane and unexciting in style or that the experimental story is always extremist and alienating in its methods. The traditional short story, as Achebe's stories demonstrate, are quite often exciting. As a rule, the more experimental the traditional story becomes and the more moderate the experimental story is in its devices, the more aesthetically pleasing the result. Hence, Achebe's stories such as "The Madman" and "Civil Peace" prominently stand out with their heightened ironic sense, deep philosophical concerns and consciously poeticized diction. In other words, Achebe is to an extent a modernist, just as lo Liyong is in some degree a traditionalist. Lo Liyong, for instance, is most pleasing in such stories as "Fixions," "Stare Decisis Deo," "A Prescription for Idleness" and in his folklore-inspired stories where thematic and artistic experiments are tempered with the simplicity of plot, lucidity of language, and convincingness of action.

Thus, the stories of Achebe and lo Liyong demonstrate both the dichotomy of style and the thematic and cultural dichotomy earlier discussed in the preface. While their stories contrast to produce the stylistic dichotomy between tradition and modernity, they are in agreement in their critical appraisal of Africa's past and present cultures. It is this uniform critical attitude that creates in their works, both individually and combined, the thematic and cultural dichotomy between reality and aspirations as far as Africa's cultures are concerned. In the chapters that follow, these issues will be discussed in detail.

NOTES

1. See, for instance, lo Liyong's collection of oral tales titled *Eating Chiefs*. Also, a number of the stories in lo Liyong's two collections under study are specifically written for children and are discussed in chapter 9. Achebe's oral tales are examined in my paper titled "Nigeria Folktales and Children Stories of Chinua Achebe." Both Achebe and lo Liyong have published essays on Tutuola. Achebe's is titled "Work and Play in Tutuola's The Palm-Wine Drinkard," while lo Liyong's is entitled "Tutuola, Son of Zinjanthropus" (*The Last Word* 157–170). Lo Liyong in addition dedicates his story "Lexicographicide" (*Fixions* 40) to Tutuola.

2. See, for instance, lo Liyong's essay "My father, his Life and Death, My Wife, my Art, and All That" (*The Last Word* 11–16).

3. See my analysis of the ideological orientation of this novel in the paper "Achebe's Anthills and the Reformist Ideology of the 'New Radicalism' " read at the Eight Ibadan African Literature Conference and scheduled for publication in *Ilorin Journal of Language and Literature*.

4. Technical and aesthetic considerations in terms of artistic finish must have dictated the exclusion of "Polar Undergraduate" and "In a Village Church" from the 1977 second edition of Achebe's collection *Girls at War*. The criticism in the irony of the second story, for instance, is particularly too pointed and obvious. Although the author's judgment is respected, the two stories have been included in the present study because of the light they shed on the theme of failure in moral leadership on the part of the Nigerian elites.

5. What constitutes the distinctive Achebean stamp in his folktales is discussed in detail on pages 56–61 of my essay "Nigerian Folktales and Children Stories of Achebe."

6

Girls at War and Other Stories: A Study of the Failure of the Elites in Moral Leadership

In his collection *Girls at War and Other Stories*, Chinua Achebe conducts a case study of the moral health of the Nigerian society from the precolonial era up to the years of the civil war. The Ibo community in its traditional and contemporary settings illustrates a failure in moral leadership on the part of the Nigerian elites who have always decisively influenced the state of the moral health of the nation. While the stories only imply that this failure in moral leadership was what led the traditional society into colonization, they practically demonstrate that the failure was what pushed the modern society into a civil war. As reported, significantly in the last story in the collection, the Nigerian society by the time of the civil war "had gone completely rotten and maggotty at the centre" (119).

Since society is not only molded by the individuals constituting it but in turn wields powerful influence over these individuals, Nigerians inevitably had been made to pay heavy penalties for the moral failure of their leaders through their experiences during colonization and the civil war. As the stories reveal, on both occasions, the common man has paid a heavier penalty than the elite who caused the misfortunes. The value of Achebe's study is that it does not stop at the diagnosis of the disease but also suggests the medicine for cure by, among other things, highlighting the healthy grooves in the moral fabric of the Nigerian nation that have enabled it to continue to survive.

The collection shows that failure in moral leadership is not a phenomenon peculiar to the contemporary Nigerian society but one that dates back to precolonial times. In the traditional Ibo society, for instance, intellectual, moral, and political leadership was the exclusive preserve of a class of elites comprised of the feared priests of the several local deities; diviners who were the custodians of awe-inspiring oracular shrines; herbalists who often combined the mystery of traditional medicine with the awe of the priest-diviner; war-leaders, and successful titled men who belonged to elitist hierarchies such as the honored *ozo* society of Umuofia. The power wielded by these elites of the traditional society was much more comprehensive than that controlled by today's elites, for a number of reasons. The traditional elites, for instance, placed more emphasis on their spiritual authority than on the secular. Spiritual authority is usually more subtle and therefore more effective than secular authority. Moreover, the influence of modern democracy has eroded the power of all authorities and has given ordinary citizens greater say in their own affairs.

The traditional elites were feared and respected by the people; but the evidence in *Girls at War* is that the elites systematically abused their offices and undermined their reputation. From one story to another the emphasis is on how they were dishonest, deceitful, materialistic, mercenary, ignorant, and short-sighted. It is impossible, for instance, to isolate from all the twelve stories in the collection a single honorable *ozo* man, or a single reliable diviner or herbalist. For instance, the much-respected *ozo* men in "The Madman" (1–10), cannot, or choose not to, see beyond appearance and recognize the fact that Nwibe is not a madman. Rather, they unanimously reject Nwibe's candidature for joining their rank with a show of wisdom and dignity that is comic and ironic in its lack of foundation. The tragedy is that the *ozo* men, in spite of their superficial wisdom or dishonesty and phony dignity, succeed in depriving Nwibe of respect and dignity and thus force him into a psychological state of mind that may ultimately deteriorate into real madness.

The medicine men, diviners, and traditional priests in this collection cut the most sorry figure of all. They are shown to the last man to be dishonest and deceitful. The two medicine men who appear in "The Madman" are revealed to be charlatans, the only difference between them being in the degrees of their shamelessness. While one hides his ignorance of his proclaimed profession in a show of false dignity, the other is absolutely without any integrity, his only concern being to make money for his upkeep: "If doctors were to send away every patient whose cure they were uncertain of, how many of them would eat one meal in a whole week from their practice?" (9). This rhetorical statement further reveals the prevalence of fraud and dishonesty among medical practitioners in the traditional society.

The show of occult knowledge through boastful claims and the deployment of proverbial wisdom to back up false pretenses by the medicine men in "The Madman" is repeated by the diviner in "Chike's School Days" (35–40). This diviner further protects his make-believe with a fearsome, talking calabash that is either a disguised mechanical device or the result of the theatricals of a practiced ventriloquist. The irony in all this is that the diviner holds the reputation of being "a man of great power and wisdom." He is supposed to possess an uncanny oracular prophetic vision that "saw not only the present, but also what had been and what was to be" and for which reason he is called "the man of the four eyes" (37). Nevertheless, his prescription to his client is ineffective for the very obvious reason that he is a fraud.

The medicine men consulted by Akueke's relatives ("Akueke" 29–34) are just as fraudulent and ineffective in their prescriptions. In fact, one of them actually prescribes a cure involving a plant that is out of season and that he thinks would be impossible to obtain. This way he would fraudulently sustain a reputation that, apparently, he had acquired just as fraudulently. The medicine man, who is also the priest of an oracle, runs out of luck however; the plant is located and when his order is carried out, the condition of the patient gets worse (31–32).

It is ironic that in spite of their fraud, the elites of traditional society for a long time continued to command great respect and thrust among the people. Villagers knew no better and they were fooled again and again by these elites who, much like the elites of today, maintained a conspiratorial unity so as to protect their elitist privileges. Such a situation was bound to lead to increasing social harms. The ozo men who, no doubt, fear competition from the enterprising and energetic Nwibe (rightly compared by the critic G. D. Killam (100) to Okonkwo, the great hero of *Things Fall Apart*), cunningly put their authority behind a superstition that pronounces Nwibe a madman.

It is a misconception to think that Achebe indiscriminately condemns traditional beliefs and practices. What he does is to discredit the fraudulent elites who manipulated traditional customs to their own advantage. It is obvious in "The Madman," for example, that Achebe sees the sound logic in the traditional belief that a man who goes naked to the marketplace has reached the height of madness. But it is also obvious that the ozo men of titles and the respected priests in this story ought to have known the distinction between a madman and a sane person who, in a moment of indiscretion induced by provocation, anger, and fear, commits an act associable with madness. That the priests consulted by Nwibe's relatives failed to recognize this distinction and that the *ozo* men did not, or pretended not to, perceive this difference is enough reason for them to forfeit the respect that ought to have been due to them. In other words, Achebe has enough justification in treating these ignorant or fraudulent elites with satirical irony.

Achebe always makes the distinction between the integrity of traditional customs and their fraudulent manipulation by traditional elites. For instance, the reader is expected to recognize the prophylactic reason why custom (which, incidentally, is always evolved not by society's elites but out of a common experience of a whole people together) demands that the victim of a swelling disease be removed from human habitation. The Ibo people, no doubt, evolved this practice not because some priests wanted it so, but because they must have experienced epidemics from the death of victims of the swelling disease in the past. What Achebe is ridiculing in "Akueke," therefore, is not tradition but the pretentions of fraudulent elites who in fact do not understand the tradition of which they claim to be the custodians. That they go to great lengths to hide their ignorance and fraud gives Achebe enough material for their ironic satirization.

Achebe also shows the integrity of tradition in "The Sacrificial Egg" (41–47). If the people of Umuru had followed the wisdom of *Nkwo*, the female deity of their market, they would not have allowed the town and market to grow beyond the point where sanitation could no longer be maintained. The deity in her wisdom appeared in her market only every fifth day, but the people in their ignorance held market every day. The result was that it became impossible to keep the market and town in a hygienic condition. The people paid a heavy price for their greed when the insanitary condition of the town caused a smallpox epidemic that claimed many lives. Thus, it should be clearly born in mind that Achebe does not discredit tradition itself but those who misadminister it.

We cannot, therefore, accuse Achebe of lacking in compassion when, for instance, he narrates with amusement the story of the native doctor in "Marriage is a Private Affair" (20–28). The herbalist has prepared what he claims is a love potion for Mrs. Ochuba, who ostensibly is anxious to recapture her husband's straying affection. Mrs. Ochuba secretly "tests" the medicine by adding it to the food she prepares for the unsuspecting native doctor. The latter eats the food and dies.

This anecdote is replete with ambiguity that yields amusement whichever way it is interpreted. The native doctor may be actually ignorant of the correct preparation of the love medicine, but has gone ahead all the same to concoct what turns out to be a poison in the effort to sustain a faked reputation. In this case, one would see poetic justice catching up with this member of a fraudulent elite class. On the other hand, the native doctor may have consciously prepared poison to get rid of Mr. Ochuba, perhaps to have easy access to his wife. Again it would be poetic justice. But it may well be that Mrs. Ochuba needs the love potion not to keep her husband devoted to her but actually to entice the herbalist with whom she is, perhaps, secretly in love. Thus, while she is scheming, the herbalist is also scheming, either to protect a spurious reputation or to get rid of a rival. Once again the reader would see poetic justice in two schemers defeating their own purposes.

The question may arise as to why Achebe did not present in his stories at least one example of the positive men among the elites of the traditional society. The answer is simple: Achebe is not unaware that the traditional society had its positive titled men, admirable priests, honest diviners, and knowledgeable herbalists. The unfortunate thing was that these positive men, as is always the case, were in the minority. Achebe had good reasons not to be interested in this minority but in the majority, those who were typical of their class and who actually influenced the direction of affairs. Achebe's primary objective here was to unravel the reasons why traditional African societies crumbled so easily when the white men came. If we believe in the evidence in his stories, it would appear that things fell apart in the traditional society largely because the elites, who were the moral leaders of the society, had undermined their own authority by being untrue to tradition by being fraudulent, materialistic, and selfish, and that they had remained in control only because there was no effective challenge from any quarter.

The challenge was at last presented by the white men, and the first people to abandon the authority of traditional elites were those who had been the victims of the selfish manipulation of tradition by the elites. We know, for example, from "Chike's School Days" (35–40) that Amos, a free-born, became a Christian because otherwise he could not have married Sarah, an *osu* (slave girl), in the face of the opposition presented by the representatives of the elites who advocated and enforced inhumane traditional practices such as the *osu* caste system. If these elites were as enlightened as they had pretended to be, they would have recognized the wisdom in discarding outdated inhumane customs rather than acting as their bulwark, as did the priest-diviner with the reputation of the talking calabash and prophetic oracular vision of the four eyes in "Chike's School Days." It is significant that Amos was converted to Christianity by Mr. Brown, the same clergyman who had converted Nwoye, Okonkwo's son in *Things Fall Apart*. Nwoye had converted to Christianity because he abhorred the inhumane aspects of tradition, such as human sacrifice and the dumping of twins into the so-called bad bush. He could not forget the heart-rending cries of the abandoned twins he once heard as a small boy while returning home from the forest, nor could he recover from the shock of the ritual murder of his adopted brother, Ikemefuna. The responsibility for safeguarding tradition, modernizing it so that it remained always viable, rested with the elites of the traditional society since they concentrated both secular and spiritual powers in their own hands. They failed woefully in this task, if they were ever aware of it.

Thus, the elites in our traditional past paved the way for colonization by failing in both their spiritual and secular duties. They failed as moral leaders because they were fraudulent, dishonest, materialistic, and selfish. They failed as secular leaders because they were largely ignorant of the tradition they were supposed to safeguard and because they had substituted bluff and pretense at knowledge for true knowledge. They were short-sighted as a result of their selfishness and, therefore, could not see the wisdom in modernizing the customs they administered as temporal powers. Even after it had become obvious that change was inevitable, these elites still insisted in putting up stupid resistance. This is the source of the irony in "Dead Men's Path" (70–74).

The village priest who is the antagonist of Michael Obi, the agent of modernization, is not as positive as the critic, Robert M. Wren, wants us to believe. Mr. Wren claims that in "Dead Men's Path," "the old ways are allowed their due" and that "Achebe seems in accord with the old priest, declining to argue with Obi" (3). I think G. D. Killam is more to the point when he says that "Achebe is impartial here: neither side is supported. Obi, despite his somewhat frivolous attitude and seeming paucity of his idealism, is never allowed to explain himself. Nor, on the other hand, does the priest question the validity of the religion he expounds. The force of the story lies in its suggestiveness rather than any explicit statement it makes" (100).[1]

That Obi, much like Soyinka's Lakunle in *The Lion and the Jewel*, is misguided and superficial in his conception of modernization, should not blind us to the weakness of his antagonist. The priest might be older, experienced, and practiced in the art of handling people, but he is as rash as Obi is insensitive, and as stubborn in his iron determination as Obi is unyielding in his resolve. Obi's willingness to help build a new path for the dead, skirting the school premises, is not as abominable and inconceivable as the priest takes it, granted that this offer is characteristically made by Obi in his undiplomatic manner. Physical description of character, which Achebe rarely indulges in, is used in this story to pinpoint the similarities between Obi and the priest, both of whom have stooping shoulders, the first from physical frailty, the second from old age. The stoop, no doubt, symbolizes their obstinacy as well as their moral inadequacy in playing the roles history has assigned them.

In spite of his experience and tact, the priest fails to live up to the wisdom in the proverb he quotes: "Let the hawk perch and let the eagle perch" (74). The burden of this proverb is that the idea of compromise in settling crisis is entrenched in the tradition. If he had realized this, the priest might have given adequate thought to Obi's proposal. If the living can abandon old roads and construct new ones, it is not unthinkable to contemplate creating a new footpath for the dead ancestors who themselves had established the principle of compromise. Thus, the action of the priest in rashly dismissing Obi's proposal that could have resolved the crisis, is as reprehensible as the action of the diviner who later sanctioned the vandalization of the village school where Obi is the principal. This diviner, like all the ones we have seen before him, is a fake. He ostensibly penetrates the occult world of knowledge to reveal oracular truths. The reality, however, is that he exploits people's credulity and gathers popular gossip, and his divination reveals nothing that is not already the property of common knowledge and popular gossip.

The victory of the priest and the diviner, representatives of traditional elites, in this encounter with Obi, the equally unattractive representative of the emerging modern educated elites, is ironic because it is ephemeral. It is evident that ultimate victory belongs to Obi. However, Achebe's stories show that Obi and all the other members of the modern elites whom he represents shall prove to be as unworthy as the traditional elites whom they replaced.

The white missionaries and colonial administrators who sponsored the modern elites of Nigeria started out first on the wrong foot. Their first converts were men and women who joined Christianity not out of spiritual conviction but out of necessity, out of convenience. Amos of "Chike's School Days," as already mentioned, could successfully challenge the inhumane *osu* custom upheld by the elites of traditional society only by joining Christianity. His fanatical embrace of the new religion is for this reason comic, the more so because he remains ignorant of both the essence of the new religion and of what constitutes "the way of the whiteman" that he assiduously cultivates. Being a religion of convenience, it is not surprising that Christianity was only skin-deep with the early converts who often held dual allegiance to their traditional faith and the new religion. The moment the new religion ceased to be convenient, it was easily discarded as it had been picked up. This is what Elizabeth does in "Chike's School Days." Although they considered themselves "devout" Christians, characters like Julius and Ma in "The Sacrificial Egg" do not find anything wrong in believing in superstitions such as *Mammy-Wota* (the goddess of the River Niger), *Kitikpa* (the god of smallpox), and in the efficacy of traditional sacrifices. Similarly, the "Christian" friends of Okeke, Nnaemeka's father, in the same breath both quote the Holy Book and advise Okeke to consult native doctors in "Marriage is a Private Affair" (24–25).

Belief in the new religion, as the narrator of the story "In a Village Church" discovers, is so superficial that as far as the converts are concerned, the church service is as good a place as any other to take a nap.[2] In fact, the church is no more than a parade ground for one's fine clothes, and this is amply demonstrated by the old woman who cries out in alarm at the discovery on entering the church that she has not worn her shoes. The comic aspect of this new belief is summed up in the ironic detail about the disharmonious singing that goes on between the three groups inside that church: the choir, the male, and the female congregations. And this is a church where males and females are segregated into the two sides of the aisle. The sermon, ironically presented by the narrator, reveals the materialism of hypocritical men piously masquerading as spiritual leaders:

The sermon was very thought-provoking. Never was a more eloquent argument put forward to explain why in these days "so far retired from happy pieties" men do not attain the longevity of Noah or Melchizedek. The preacher pointed out that the Jews always sent their first-fruits to the High Priest and received his blessing. "Do we do that today?" he asked. "Is it any wonder then that we are surrounded by death?" (75)

Materialism and hypocrisy remained with the church even after it had survived infancy in Nigeria, and as Achebe's stories reveal, these evils have continued to survive today. The story "The Voter," for instance, shows that the church colludes with corrupt politicians and gives its blessings to the latter's exploitation of the common man. The new house that Marcus Ibe, the corrupt minister of culture, builds with ill-acquired wealth is opened during an ostentatious ceremony by no less a personality than the archbishop of the province himself. The selfless dedication of a Catholic priest during the civil war described in the story "Sugar Baby" was the exception. The order of the day was the materialism and immorality manifested by the Protestant clergyman who during that war "wangled himself into the venal position of controlling and dispensing scarce materials imported by the government, especially women's fabrics." The narrator complains bitterly that "this wretch" once asked his "girl friend when she went to file an application to buy a bra to spend a weekend with him in some remote village!" (99).

The inadequacy of the new faith is also evident in "Vengeful Creditor" (48–69). A close examination of this story shows that religion is callous where it needs most to be sympathetic and understanding. Martha's pathetic fate is dismissed with easy platitudes. Her husband who dies prematurely, leaving her and their children in miserable poverty, is said to have been called to "higher service" (58), when it is obvious that his "higher service" actually lay in remaining alive to cater to the needs of his family. His death plunges his dependents into misery and subjects them to degradation and callous exploitation at the hands of the modern elites, represented in this story by the Emenike family. The much vaunted advantages of Christian and colonial education are revealed in this story not to be the result of a conscious plan for the advancement of the black man, but the accidental byproducts of a basically paternalistic objective: Martha's husband was trained "by white artisan-missionaries at the Onitsha Industrial Mission, a trade school founded in the fervent belief that if the black man was to be redeemed he needed to learn the Bible alongside manual skills" (58).

The irrelevance of colonial Christian education is the subject of "Chike's School Days" (35–40). At home the child, Chike, is taught "the way of the white man" by his acculturated father, and at school he is tutored by a teacher who reveals his ignorance by teaching about Caesar during catechism lessons and by his love for highfalutin phrases that he always misuses. Nothing that Chike learns relates to his African environment; rather, everything concerning the white man's country appears in rosy colors while Africa is presented with a Tarzanian stereotype: "Once there was a wizard. He lived in Africa." (40) The colonial school administrators, as "Dead Men's Path" reveals, are remarkable for their ignorance of the realities of Africa. The white school inspector who writes an uninformed but destructive report on Michael Obi is doubtlessly considered an expert on the African school system, otherwise he would not have been so appointed. Nonetheless, he is so abysmally ignorant of how Africa operates that his paternalism looks pitifully ridiculous for its hollowness. He, an Englishman, for that matter, describes the misunderstanding between Obi, the school principal, and the village priests as amounting to a "tribal-war situation" (74).

It is obvious from all this that the Christian missionaries and colonial administrators were not the right people to select and train modern replacements for the elites of traditional African societies. It is the misfortune of Africa, however, that it was precisely the task these missionaries and administrators were morally ill-equipped to perform that they actually performed. It was therefore a foregone conclusion that modern elites, be they in the bureaucracy, business, politics, religion, or the academics, were going to misuse power perhaps even worse than did their predecessors in the traditional society.

We gain an insight into how the new elites received their higher education and prepared themselves for the onerous task of leadership in a story titled "Polar Undergraduate."[3] The story shows that for these future leaders, university studies are characterized by irresponsibility, lawlessness, and a practiced pretense at studies rather than studying.

It is no wonder that after graduating these elites in essence still remain uneducated, shallow and worthless and have to seek for meaning to their empty lives in precisely those things that are incapable of enhancing the intrinsic value of a man: wealth, material acquisition, and external trappings such as hollow titles. Because of the shallowness of his educational preparation, the modern elite, as a rule, is ill-equipped to efficiently perform on any kind of job even when he brings to this job the zeal of a man with a mission. For example, even though Michael Obi, the major character in "Dead Men's Path," passionately believes in modernization, his understanding of modernization is shallow and inadequate. Moreover, he lacks the humility and wisdom produced by a good education, indispensable in handling a man like the village priest. He ends up spoiling everything and ruining even his own career in the educational field, just as his counterparts in religion, politics, administration, and business also do through greed and corruption.

Achebe's stories show that the modern elite, as a rule, is not idealistic even in the misguided manner of Michael Obi. He is materialistic and corrupt and he pursues his objectives with singleminded ruthlessness, even if this is the exploitation of the common man. The joint exploitation of Martha and her daughter, Vero, by the permanent secretary, Mr. Emenike, and his wife in "Vengeful Creditor" (48–69) is a classic example. The way the elites collaborate not only between themselves but also with foreign neocolonial forces to protect their privileges at the expense of the exploited masses is also a major subject in "Vengeful Creditor." The controversy surrounding the withdrawal of the free primary education scheme exposes the fraud, hypocrisy, and deceit that characterize the collaboration existing between the business, bureaucratic, and political elites and their neocolonial external sponsors represented respectively here by Mike Ogudu, Mr. Emenike, the finance minister, and the newspaper, *New Age* (50–57).

With her love for cars, public displays of affluence, array of five house maids and servants, her superficiality, lack of interest in serious issues of public concern, and her callousness to her maids, Mrs. Emenike is a good example of the crass materialism and insensitivity that characterize members of the modern elite who are totally Machiavellian in the tactics they adopt to safeguard their privileges. They lie and falsify facts as happens, for instance, during the debate on free primary education. The truth is that free education encroaches on the privileges of the elites by depriving them of easy access to housemaids and servants. It provides opportunities for the common men to elevate themselves through education and thus become competitors with the members of the elite class. Moreover, it threatens the chances of the reelection of the political elites because it requires increased taxation, which the population resents. Rather than admit these facts openly,

the elites—"lawyers, doctors, merchants, engineers, salesmen, insur-
ance brokers, university lecturers, etc." (51)—use the *New Age* (the
platform provided by their external neocolonial sponsors) to publish
vicious criticisms of the scheme. For instance, Mike Ogudu, the business tycoon, claims that "free primary education is tantamount to naked
communism" (52); the *New Age* calls the proposal a "piece of hare-
brained socialism" that is "unworkable in African conditions" (55); the
finance minister pretends he is protecting "our long-suffering masses"
from further taxation by advocating the cancellation of the program
(55–57); and Mr. Emenike is all regrets that civil servants are prohibited
from writing to the papers—otherwise, he would have liked to make it
known that "we are not a nation of Oliver Twists" for whom free education has to be provided (51).

Both "Vengeful Creditor" and "The Voter" give a good picture of how
the modern political elites operate. To win elections they use false
promises, bribes, thugs, and tribal sentiments. After elections they rob
the national coffers both "to retire" their "election debts" (56) and to
provide themselves with luxuries. For example, Marcus Ibe, "a not too
successful mission school teacher" who joined politics "just in time to
avoid imminent dismissal arising from a female teacher's pregnancy,"
has become a minister who, after only five years in politics, is so rich
that he has "two long cars" and "the biggest house anyone had seen in
these parts" (12). Not surprisingly, political corruption breeds moral
corruption among the people, who are no longer prepared to vote for
free but to sell their votes to the highest bidder (12).

In order to have enough money to give bribes, sponsor his thugs,
and foot the other bills of the election, Marcus Ibe "had drawn five
months' salary in advance" (15) and "no one knew for certain how
much money POP [the party of the opposing candidate] had let loose
in Umuofia but it was said to be very considerable. Their local cam-
paigners would end up very rich, no doubt" (15–16). While Ibe's cam-
paigners give shillings as bribes, POP's electioneerers distribute pounds.

The collaboration of the religious elites with their political counterparts is expressed in a vivid image of bribery. Marcus Ibe's campaigner,
Rufus Okeke, has offered the elders two shillings each, but the latter
refused on the ground that the bribes were too small. After vainly
pleading with the elders to accept the two shillings, Rufus Okeke increased the amount and "then bent down *like a priest distributing
the host* and gave one shilling more to every man" (15; emphasis added).

The linking of Rufus to the priest is justified because Marcus Ibe's
corruption is promoted and protected as much by the churchmen as
by Rufus. It is the provincial archbishop, as earlier noted, who opens
Marcus Ibe's mansion built with public money, fraudulently acquired.

While the corrupt politicians receive the spiritual blessings of the elites of the church, their illegal wealths are protected by the legal elites. For instance, Marcus Ibe's protege, Rufus Okeke, wins a land case "because, among other things, he had been chauffeur-driven to the disputed site" (14–15). The "among other things" is, no doubt, a subtle reference to the bribes the judges must have been given; and, of course, the car and the driver are those of Marcus Ibe.

Once the politicians are in government, they want to remain there, if possible, forever. That they are ready to do everything possible, legal or illegal, moral or immoral, to achieve this end is amply demonstrated in both "The Voter" and "Vengeful Creditor." A minister who has "drawn five months' salary in advance," as did Marcus Ibe, will rig an election if that is all it takes to assure his return to office. The practice of election rigging is, no doubt, implied when the narrator with a subtle touch of irony tells us that "Chief the Honourable Marcus Ibe, was Minister of Culture in the out-going government (which was pretty certain to be the in-coming one as well)" (11). Election rigging is similarly the point of allusion in a passage in "The Voter." The policeman wonders aloud why Rufus Okeke stays for so long inside the polling booth: "Abi na pickin in de born?" (Is he delivering a baby?) (19). It was a common practice of election rigging during the first republic for men to fill the pockets of their rich agbadas and women to pack the folds of their voluminous wrappers with stolen ballot papers, which made both men and women look pregnant as they proceeded into the secrecy of the election booths, where they "delivered" their ballot babies.

The way the modern elites carried on, it was inevitable that they would lead the nation into disaster, just as did their predecessors in the traditional society. The elites of the past weakened their authority, demoralized the society by their materialism, greed, and corruption, and consequently paved the way for colonization. The modern elites followed the footsteps of their predecessors and led the country into a civil war.

Three of Achebe's stories deal with the Nigerian civil war of 1967–70 and the early days of reconstruction immediately following it. The stories are an indictment of the elites not only for causing the war but also for proving to be villains in the prosecution of the war. Having become so used to luxury, the elites find the hardship of the war unbearable. Cletus, the character under focus in "Sugar Baby," is so helplessly addicted to sugar that no degradation is beneath him, as long as he can satisfy his addiction. Although a radio war propagandist, Cletus abandons his war duties and keeps to his bed for days because he cannot secure sugar. That the absence of sugar, an easily dispensable luxury, especially during the war, could completely wreck an administrative-intellectual elite like Cletus, is a sorry comment on his class.

The major story about the war, "Girls at War" (103–123), shows how the elites, with their usual propensity for exploiting every situation for self-aggrandizement, demoralize idealistic youths who are prepared to sacrifice their lives for patriotic ideals. While the common men die daily in the front and at the rear and foreign pilots plunge to death flying in relief aids, the elites become "attack-traders" and contractors "who receive piles of money daily for food they never deliver to the army" (119). Even during the war, the elites would not surrender any of their privileges. They receive their rations regularly and have enough money and material to throw expensive birthday parties while the common men die of hunger. The treasonable corruption and immorality of military elites like Captain Joe, intellectual elites like Cletus, and business elites like the "attack-traders" are responsible for the fall of Gladys and many other girls like her from the height of patriotic idealism to the depth of moral corruption and materialism.

It is significant that in the end Gladys, a representative of the common man, redeems herself by dying a heroic death while Mr. Nwankwo and his like fail to rise above moral pettiness. The moral superiority of the common man, which enables him not only to survive the war and the hectic days following it but to actually prosper under harsh conditions, is the subject of "Civil Peace" (82–87). Jonathan Iwegbu lives by the traditional beliefs and values of humility, implicit trust in God, honesty, native wisdom, enterprising ingenuity, and hard work. These are the qualities that have carried Jonathan through thick and thin and have marked him as a man who will prosper. There is indeed a lesson intended here by Achebe for the elites of the Nigerian society who have repeatedly failed as leaders. This lesson is the central objective of Achebe's collection.

Achebe has consciously made a virtue of ambiguity in several of his stories, which are therefore subject to multiple interpretations. Although it is obvious that Nwigbe, the protagonist of the story "The Madman," is sane, one has to admit that a man who out of anger, fear, and desperation loses control of his senses at a most critical moment in his life cannot be regarded as perfectly sane. Similarly, the claim of the hero of "Uncle Ben's Choice" (75–81) that he saw the folk goddess, *Mammy-Wota*, is never denied by the narrator, just as we are never sure whether the breaking of the egg by Julius in "The Sacrificial Egg" (41–47) has anything to do with the subsequent death of his fiancée and her mother. Our rational explanations for these events may be sound, but in the end they may not be the only ones that are applicable. How, for instance, does one explain the many coincidences of meeting between Gladys and Reginald Nwankwo in "Girls at War"? Indeed, in composing the stories that deal with the supernatural, Achebe gives room for the reader to think that he, Achebe, believes in them; and it is a mark of his artistic maturity—to quote the critic Michael Echeruo—that he does so "without that 'superior' pose which very often mars fiction of that kind" (6).

A story like "Akueke" is all the more interesting for its ambiguity. Is Akueke actually sick of the swelling disease? Is she the random victim of cosmic irony? After all, according to her grandfather, "We are god's chicken. Sometimes He chooses a young chicken to eat and sometimes He chooses an old one" (31); and as Shakespeare puts it in *King Lear*: "As flies to wanton boys, are we to the gods / They kill us for their sport." In spite of its harshness, the removal of the victim of the swelling disease to the bush is necessary since its purpose is to prevent the spread of epidemic infections. But what happens when someone is wrongly diagnosed with the swelling disease? This seems to be the central concern of this story and the fate of its young heroine, Akueke, a village beauty.

The objective of the narrator, however, might be to present Akueke's experience as a mystery that defies understanding, which the love of her brothers is powerless to prevent and which even the oracles cannot unravel. But it may well be that there is no mystery to unravel and that a very mundane explanation exists for Akueke's situation. Achebe is never gratuitous with his use of details; and it would appear, therefore, that we should pay closer attention to the aspects in his heroine, which invite comparison with the heroine of Tutuola's famous mythical fable, "The Complete Gentleman." Like Tutuola's heroine, Akueke's beauty was a sensation that attracted several suitors, all of whom she rejected. Worried, her brother had to remind her that "proud girls who refused every suitor often came to grief, like Onwuero in the story, who rejected every man but in the end ran after three fishes which had taken the form of handsome young men in order to destroy her." (33).

This would appear to be a modern variation of the fable common to the folklore of several peoples of Africa. We are never told exactly from what Akueke suffers. We only know for certain that it is not the abominable swelling disease, a fact which makes her grandfather ask her brothers in anger, "If you don't know what the swelling disease is why did you not ask those who do?" (33). It is significant that from the beginning Akueke resents the idea of being carried to the so-called bad bush, where victims of the disease are usually dumped. This could be because she is determined to fight and not succumb to her disease. But it could equally be because she knows that she is not suffering from the dreaded disease. In which case it would appear she knows what her disease is but is not prepared to share her secret with anyone. An important factor in not voicing her meditated request to be taken to her grandfather is her pride: "Her pride forbade her to speak" (29). If she had made the request to be taken to her grandfather she would have needed to explain why she was certain she would be cured. In other words, she would have needed to explain why she believed that she did not have the swelling disease. It appears the explanation would have revealed a truth that would have hurt her pride.

We are told that Akueke, much like Tutuola's heroine, had several suitors whom she rejected out of pride. Her brothers sternly warned her she might come to grief. And she did, and again like Tutuola's heroine, although the nature of her misfortune was different. It is significant that she felt she had been stricken with this disease because "her protective spirit" had despaired of her (31). What would make her personal *chi*, her protective spirit, despair of her, take sides against her? Could she have committed some infringement, a social or moral abomination? It could be that, unknown to her brothers, Akueke had her "complete gentleman," a secret lover with whom she has had her fun, therefore, the "swelling disease," which significantly is in her stomach, might be nothing other than a miscarried pregnancy. This might be the secret her pride forbade her to reveal.

Again it might not; but whatever the explanation for the mystery, it is certain that the ambiguity, rather than lessen our enjoyment of the story, has in fact enhanced it with broadened levels of interpretation. Achebe is for a good reason ambiguous in his stories about the supernatural: no ordinary man can claim knowledge of the mystery of the supernatural. Hence, Achebe has no sympathy for charlatans who parade themselves as spiritual leaders. When it comes to the pretensions and vices of the African elites, both traditional and modern, Achebe is not only unambiguous but also unsparing in the way he uses irony to satirize them.

NOTES

1. I also think Robert Wren has misjudged another of Achebe's stories, "Marriage is a Private Affair," when he asserts that "the story shows no sense of community with the past" and that in it "tradition has so little strength that the single idea, 'grandson,' crushes it." He therefore concludes that the story is "immature" and its happy ending is "unrealistic" (2–3). Wren would not have come to this conclusion had he taken cognizance of the importance tradition attached to the male child among the Ibo and other communities in Nigeria. Moreover, the happy ending is in part due to the maturity, tact, determination, and courage with which Nnaemeka handled the situation. These are precisely the qualities lacking in Obi Okonkwo, the protagonist of *No Longer at Ease*, who fails in a similar situation. Although Obi was up against greater odds since marrying an *osu* girl was a greater taboo than marrying a stranger, his story would have had a similar happy ending if he had had the qualities of Nnaemeka who, though respectful of tradition, was firmly resolved to make tradition accommodate the new. Obi Okonkwo, though well-intentioned, was a weak character who did not possess such a firm resolve backed with appropriate courage and diplomacy.

2. "In a Village Church" first appeared in *The University Herald*, Ibadan, in 1951 and was included in the first edition of *Girls at War and Other Stories* published by

Heinemann in 1972 (74–77), but was subsequently excluded from the 1977 second edition.

3. "Polar Undergraduate" has the same story as "In a Village Church." It was first published in 1950 in *The University Herald* and was included in the 1972 collection (48–51) but was later dropped in the 1977 edition.

7

The Poetry of Irony in *Girls at War and Other Stories*

INTRODUCTION

The predominant element of style in Chinua Achebe's short stories is irony, which, to rephrase the definition earlier given, is the conscious exploitation for artistic effect of the incongruity between characters' beliefs, actions and statements on the one hand, and actual reality that is at variance with these beliefs, actions, and statements on the other hand. In other words, one can recognize in Achebe's short stories "a reality different from the masking appearance" (Holman 236). While readers are conscious of this incongruity, this distinction between appearance and reality, Achebe's characters remain ignorant.

Two things are meant by the term "poetry of irony." First, that Achebe consciously renders an ironic story poetic through the use of the poetic elements of imagery, rhythm, and sound devices and in consequence some of his passages read as prose-poems. Second, that there is a high level of perfection in the artistic execution of irony in Achebe's stories. In other words, Achebe's stories give aesthetic pleasure because of the effective way they combine the titillating humor inherent in irony with the intellectual and emotional satisfaction derivable from reading a passage of prose-poem.

This chapter examines the nature of irony in Achebe's stories, the objective of the irony, and its mode of poetic realization. This is done in order to reveal the secret behind the artistic success of Achebe's stories. Since this is an application of the general principles discussed in Chapter 4 to a particular writer, the basic ironic patterns, except for the difference already noted in that earlier chapter, are here repeated. Similarly, some of the illustrations used in Chapter 6 are repeated in the present chapter but in each case to establish a different point.

THE NATURE OF IRONY IN ACHEBE'S STORIES

An Achebe story is generally constructed around a *situational irony*; and this is when incongruity exists between belief and reality, or between "expectation and its fulfillment" or between "the appearance of a situation and the reality that underlines it" (Beckson and Ganz 119). As pointed out in Chapter 4, this dominant type of irony in Achebe's stories is followed in importance by *rhetorical* or *verbal irony*. In this case, there is a discrepancy between what a statement is meant to convey and what it actually expresses. Used less frequently by Achebe is *structural irony*, which is when an author "introduces a structural feature which serves to sustain the duplicity of meaning" inherent in an irony (Abrams 81). The structural feature Achebe uses is narrative. In most cases, he selects an objective third person narrator who is so detached that he completely effaces himself and allows narration to filter through the point of view of his character. The character invariably "manifests a failure of insight, viewing and appraising his motives, and the motives and actions of other characters, through the distorting perspective of his prejudices and private interests" (Abrams 81–82).

Whether situational, rhetorical, or structural, an irony in an Achebe story is always tragi-comic. On occasions, it is more comic than tragic and it induces pronounced humor in spite of tragic undertones. Such a style of conveying irony is best described using the Gogolian formula: "laughter through tears." On the other hand, when tragic overtones predominate and we are moved to tears despite the existence of humor, the reverse of the Gogolian term becomes appropriate: "tears through laughter" (Poggioli 315).

SITUATIONAL IRONY

The greater percentage of the ironies in Achebe's stories belong to this category. By far the most significant unit under this category, and in fact in the three types of ironies, is the irony that is built on the incongruity between a character's religious beliefs (traditional or Christian) and actual reality. Often a community or individuals would act on the basis of certain religious convictions with the intention of solving a particular problem only to end up further aggravating the problem because their beliefs are at variance with reality. The consequences of such ill-informed actions are invariably tragic, and even though the reader may laugh because of the underlying irony, it is "tears through laughter." In the majority of cases, traditional religious beliefs constitute the source of this type of irony, although the Christian belief is sometimes the origin.

The traditional belief in gods, goddesses, and spirits, for instance, is responsible for the ironic situations in stories such as "The Sacrificial Egg" (41–47), "Dead Men's Path" (70–74), "Uncle Ben's Choice" (75–81), "The Voter" (11–19), and "The Madman" (1–10). For instance, rather than recognize the unhygienic situation of the market as the cause of the smallpox epidemic, the characters in "The Sacrificial Egg" resort to making sacrifices to appease the feared god of smallpox. Similarly, the characters in "Dead Men's Path" believe that dead men require a special path to communicate with the living. Consequently, when Michael Obi blocks the track identified as such a path because it trespasses his school compound, villagers pull a school building down and destroy flower beds in the conviction that the closure of this path is responsible for the death of a baby at birth. The belief that female spirits take the form of beautiful women to entice men unto ruin or fortune is the subject of "Uncle Ben's Choice" and "The Sacrificial Egg."

Medicine men and diviners who profess occult powers are subjected to biting ironic criticism in "The Madman," "Marriage is a Private Affair" (20–28), "Chike's School Days" (35–40), "Dead Men's Path," and "Akueke" (29–34). In every case the claim of the diviner or medicine man is shown to be fraudulent. The diviner either divines the obvious by exploiting popular gossip as in "Chike's School Days" and "Dead Men's Path" or recommends cures that aggravate the situation of the sick as in "Akueke." It is ironic that the charlatans are feared and obeyed even when their fraud is exposed or they suggest steps that lead to great evils, as in the case of the village reprisal against Michael Obi for closing the so-called path for dead men. Hence, the reader sees it as a befitting irony that the medicine man in "Marriage is a Private Affair" should die after eating the love potion he had prepared for a client, and which the wise client secretly tested on him. The reader is similarly amused by the great discomfort of the character called Rufus in "The Voter." Rufus is torn apart by indecision for not knowing how to vote, having sworn an oath on a feared *Juju* to cast his ballot for the opposition candidate. Rufus accepts bribe money to vote for the opponent despite the fact that he is the chief campaigner for his party's candidate. He resolves his dilemma by tearing his ballot paper into two and casting one half into each ballot box. He feels relieved, and it does not even cross his mind that his vote will be nullified. The most tragic instance of this type of irony is in the story "The Madman," where a sane man is treated as a madman simply because he breaks a local taboo when he temporarily loses self-control out of anger and desperation.

At least five stories exploit the irony inherent in the duality of the faith of ambivalent Christian converts. For instance, even though Julius, the major character in "The Sacrificial Egg," is a Christian who sings in his church choir, he does not stop believing in gods, goddesses, spirits, and in the efficacy of traditional ritual sacrifices. On one occasion, after accidentally stepping on and breaking an egg laid out in sacrifice at a crossroad, Julius becomes greatly worried, fearing he has inherited the misfortunes the sacrifice is meant to transfer. Similarly, despite the fact that the character called Ma considers herself "a very devout Christian convert," she continues to see nothing wrong in advertising her belief in *Kitikpa*, the dreaded god of smallpox, and in *Mammy-Wota*, the goddess of the big River Niger, who supposedly ensnares victims with her exceptional beauty.

Also Elizabeth, a Christian convert in "Chike's School Days," has no scruples in consulting a diviner and performing traditional ritual sacrifices to prevent her Christian son, Amos, from marrying Sarah, an *osu* girl, and thus breaking a pagan taboo. One would have thought that as a Christian, she would have given moral support to her son who is proving himself to be a good Christian by refusing to be influenced by pagan beliefs. On the contrary, Elizabeth finds the marriage of Amos to Sarah to be too much of a sacrilege against the pagan gods she has ostensibly abandoned and she immediately "renounced her new Christian religion and returned to the faith of her people" (37). Okike's "Christian" friends in "Marriage is a Private Affair" are likewise perfectly at ease with their conscience when they advise him to consult a native doctor and apply *Amalile*, the love medicine, so as to prevent his son, Nnaemeka, from marrying a girl from a different language group.

Even the converts who seem to be strong believers in the new faith such as Okeke ("Marriage is a Private Affair"), Amos ("Chike's School Days"), and even the Christian missionaries themselves ("Vengeful Creditor") are not spared the sting of Achebe's ironic satire. For instance, Okeke's belief that a good Christian woman is forbidden to teach in school is as ironically exposed for its humor as Amos's understanding of what constitutes the "ways of the white man," which he assiduously imitates by using "a tiny bell with which he summoned his family to prayers and hymn-singing first thing in the morning and last thing at night" (35). The white missionaries who felt that "if the black man was to be redeemed he needed to learn the Bible alongside manual skills," are also ironically satirized for not knowing the damage they were doing to their cause by applying callous platitudes to human tragedy such as the premature death of Martha's husband, whom they claimed "was called to higher service" ("Vengeful Creditor" 58). As already explained in the preceding chapter, the story makes it explicit that Martha's husband's "higher service" was in remaining alive to take care of his family, which lives in poverty and misery after his death. In this story irony actually reaches the height of atheistic revolt against the all-loving Christian God who apparently takes delight in heaping misfortune after misfortune upon Martha. It is therefore not surprising that Martha would finally revolt against her callous destiny as the victim of "cosmic irony."[1]

It is inaccurate to interpret all stories in this category as reflecting the ironic consequences of remaining faithful to traditional beliefs while proclaiming adherence to the new Christian faith. In other words, they cannot be given the blanket thematic identification as stories depicting ironic situations in the clash of cultures. In fact, in only three instances out of a total of eight is such a clash clearly defined: "Marriage is a Private Affair," "Chike's School Days" and "Dead Men's Path." In the remaining five stories ("The Madman," "Akueke," "The Sacrificial Egg," "The Voter," and "Uncle Ben's Choice") traditional beliefs are not challenged, but reign supreme.

The majority of the situational ironies are too pathetic to be freely amusing in spite of their humor, and hence they can be described as "tears through laughter." The stories with the grimmest or most tragic ironies are "The Madman," "Akueke," "The Sacrificial Egg" and "Vengeful Creditor."

The incongruity or disharmony between expectation and fulfillment constitutes the source of the irony in "The Madman," "Marriage is a Private Affair," "Vengeful Creditor," "Dead Men's Path" and "Civil Peace." In the first story, Nwibe runs naked after the madman to retrieve his own clothes so that he would not go through town naked and be mistaken for a madman. Ironically, the very tragedy he tries to prevent overtakes him. In the second story, Okeke strongly opposes his son's marriage mainly because he wants his son to have a happy family. Ironically, it is the very marriage that would ensure his son's happiness that he opposes. In the third story, Mrs. Emenike herself provides the information that Vero, her housemaid, later abortively uses in an attempt to kill Mrs. Emenike's son. She tells Vero that red ink is poisonous because she wants to scare her from using it as a cosmetic. However, when Vero decides to get rid of Mrs. Emenike's son, who constitutes the impediment to her going to school, she gives him red ink to drink. In the fourth story, the event that is to have helped Obi achieve his long-planned educational modernization and that in turn would have enhanced his future progress, turns out to be the cause of the abrupt end to his career. He has planted beautiful flower gardens on the school grounds and in the areas that the villagers called "dead men's path" because he wants to impress the expected white school inspector. The action ironically leads to both the destruction of school property and his receiving bad reports from the inspector. In the last story, a man who survives the terrible ordeals and dangers of civil war nearly gets killed by armed robbers in the "security of his home" in peace time.

Mostly the same stories can be used to illustrate the irony built on the incongruity between "the appearance of a situation and the reality that underlies it." The irony of "The Madman" is that of mistaking appearance for reality, taking a sane person (Nwibe) for a madman. The old men in "The Voter" seem justified in squeezing out bribe money from candidates for election, because elected candidates soon get rich and forget about the electorate. The irony of the situation, however, is that the more money elected candidates spend bribing the electorate, the more money the candidates will embezzle from the public purse after election in order to replenish depleted savings. The old men are thus ignorantly and ironically abetting a crime that further worsens their condition of living.

Akueke is believed dead and her brothers are performing purification rites, only to discover that she is alive. Moreover, she was treated for the so-called "swelling disease," whereas she probably had a miscarriage! The well-educated Emenikes believe themselves wise but they turn out not to be as wise as their servants, who repeatedly outwit them. Also, they believe they are superior to their domestic servants and to the poor people like Martha, but in actual fact they are shown to be morally inferior for their heartless exploitation and lack of compassion. Jolly Ben believed he saw *Mammy-Wota*, the mischeviously beautiful female spirit of River Niger, on his bed, whereas he was having a delusion and a nightmare caused by too much drinking.

As is obvious from the enumerated examples, the ironies built on both the discrepancies between expectation and its fulfillment on the one hand, and between appearance and reality on the other, are generally more lighthearted and tend to be more comic than tragic even though there are elements of both moods. Stories like "The Voter," "Uncle Ben's Choice," and "Marriage is a Private Affair" are obvious cases of "laughter through tears" with subdued tragic undertones. An obvious exception is the story "The Madman" where the tragic elements outweigh the comic and induce "tears through laughter."

RHETORICAL IRONY

Each of the twelve stories in *Girls at War and Other Stories* has a number of verbal or rhetorical ironies. These are less subtle and more easily recognizable, unlike the situational ironies already discussed. However, rhetorical irony contributes more than other types of irony in making Achebe's stories humorous. At the same time, apart from a few instances, the incongruity, and therefore the humor, in a rhetorical irony is made obvious only in the context of either the situational or structural irony. Except, for example, that one is aware of the situational irony that has made it possible to treat a sane man as a madman, one is not likely to recognize the verbal irony nor the humor in this brief conversation from "The Madman":

"They've got his cloth he says."
"That's a new one I'm sure. He hardly looks mad yet. Doesn't he have people, I wonder." (7)

The irony of these statements is, of course, obvious as they reveal the tragic situation when Nwibe enters the market naked while pursuing a madman to recover his loin cloth stolen by the madman. Since appearance has been mistaken for reality, Nwibe's claim that his cloth has been taken is not believed, and he is considered mad even though he is not.

The protagonist of "The Voter" abbreviates his name Rufus to "Roof" without recognizing the comic dimension he has added to his personality. He is also said to be a patriotic person because he has abandoned "a bright future" to return home and "guide" his people (11). The irony becomes apparent when we realize that the "bright future" he abandons is in fact the impecunious profession of bicycle repairing. Furthermore, his immorality disqualifies him from guiding anybody. Finally, coming home is actually a shrewd decision on his part because it ensures him a good income and a promising political career as the protégé of Marcus Ibe, the elected representative in Umuofia. Ibe calls his exclusively private house, built with dubiously acquired wealth, "Umuofia Mansions," as if it were the common property of the people of Umuofia. Ironically, his name remains as "Chief the Honorable Marcus Ibe, Minister of Culture" and he is certain to be returned at the next elections!

In his letter, Okeke explains the reason he believes Ugoye Nweke will make a good Christian wife for his son, Nnaemeka, affirming that he bases his judgment on a solid reason: "Her Sunday School teacher has told me that she reads her Bible very fluently" ("Marriage is a Private Affair" 22). The ironic significance of the words of Akueke's grandfather when he says, "As for your purification rites you may carry on because Akueke is truly dead in Umuofia" ("Akueke" 34) becomes apparent only after understanding the circumstances that necessitated the statement. Although the brothers loved their only sister, Akueke, a great deal, they had been compelled by Umuofia tradition to dump her in the so-called bad bush since she was diagnosed with the "swelling disease." Akueke, however, managed to reach her grandfather living in another village and was cured, after which the grandfather invited her brothers to come and see him. When he asked about Akueke, the brothers affirmed that she was dead and explained they had not informed the old man because they wanted first to complete the purification rites.

In order not to incur the wrath of the feared god of smallpox, *Kitikpa*, the people of Umuru do not say that smallpox has killed a person but euphemistically say that the victim has been "decorated" ("The Sacrificial Egg" 44). The white school inspector in "Dead Men's Path," no doubt, would congratulate himself for his objectivity, accurate insight and, generally, for a job well done after describing the misunderstanding between the school and the village in Ndume as a developing "tribal war situation" (74). Not only is such a misuse of words ridiculous, particularly coming from an Englishman, but it is also tragic since it exposes the ignorance of one who occupies such a responsible post and is considered an expert on Africa. The situation, however, is one that invites laughter through tears because of its underlying humor. Jolly Ben, the protagonist of "Uncle Ben's Choice," considers German doctors great experts and he enthusiastically describes how efficient they were in words that reveal how bad they actually were: "Those German doctors were spirits. You know they used to give injections in the head or belly or anywhere. You just point where the thing is paining you and they give it to you right there—they don't waste time" (77). While exaggerating with the intention of showing how good German doctors were, Jolly Ben ironically made them look more dangerous than they probably were.

Cletus goes through a theatrical act of throwing a handful of sugar out through the window because as he says it is "only to show sugar that today I am greater than he, that the day has arrived when I can afford sugar and, if it pleases me, throw sugar away" ("Sugar Baby" 90). The words actually end up showing how much of a slave Cletus still is to sugar. During the war, when sugar was hard to get, he disgraced himself on several occasions because of his addiction. The only way he could have shown his victory over sugar would have been to do without it, but it is obvious that he is still very much addicted to it. Gladys in "Girls At War" says "I am all right, sir," when she actually means she is through with her task (104); and a contingent of school girls march behind a banner that says: WE ARE IMPREGNABLE! when they mean invincible (105).

John, a forty-year-old man who works as a carrier in a supermarket is called "boy" by his juniors ("Vengeful Creditor" 49). In the same story, the minister of finance fails to see the ironic contradiction in his words when he advocates the withdrawal of the free education scheme in order not to overburden "our long-suffering masses" with taxes, whereas the common man sees education as the only way to end his sufferings (56). In trying to pacify Martha for the bad way things have turned out between his family and Martha's, Mr. Emenike says that "It is the work of the devil, I have always known that the craze for education in this country will one day ruin all of us. Now even children will commit murder to go to school" (68). The ironies here are multiple. First, the actual "devil" is the speaker himself who collaborated with other members of the elites to withdraw the free education scheme. Second, Mr. Emenike thinks that he can deceive Martha with his false consolation but the irony is that the provincial poor widow sees through the deceit of the urbane permanent secretary, for she afterwards thought to herself: "And that thing that calls himself a man talks to me about the craze for education. All his children go to school, even the one that is only two years; but that is no craze. Rich people have no craze. It is only when the children of poor widows like me want to go with the rest that it becomes a craze" (69).

The most spectacular story in this category is "Civil Peace," whose verbal ironies are as devastating as they are entertaining, as tragic as they are comic. The story is a rare achievement in the combination of opposites. The balancing is so aesthetically pleasing as to make this story stand in the same category as "The Madman," "Girls At War," and "Vengeful Creditor" as the best stories in the collection. Jonathan and others call their ex gratia awards "eggrasher" (85) without any awareness of the absurdity of their coinage. The paralyzing awareness that civil peace is more dangerous than civil war is brought home by the cynicism of the armed robbers who visit the Iwegbus at night. After Jonathan and his family have shouted in vain for help, the chief of the robbers offers to assist in calling for help. And indeed the robbers themselves start hollering into the night, asking for assistance against armed robbers. The irony of the situation is further heightened when the robbers initiate a conversation that resembles more of a business transaction than the molestation of robbers. This is followed by a false show of compassion on the part of robbers, who urge Mrs. Iwegbu not to cry for, as they claimed, "We no be bad tief. . . . We just take our small money and go nwayorly. No molest. Abi we de molest?" (87–88). It is ironic that thieves should speak of themselves in this fashion when they are actually molesting defenseless people and that they should refer to the money they were stealing as if it were their own. But the greatest irony is that even though, strictly speaking, there could be no good thieves, we are forced to admit that these were good thieves of sorts. This irony becomes more obvious in the light of contemporary reality in Nigeria, where armed robbers daily gun down their defenseless victims.

As this last story shows, rhetorical irony is intimately linked with situational irony and, as already stated, the former cannot be understood without the latter.

STRUCTURAL IRONY

Structural irony is the most subtle form of the ironies employed by Achebe. It is associated with the selection of a narrator who creates discrepancies between point of view and objective reality by coloring his narration with his prejudices. It is used in varying degrees in the few stories where it occurs and it appears mostly in the latter stories published in 1971 and 1972: "The Madman" (1971), "Uncle Ben's Choice" (1971), "Sugar Baby" (1972), and "Girls At War" (1972). Except in "Uncle Ben's Choice," where the first-person narrator is used, structural irony seems a further refinement on the use of a third-person narrator who, having reached the limit of objective detachment, renders the story through the subjective perspective of the characters.

In "The Madman," for instance, the narrator completely effaces himself and tells the story from the angle of vision of the character under focus at every given point. This enables the narrator to reflect faithfully the psychology, vision, and prejudices of the three major characters in the story: the madman, Mr. Nwibe, and the community. The result is a motley of conflicting and contradictory views, each of which is allowed its freedom of expression. This appears to have been purposely done by Achebe who, it would seem, wants to question human ability to accurately perceive reality. In any case, this type of narration builds ambiguity into the narrative fabric of the story, which is thus enriched by expanding multiple interpretations. This story, "The Madman," will no doubt be recognized by the school of new criticism as belonging to the highest order of poetry (art) for having expertly "incorporated the poet's own 'ironic' awareness of opposite and complementary attitudes" and for demonstrating "that kind of 'wit' absent in the Romantic poets, which is an 'internal equilibrium' that implies the 'recognition,' in dealing with any one kind of experience, of other kinds of experience which are possible" (Abrams 83–84).

The sociological critic, too, would be full of praise for the story, for its ambiguity enables it to put a strong case forward advocating humane treatment of the unfortunates in our midst, because ultimate responsibility for their misfortunes rests with the society. The fates of Nwibe and of the madman demonstrate this fact because the real madman, whom we meet at the beginning of the story, probably got to his present state of madness by receiving a treatment similar to that being meted out now by the society to Nwibe. This would explain the symbolic exchange of identities between the two characters.

Another successful use of the mode of structural irony is in "Girls At War." Here there are no shifting multiple viewpoints creating ironic and poetic ambiguity. The third person narrator sieves events through the dominating point of view of Reginald Nwankwo, a sensitive intellectual working in the Biafran Ministry of Justice. However, in spite of his sensitivity, intellectual patriotism, and general good will, he is ultimately incapable of rising above the level of those he detests for their materialism, corruption, and immorality. Although he is not completely satisfied with himself and actually goes into moments of self-reproach, he nonetheless believes he is better than the generality of people in his class. The irony, however, is that his greater insight into the nature of things imposes greater responsibility on him, but he lacks the moral courage and heroism to meet this challenge. As a result, our respect for him is much lower than he actually believes he commands. In fact, he thinks he is very high in our estimation because he is one of those who love to appear impressive and important. In reality he is neither, and hence the structural irony his vision engenders.

Mike, the character whose point of view informs the third person narration in "Sugar Baby," fares even worse than Mr. Nwankwo of "Girls At War" because of the extreme seriousness with which he takes himself and his patronizing attitude to Cletus and others. The fact that he attaches so much importance to himself makes us rate him lower than even Cletus; and this is ironic because he is in fact a better person in several respects than Cletus, the sugar addict.

Jolly Ben, who tells his own story in the first person in "Uncle Ben's Choice," is also a boastful character who is not aware of the counter effect his boastfulness has on the rating we give him. He seriously undermines his own personality by revealing how shallow he is through his belief in superstitions and his inability to realize that it was his drunken state that induced his fantastic hallucinations. The irony is that he tells his story purposely to younger people to show how shrewd he was, how he respected traditional values, and how important it was for the younger ones to imitate his example.

Structural irony intensifies the situational and rhetorical ironies that already exist in any given story and, by so doing, reinforces the story's thematic focus.

Achebe's objective in these stories is satiric. In "Uncle Ben's Choice," the empty boast of a shallow individual is deflated; "The Madman" satirizes both the callousness of the insensitive society and man's presumptuous claim to perceive true reality. Both "Sugar Baby" and "Girls At War" reduce the Nigerian intellectuals, who grossly overrate their own importance, to true pony size, because they fail to match vision with performance and thus disappoint expectations.

THE POETIC REALIZATION OF IRONY

The ways Achebe employs poetic elements to enhance the aesthetics of irony in the most consciously poetic of his stories, "The Madman," is the subject of the next chapter and shall therefore be left out of the present discussion to avoid repetition.

As the American writer Edgar Allen Poe pointed out, selecting the right size for a poem or a short story is a crucial aesthetic consideration. The effect of a story can be ruined by inappropriate length just as it can be considerably enhanced by observing correct proportions.[2] Generally, terseness is highly prized in short stories because it aids intensity of effect. Achebe usually succeeds in executing his story in an appropriate length and he is highly disciplined in his choice of diction. Words and phrases are carefully selected with a view to achieving utmost conciseness in length. As a result, the most successful of his stories, such as "The Madman" and "Civil Peace," display a linguistic discipline as strict as that found in poetry.

Achebe's stories do not just resemble poetry by being concise but actually employ the elements of poetry with respect to the use of proverbs, imagery, rhythm, and sound devices.

Apart from their inherent poetic quality as concise, witty images, often embellished with sound effects, proverbs sometimes play the poetic role of leitmotif in Achebe's stories. In "Uncle Ben's Choice," for instance, proverbs occur at regular intervals and each time a proverb is used it is to reveal Jolly Ben's boastful attitude. He is always at pains to show how meticulously he remembers his father's wise advice, cast in the form of proverbs: "I must always keep my sense with me. My father told me that a true son of our land must know how to sleep and keep one eye open" (76); "I had seen many young men kill themselves with women in those days, so I remembered my father's word: Never let a handshake pass the elbow" (76); "My father used to say that the cure for drink is to say no" (77); "Then I said to myself: How can you be afraid of a woman? Whether a white woman or a black woman, it is the same ten and ten pence" (79); "Our fathers never told us that a man should prefer wealth instead of wives and children" (80); "For where is the man who will choose wealth instead of children?" (81).

The proverbs reoccur at regular intervals from the first page to the last page, thus serving almost like a refrain in the same way his beloved phrase: "like this," adds a rhythm of its own apart from its role as a character-depicting element. The proverb is a proud heritage, highly respected among the Ibo and all African people, and its use ought to be commensurate to the occasion. In these examples, however, proverbs serve the purpose of self-advertisement, which is not noble. Thus, Achebe uses proverbs in this story not only for poetic effect but for ironic satire.

The use of proverbs in "The Voter" serves the same poetic and ironic intentions. Those who look at Marcus as not comparable to "the little bird who ate and drank and went out to challenge his personal spirit"

(13) or those others who affirm that Marcus "Our Son is a good man; he is not like the mortar which as soon as food comes its way turns its back on the ground" (13), are shown to be ignorant of the true state of affairs. But more than that, their objective is to achieve favors through flattery. In fact, the old men who are doing everything to preserve their dignity in a circumstance that already denies them dignity (since they are negotiating how much bribe money to take), only make themselves more distasteful by "sanctifying" their corrupt deals with proverbs such as these: "Who would leave an *ozo* feast and go to a poor ritual meal? ...We have climbed the iroko tree today and would be foolish not to take down all the firewood we need" (14). The poetry of the metaphor in the last proverb is unmistakable but so is its ironic deployment, for the firewood they are harvesting is bribe money, which, as earlier explained, only further aggravates the vicious cycle of their exploitation by politicians like Marcus and Rufus.

Thus, proverbs in these two stories, as in others, serve two purposes: poetic and ironic. They enrich the stories with their poetic imagery, they serve the poetic role of leitmotifs and refrain and they intensify aesthetic appeal with the humor they elicit by being ironic.

The role of leitmotif is served, ironically, by curses in "Akueke." Akueke's curses, which punctuate the narrative, show her determination not to succumb to her disease and they also serve to repel her brothers who have allowed themselves to be persuaded by villagers to dump her in the bad bush: "Let them dare" (29), "Let them eat shit" (29); "Let them all eat shit" (30). The pleasant-sounding alliterated "b" in the "bad bush" cannot escape the ear and the eye, just as the repetitions with variations in these curses achieve intended sound satisfaction. This story begins with a beautifully merged image and a metaphor: "Akueke lay on her sick-bed on one side of the wall of enmity that had suddenly risen between her and her brothers" (29). There is the visual image of a person lying on one side of a sick-bed and there is also the metaphor of lying on one side of the wall of enmity. This type of merging of images not only enhances the poetry of this ironic story but also promotes brevity, which is an outstanding quality in this five-and-a-quarter-page-long story.

Pages 48, 49, and 62 of "Vengeful Creditor" demonstrates a more intense and consistent effort to turn a prose work into prose-poem. A regular rhythmic effect is achieved on pages 48 and 49 by: (a) the regular repetition of two words: "Sang" and "and"; and (b) parallel syntactical units based on those two words. A pair of illustrations suffices here:

(1) "Madame, this way," / sang the alert, high-wigged sales-girl / minding one of a row of cash machines in the supermarket.

(2) "Good afternoon, Madame," / sang the sweet-voiced girl / already loading Madame's purchases on to her counter.

The two sentences have exactly the same structural patterns, each of which is divided into three similar syntactical units. The obvious intention of such an arrangement is to create a recurrent rhythm to stimulate auditory pleasure. The same approach is obvious in these examples:

(1) She punched the prices as fast as lighting *and* announced the verdict.
(2) Mrs. Emenike opened her handbag, brought out from it a wallet, unzipped it *and* held out two clean and crisp five-pound notes.
(3) The girl punched again *and* the machine released a tray of cash.
(4) She put Madame's money away *and* gave her change and a foot long receipt. (emphasis added)

Units 1, 3, and 4 of the second set of examples are almost exactly the same in structure while unit 2 introduces minor variations into the same basic pattern. The alternating arrangement with the introduction of variations are meant to prevent monotony.

The passage on page 62 is a little more complex, although the same principles of repeated words and phrases with variations is at work. The rhythmic cadence of the passage is derived from the repetition of the words "very" and "and"; and of phrases such as "going away," "going away from," "in fine dresses," and "in dainty little school bags."

The choice of words is also poetically imaginative: "little daily departures." The passage is constructed on the principle of expanding elaboration. An idea is introduced in a unit sentence and every successive unit is a further elaboration on the preceding one. The arrangement of the passage makes it sonorous, lyrical, and pleasing to hear. The poetic beauty of the passage, however, is incongruous with the reality it describes. A disappointed aspiration is captured in a beautiful poetry and this further serves to underscore the tragedy of the disappointment:

Every morning as the older Emenike children—three girls and a boy—were leaving for school in their father's Mercedes or their mother's little noisy Fiat, Vero would bring the baby out to the steps to say bye-bye. She liked their fine dresses and shoes—she'd never worn shoes in her life—but what she envied them most was simply the going away every morning, going away from home, from familiar things and tasks. In the first months this envy was very, very mild. It lay beneath the joy of the big going away from the village, from her mother's drab hut, from eating palm-kernels that twisted the intestines at midday, from bitter-leaf soup without fish. That going away was something enormous. But as the mouths passed the hunger grew for these other little daily departures in fine dresses and shoes and sandwiches and biscuits wrapped in beautiful paper-napkins in dainty little school bags (62).

The poetry of passages such as the above is often enhanced by the accompanying beautifully rhythmic songs spontaneously composed by Vero, the housemaid (62, 63). Thus, Achebe's stories are poetic literally by exploiting the poetic qualities of proverbs; using proverbs as leit-motifs and as refrains; employing imagery such as metaphor and simile; sound effects such as alliteration and repetition; and achieving definite rhythmic cadence through parallelism produced from repeating similar words, phrases, and sentences, often with variations. The beauty of the poetry is further emphasized by the introduction of situational irony into their use.

OBJECTIVE OF IRONY

The ironies in Achebe's stories fulfill two functions. First, they make the stories more humorous and intellectually more entertaining. Second, they satirically draw our attention to human and social weaknesses and to inadequacies that they invite us to laugh at in the hope that we would learn to correct them. Irony in Achebe is thus educative, satiric, and entertaining. In order for us not to become cynically complacent, the irony is mostly underlined with tragedy. We often laugh "ha ha" through our tears, comically, but many other times we cry while laughing and tears drop through our laughter as we are moved to compassion for the sufferings of fellow human beings. We value Achebe's stories, therefore, not only for their poetically ironic aestheticism but also for their humane values.

NOTES

1. M. H. Abrams defines "cosmic irony" or "the irony of fate" as referring to "literary works in which God, or destiny, or the universal process, is represented as though deliberately manipulating events to frustrate and mock the protagonist" (83). For a detailed discussion of Martha's revolt, which recalls the atheistic revolts of Ivan, Dmitri, and Aljosha in Feodor Dostoevsky's novel, *The Brothers Karamazov*, see my paper, "Russian and Nigerian Literatures" (493–94).

2. Edgar Allen Poe repeatedly discussed this question in his essays "Twice Told Tales," "The Philosophy of Composition," and "The Poetic Principle" (Davidson). Poe said that for a literary work of art to be aesthetically pleasing, it must achieve "unity of impression" (454), which he also called "totality of effect or impression" (464). To achieve this effect or impression, the work must have what he called the "proper length" (455) and must neither be too long nor too brief (447). Poe considered poetry to be the best form of literary art because, more than any other genre, it is capable of achieving the "proper length." Next to the poem, he put the short story, which was then called "the brief prose

tale." He wrote: "Were I called upon, however, to designate that class of composition which, next to such a poem [which belongs to "the noblest order of poetry" (447) for having the "proper length"], . . . should best fulfill the demands and serve the purpose of ambitious genius, should offer it the most advantageous field of exertion, and afford it the fairest opportunity of display, I should speak at once of the brief prose tale" (448).

8

"The Madman": A Poetic Realization of Irony

THE IRONIES

Chinua Achebe's story, "The Madman," is a poetic realization of an irony. The irony centers on Nwibe, the protagonist, a successful farmer who has so distinguished himself that he is about to be received into the select, dignified society of the men who hold the highest title in the land—the *ozo* men. Returning from an early morning work on his farm on a fateful market day, Nwibe stops to have a bath at the local stream. Meanwhile, a madman comes along to quench his thirst at the same stream; he sees Nwibe's loin cloth, gathers it, and wraps it over his nakedness.

Significantly, this involuntary but tragic exchange of identities between a sane person and a madman, an exchange symbolized by clothing, is registered by the jeering, ironic laughter of a taunting madman. Nature, which seems to be participating in this tragic irony, solemnly echoes the madman's mocking laughter: "The deep grove of the stream amplifying his laughter" (6).

Nwibe, who has been appropriately compared to Okonkwo of *Things Fall Apart* as a man of fierce temper whose "judgment deserts him when he is under its full sway" (Killam 100), fully recognizes not only the outrageousness of the madman's affront, but, more significantly, he understands the ominous import of the sacrilegious challenge. The words Nwibe screamed out to the madman, "I will kill you,...I will whip that madness out of you today!" (6), convey in fact more than the obvious threat. They also carry the veiled desperation of a man who realizes that his life is about to take a sudden tragic turn if nothing is immediately done to avert the impending disaster. The situation in which a stark-naked sane person pleads through a threat with a clothed madman for, of all things, clothes to cover his nakedness, is ripe with obvious irony.

In his stark-nakedness Nwibe pursues the fast retreating clothed madman who is "spare and wiry, a thing made for speed" (7). In a short while what Nwibe has dreaded swiftly becomes a merciless reality in the irony of mistaken identities. The involuntary transfer of clothes that only threatens possible disaster—which, in fact, is still laughable while it remains a private matter between Nwibe and the madman—suddenly assumes a tragic dimension the moment the first witnesses appear on the scene: "Two girls going down to the stream saw a man running up the slope towards them pursued by a stark-naked madman. They threw down their pots and fled, screaming" (7). With this, the exchange of identities is complete and the irony that makes possible the acceptance of appearance for reality is triumphant.

As if fate has decided that day to crush Nwibe completely, the pursuit of the madman to retrieve his loin cloth leads Nwibe to the highway and, worse still, into the marketplace, seen by everyone. Now Nwibe is no longer just an ordinary "madman" but an incurable one, for local tradition holds the belief that a madman who sets foot into the "occult territory of the powers of the market" (8) can never be cured again: "Such a man is marked for ever" (10). Indeed, tradition proves to be only too true in the case of Nwibe, who even after he has been supposedly "cured" remains a shadowy ruin of his former promising self. His efforts to regain respectability are continually frustrated by those who matter in the society.

Once the central irony of mistaken identities has firmly established itself, several other minor ironies inevitably follow. There is, for instance, the situational irony involving Nwibe, who stands stark-naked in a crowded market and starts shouting: "Stop the madman,...he's got my cloth!" (7). No one, of course, believes him and the response he receives registers another situational irony, for he is certified as a madman except for the sympathetic concession that he is "a new one" (7).

From this central irony of mistaken identities also emerges the ironic situation whereby a "reputable" medicine man (psychiatrist) loses his fame while a mere charlatan overnight acquires the reputation of the best "mad-doctor" in town. The "reputable" doctor appears to be a man of integrity who would not waste his time or his client's money on an obviously bad case, as he has categorized Nwibe's "madness." The other doctor is not as fastidious and he accepts to treat Nwibe. Even though he too sees the case as hopeless, he has no qualms about making some money out of his new patient.

Nwibe, of course, only needs time to recover from the shock from his traumatic experience, but when he does, the credit for his "cure" ironically goes to the charlatan, who "became overnight the most celebrated mad-doctor of his generation. They called him sojourner to the Land of the Spirits" (9).

There is further irony in this situation because the distinction set up between the two medicine men does not exist in reality. The first medicine man is as ignorant as the second, and hence none of them could correctly diagnose Nwibe and recognize the fact that he is not mad. The only difference between these two charlatans is in the degree of their shamelessness. While the first has "some kind of integrity," which he protects with false pretenses, the second absolutely has no conscience, no shame, being most cynically realistic: "If doctors were to send away every patient whose cure they were uncertain of," he rhetorically asks, "how many of them would eat one meal in a whole week from their practice?" (9).

Perhaps the most devastating irony that emerges from this story, however, concerns the fact that the foundation has suddenly and effectively been removed from under our self-assuredness as cognitive beings who can distinguish fact from fiction. Suddenly we are made to entertain doubts concerning our perception of the nature of reality and we begin to credit the philosophical doubt that affirms illusion and reality to be the same. And if indeed we cannot distinguish truth from untruth, reality from illusion, a sane man from a madman, then we must confront the existential question as to whether we actually exist, because the philosophical evidence of our existence as human beings is: "I think, therefore I am."

The situation whereby a sane person is identified and treated as a madman not only underscores the precariousness of the claim of every sane person to sanity within the society, but also pinpoints the basic subjectivity of existence and human judgments. In fact, we cannot be sure of anything. We cannot, for instance, be sure of who is actually sane in the context of this story. Is "the madman" really mad? Is Nwibe truly sane? Can we vouch for the sanity of the people of Olu and Igbo? Would a sane person allow anger and desperation to rob him of his better judgment and run naked for whatever reason into a crowded market? But perhaps what the story has done is to equate extreme anger with insanity. The psychiatrist will accept this view, but that makes every one of us a madman because we are all capable of or have actually experienced extreme anger. If we are all insane, what right do we have to certify only some people as mad? The extreme clarity of the logic of the madman as he walks on the highway seems to suggest that he is perfectly sane; and if he is actually sane, then is it not the society that labels him mad that is actually mad? The story might not be inviting us to abandon our own logic and judgment of sanity, but it certainly introduces doubts into the authenticity of our perception of reality.

The moral implication of the story is obvious, for it shows that it is the society that creates its madmen and it is the same society that treats these so-called madmen shabbily, as if they were not human beings. If at first we are comfortable with the way the madman who opens the story is ill-treated, by the time the story closes and we are familiar with the fate of Nwibe, we certainly can no longer be complacent about the treatment of this or any madman. More than that, we are awed by the realization that Nwibe's troubles have only begun by the time the story ends. The suggestion is that Nwibe might in the end become a true madman. This situation certainly urges us to the belief that the madman who opens the story might have become a madman through an experience similar to that of Nwibe. This is a shattering indictment of society.

The indictment is addressed not only to the primitive society ridden with superstitions and taboos such as the society of Nwibe, but also to the modern society, because Nwibe's village is in the end only a microcosm of the human society at large. The extreme vulnerability of the individual within the society is thus the major concern of this story. Man is revealed to be ultimately alone and alienated in a society that is supposed to exist for his advantage but that ironically seems to exist to destroy him. In spite of the solicitude of relatives, the existential tragedy of Nwibe is his alone.

Consistent with the system of ironies in this story, water, which is a universal symbol of life, becomes the source of human tragedy. The local stream that invites Nwibe to cleanse and purify himself from dirt has also invited the madman to quench his thirst and rejuvenate his tired body. Yet these invitations lead to a tragic collision. Similarly ironic is the fact that the road, which is a universal symbol of life and of human quest for knowledge, is also that which has tragically crossed the paths of Nwibe and the madman.

As the story begins, Nwibe is surely a representative of the society, with all its boasts to success and sanity. The madman, on the other hand, stands for the victims of society. In the tragic collision of these two and in the symbolic fate of Nwibe, therefore, we can read the poetic justice visited on the callous society by nature, which seems to have taken sides with the victim. The fact that Nwibe is the unhappy representative of the society, which creates its madmen and treats these same creations callously, is confirmed by the fact that the madman sees Nwibe as the embodiment of all the social injustices he suffers. Hence he identifies Nwibe with everybody who had ever ill-treated him. In the madman's symbolic eradication of individual differences, Nwibe is remembered first as "the same hefty man who brought three others like him and whipped me out of my hut in the Afo market." Second, Nwibe merges with "the same vagabond who descended on me from the lorry in the middle of my highway." And third, Nwibe becomes the "fellow who set his children to throw stones at me and make remarks about their mothers' buttocks, not mine" (5–6).

Thus, the story not only casts doubts on the sanity of the "sane" society, because no sane society would be so callous, but also issues a serious warning of the possible consequences of social callousness, for, as we have seen, the callous society ends up destroying itself.

The story is consequently a call on society to uphold humane principles in the treatment of every individual. It is also a special appeal to society to treat social victims such as the madman with extra humane care. Hence, the sympathy of the unintrusive narrator is throughout on the side of the victim. Indeed, the story is structured in such a way as to ensure the permanent sympathy of the reader for the victim. Thus, the first part of the story is centered on the madman and it is the madman's point of view that guides the reader. In fact, as we follow the reasoning of the madman, his logic appears impeccable, a fact that further casts doubt on the sanity of the "sane" society: "He had got himself this cudgel lately to deal with little beasts on the way who threw stones at him and made fun of their mothers' nakedness, not his own" (2). The moment Nwibe switches role from a representative of the society to become its victim as a "madman," the narrative sympathy immediately switches to his side. In fact, to make sure that our sympathy in undivided and solely enjoyed by Nwibe, the first object of our sympathy—the madman—disappears completely from the scene.

The story is a perfect example of complete narrative objectivity. Although the third-person narrator appears to be limited, since events are conveyed through the points of view of the protagonists, the reader nonetheless knows that the narrator is omniscient, that he knows everything but has only selected to efface himself. This enables the narrator to remain true both to the psychology and logic of the madman as well as to the logic of the "sane" society. It is by using this objective point of view that the ironies of the story are allowed to have their full impact. While the reader knows the truth of every situation, the character whose view is being conveyed is invariably ignorant, yet it is this ignorance that is allowed to prevail and decide the course of events. The reader, for instance, knows that Nwibe has only temporarily lost his "sanity" because of extreme anger and shock, yet society treats him as a complete madman. On this mistaking of appearance for reality, which is allowed to exist through objective narrative, rests the system of ironies in the story.

THE POETRY

The most artistically successful of Achebe's short stories is undoubtedly "The Madman." It is a consciously made piece of fiction. It is so consciously made and so poetic that it is, in fact, a poem—a prose-poem whose seven brief divisions, which move with cinematographic rapidity, sound like the seven stanzas of a poem. The story actually sustains a consistent poetic cadence based on repetitions, alliterations, rhythmic dialogues, rhythmic descriptions, syntactical parallelisms, paradox, irony, and a metaphoric proverbial diction.

The story opens with a beautifully constructed parallelism which gives a panoramic view of the geographical area of the wanderings of the madman. The poetically repetitive and contrastive words, "not/but," "and not/but," form the cornerstone of the rhythmic parallelism of compound constructions. Each of the two halves of the first parallel sentence can be segmented into three rhythmic units as follows:[1]

He was drawn to straight roads.

Not any tiny neighborhood market	(1)
where a handfull of garrulous women might gather at sunset	(2)
to gossip and buy ogili for the evening soup	(3)
but a huge, engulfing bazaar	(1)
beckoning people familiar and strange	(2)
from far and near.	(3)

The first unit in each of the halves of the contrastive parallel has two adjectives of size: "tiny neighborhood" (market) and "huge, engulfing" (bazaar) which contrast as they modify two nouns that are synonyms: "market" and "bazaar." The second unit in each half of the parallel is built around a verb of action: "(might) gather" and "beckoning." The third unit in each case has the coordinating conjunction "and" that further generates an internal parallelism ("gossip and buy": "far and near") which enhances the over-all rhythm.

The first parallel construction is immediately followed by another rhythmical compound sentence built on the same principles. Here also "and" contrasts with "but." Similarly, two sets of three adjectives of quality ("any, dusty, old" and "broad, black, mysterious") modify two noun synonyms that contrast in quality: "footpath" and "highways":

And not any dusty, old footpath   (1)
      *** ***** *** =========
beginning in this village,   (2)

and ending in that stream,   (3)

but broad, black, mysterious highways   (1)
      ***** ***** ********** ========
without beginning   (2)

or end.   (3)

Part of the rhythmical beauty of this parallelism emanates from the words "beginning" and "ending," both of which operate as post-position gerundial adjectives in lines 2 and 3 of the first unit of the parallelism. Similarly, the words "beginning" and "end," which operate as a gerundial noun and as a noun respectively in lines 2 and 3 of the second unit of the parallelism, contribute greatly to the poetic beauty. Apart from creating a notionally contrastive internal parallelism ("beginning": "ending"), these words produce a definite rhythm that runs through the two units of the parallelism in the repetition of the verbal suffix "ing."

This second parallelism is followed yet by a third with an internal rhyme becoming almost an end-rhyme built on the words "much" and "such":

> After *much* wandering he has discovered
> two *such* markets
> linked together by
> *such* a highway.

A fourth parallel construction using the contrastive syntactical structure "the one . . . ; the other . . ." still follows to sustain the rhythm:

> One market was Afo,
> the other was Eke.

Not far from this fourth parallelism is a sentence with a rhythmic cadence based on the alliteration of the consonant "b":

> . . . *b*easts of the *b*ush.

The first of the seven divisions (stanzas) of this story ends with a set of two sentences, each of which ends with a similar rhythm:

> He had got himself this cudgel lately to deal with little beasts on the way who threw stones at him and made fun of *their mothers' nakedness, not his own.*

> They said their lorry very nearly ran over *their mother, not him.*

These rhythms are once again created out of notional contrasts ("their mothers' . . . not his;" "their mother, not him") and out of similar syntactical structures. The phrases "their mothers' nakedness, not his own," "their mother, not him" are both object complements to the verbs "made fun of" and "ran over," respectively.

The parallelisms, repetitions, alliterations, and other poetic elements of the first "stanza" of this prose-poem, combine to create a mellifluous, pleasant, smooth rhythm that accurately reflects the contentment and serenity in both nature and man prior to the tragic collision between Nwibe and the madman. This serenity will later be shattered after the fateful encounter between the two characters. Meanwhile, what is emphasized is the serene contentment of the madman, who is shown to have established a harmonious relationship with his world as he walks the road, "holding it in conversation." It must be noted, however, that even at this stage there are hints concerning the latent antagonism between the madman and the "sane" society as we read about the "two fat-bottomed market women" and their "four hefty beasts of the bush" who threw the madman out of "his" market stall, the "little beasts" who threw stones at him, and the "vagabond" driver of a mammy-wagon and his mate who ill-treated the madman on the road.

It is also significant that the harmonious rhythm of the many parallelisms of this opening "stanza" emerges out of notionally contrastive syntactical structures. This, no doubt, reflects the central thematic irony of a story that permits the mistaking of a sane man for a madman.

The second division (stanza), which is very brief, bases its rhythm on the simple device of repetition. The adverbial phrase "then he saw," the adverb "then," and the hyphenated noun "water-pots" are repeated at strategic places in the paragraph to sustain the rhythm: "*Then he saw* some young ladies with *water-pots* on their heads coming towards him. . . . *Then he saw* two more *water-pots* rise out of a sloping footpath. . . . He felt thirsty *then* and stopped. . . . *Then* he set down his basket on the roadside and turned" (2).

It is interesting to note that the first time the noun "water-pots," which plays a significant role in the rhythm of this passage, occurs, it is overshadowed by the noun phrase in object position—"some young ladies." Here the noun "water-pots," is only a complement to the noun phrase, "some young ladies." By the time this hyphenated noun "water-pots," appears the second time, it has already gained in prominence, having graduated from being a mere complement to becoming a noun in object position: "Then he saw some water-pots." Here the "water-pots" have become personified objects able, like human beings, to "rise out of a sloping footpath." The emphasis on this noun, "water-pots," through graduation in grammatical function (complement-to-object) and figurative role (personification) is justified because the noun has a symbolic value. The pots contain water, a universal symbol of life. It is not surprising, therefore, that the madman instantly sets out in search of the stream that is the source of the water in the pots. His intention is to quench his thirst and refresh his body. Similarly, Nwibe, on his way from the farm stops at the same stream to wash away farm dirt and rejuvenate his tired body after the morning work. This stream, this "water of life," we might say, ironically becomes the cause of the subsequent tragic collision between Nwibe and the madman, a collision that would ruin the life of the highly respected and prominent Nwibe. This is an example of the careful consideration put into the selection of words to perform multiple phonetic and semantic functions in this poetic short story.

The third division (stanza), which covers pages three to five of the short story, varies the nature of the rhythm in its language of prose-poem. It employs strategically placed, cryptic, weighty phrases, rhetorical sentences, and proverbs—all of which are pregnant with symbolic meaning: "When we see we shall believe" (3); "and where is the man to hide his face who begins the *ozo* dance and then is foot-struck to the arena?" (3); and "but our people say the man who decides to chase after a chicken, for him is the fall" (5).

The first phrase creates a weighty suspense: "When we see, we shall believe." The ominous load of this suspense is foreshadowed in the tragic image of the hypothetical man who cannot successfully complete the *ozo* dance and also in the equally tragic fate of the proverbial foolish man who falls chasing after a chicken. The cadence of the rhythm of these types of cryptic phrases, rhetorical sentences, and proverbs with their emphasis on the consonant sounds, s, c, sh, and ch ("see," "shall," "is," "his," "face," "begins," "dance," "stuck," "say," "decides," "chase," "chicken") is combined in this third division (stanza) with the simple device of repetition. The repetition is based on the recurrence of words and phrases such as "crazy," "mad," "the great judge has spoken," "thank you, great judge," "Udenkwo is mad," and others: " 'If Udenkwo is *crazy* must everybody else go *crazy* with her? Is one *crazy* woman not enough . . . '*The great judge has spoken*,' sang Udenkwo in a sneering sing-song. '*Thank-you, great judge. Udenkwo is mad, Udenkwo is always mad*' " (5).

There is also a beautiful alliteration on "s" in the unforgettable phrase: "sang Udenkwo in a sneering sing-song." The foreshadowing in this division is unmistakable in the use of the words "crazy" and "mad" and especially in the sentence with repetitions and with the "sh" alliteration that Nwibe uses to caution his "crazy" wife: "*Shut your mouth*, *sh*ameless woman, or . . . When will you learn to keep your bad-ness within this compound instead of *sh*outing it to all Ogbu to hear? I say *shut your mouth*" (5).

It is because Nwibe could not follow his own counsel that he would later act like the proverbial foolish man who chases after the chicken and by so doing courts "the fall." Nwibe runs after the madman, who in the estimation of that society is as insignificant as a chicken, and he "falls" in the process. Moreover, his "fall" is in public and he has therefore failed to keep his "badness" ("madness") within his compound. The foreshadowing itself, as we can see, is pregnant with irony.

More than any other quality, however, the poetic rhythm of this division emanates from a poetically constructed rhythmic dialogue that uses repetitions, alliterations, balanced brief parallelisms, and run-on lines:

"*What has a little dog done to you?*" she screamed loud enough for half the village to hear. "*I ask you, Mgboye, what is the offence of a puppy this early in the day?*"

"*What your puppy did this early in the day,*" replied Mgboye, "is that he put his *shit-mouth into my soup-pot.*"

"*And then?*"

"*And then I smacked him.*"

"*You smacked him!* Why don't you cover your *soup-pot?* Is it easier to hit a dog than cover a *pot?* Is a small puppy to have more sense than a woman who leaves her *soup-pot* about . . . ?*"

"*Enough from you,* Udenkwo."

"*It is not enough, Mgboye, it is not enough.* If that dog owes you any debt I want to know. Everything I have, even a little dog I bought to eat my infant's excrement keeps you awake at nights. *You are a bad woman. Mgboye, you are a very bad woman!*" (4)

The effective use of repetition is quite obvious in this division, especially in the section with the run-on lines that graphically divides the dialogue into two halves:

"And then?"

"And then I smacked him."

"You smacked him! Why don't you . . . "

Furthermore, the rhythmic phrase "put his shit-mouth into my soup-pot" seems to concentrate in itself many of the sound characteristics of this poetic dialogue. There is the repetition of notionally contrastive balanced phrases: "shit-mouth" and "soup-pot." Moreover, the words "soup" and "pot" reoccur several times in the dialogue as a leitmotif to emphasize the domestic nature of the setting.

The fourth division (stanza), covering pages five to eight of the story, once again reverts to the simple device of repetition to achieve its rhythm. In the end the repetition helps to create a passage of parallel syntactical structures, each of which has three units:

And then remembered:	(1)
This was the same hefty man who . . .	(2)
He nodded to himself	(3)
And then remembered again:	(1)
This was the same vagabond who . . .	(2)
He nodded once more	(3)
And then remembered again:	(1)
This was the same fellow who . . .	(2)
Then he laughed	(3)

In the succeeding threatening exchange between Nwibe and the mad-man, there is a preponderance of phrases with the first person pronoun as subject: "I have caught you naked."; "I say, I have caught you naked."; "I can see you are hungry for a whipping."; "I say drop it!" "I will kill you. . . . I will whip that madness out of you today!" (6).

Apart from creating a rhythmic repetition, the pronoun "I" is obviously a device to reflect the contending egos of the two personalities seeking dominance in a tragic contest.

The fifth division (stanza) of the story, in keeping with the ominous silence of the occasion, is very brief. Appropriate words and phrases are selected to emphasize frantic rapid actions and to reflect the solemn tragic mood that prevails. Even the balancing of rhythmic syntactical units are structured especially to produce the effects of rapid actions and to reflect the solemn tragic mood: "Two men from Nwibe's village recognized him and, throwing down the one his long basket of yams, the other his calabash of palm-wine held on a loop, gave desperate chase." (8).

Even though the sixth division (stanza) avails itself of the rhythmic beauty of the repeated phrase, "Don't blame us too much," "Don't blame us too much" (9), this division primarily exhibits the poetic beauty of the metaphorical statement, the simile, and the cryptic paradox uttered by solemn mysterious medicine men. This division is thus like the second division analyzed earlier: "Never have I professed to bring back to life a man who has sipped the spirit-waters of ani-mmo. . . . They have already embraced him. . . . He is free and yet no power can break his bondage" (8–9).

To emphasize the hopelessness of Nwibe's situation, the medicine man in his culture-based comparison uses a metaphor that identifies Nwibe as a dead man: "A man who has sipped the spirit-waters of ani-mmo." To show recognition of the great powers supposedly possessed by the medicine man who is requested to cure Nwibe of his dumbness, Nwibe's relations use a metaphor that emphasizes physical action: "Can you do nothing at all then, not even to *untie his tongue*?" The beautiful paradox of the man who is at the same time free and eternally bonded underscores the cultural perception of death in this Ibo community.

Death is not a physical extermination but a metaphorical crossing of the boundary that separates the living from the dead. This crossing into the spirit world is succeeded by taking actions normally associated with the living: drinking the spirit-waters of *ani-mmo*, being embraced by the divinities of the marketplace, delivering oneself to the deity called *Alusi*. Furthermore, the paradox of the man who is free but eternally bonded proves to be only too true for Nwibe. Even though Nwibe is supposedly cured of his "madness," he is nonetheless treated as a madman by the people who matter in the society—the *ozo* men.

The foolishness of Nwibe as a man who is partially the architect of his own misfortune is subtly hinted at in the simile that compares him to the proverbial character who jumps from the frying pan into the fire by offering himself as a slave (*osu*) to the deity *Alusi* in an effort to escape the oppression of his fellow men. It would seem the medicine man is of the opinion that a man should maintain his sanity irrespective of the provocativeness of the situation in which he finds himself, because failure to do so might lead to culpable tragic consequences. Viewed in this light, the medicine man would appear to be right, inasmuch as Nwibe would not have been in his present tragic predicament had he judiciously considered his options and resisted the precipitate action of pursuing a madman in stark nakedness.

Complementing the poetry of the metaphor, the simile, and the cryptic paradox in this division is the beauty of the supreme irony with which the narrator treats the other medicine man, the charlatan, parading as an understanding physician, who suddenly becomes "that humble practitioner" that "performed miracle" and "became overnight the most celebrated doctor of his generation" (9). Here, too, is the beauty of an appropriately used personification, followed by well-selected metaphors: "It remains true that madness may indeed sometimes depart but never with all his clamorous train. Some of these always remain— the trailers of madness you might call them—to haunt the doorway of the eyes" (10).

The metaphor—"the doorway of the eyes"—is unique, original, and beautiful. The aftermath of Nwibe's supposed "madness," metaphorically called "the trailers of madness," is public knowledge and is, no doubt, a source of popular gossip and disgrace in the community. Consequently, its symbolization in the metaphor of "clamorous train" is most appropriate. Furthermore, inasmuch as Nwibe's experience of "madness" is comparable to the vanquishing visit of a superior enemy, it is the genius of appropriateness to have personified madness: "Madness may indeed sometimes depart but never with all his . . . "

Achebe's prose-poem ends most appropriately in the seventh division (stanza) with an epilogue in a subdued voice recording the aftermath of the tragic drama of the most crucial day in the life of Nwibe. The solemn tragic mood of this conclusion is again appropriately charged with the caustic irony of the social criticism in the very last sentence of the story-poem. The last chance Nwibe has of regaining his integrity is casually dismissed by the dignified *ozo* men who epitomize the vanity, ignorance, and blindness of the callous inhumane society. The self-assuredness of these *ozo* men who, "dignified and polite as ever, deftly steered the conversation away to other matters" (10), creates an ironic contrast with the fact that these men are indeed revealed to be super-stitious, superficial, callous, and inhumane. In the most damning con-demnation of these pretentious men who symbolize the callous society, the narrator's voice is as usual restrained, indeed casual: "Had they received him perhaps he might have become at least partially restored" (10).

Further studies will discover in Achebe's prose-poem more poetic qualities than have been revealed in this analysis. What has been seen, however, is enough to show that "The Madman" is indeed a consciously written, beautiful piece of prose-poem. A good quality of this short story is that it is not poetically ostentatious even though it is consciously poetic. Indeed what is quite obvious at the first reading is the elegance of its prose. It is only when one listens attentively to the beautiful resonance of this prose at the second reading that one begins to hear the captivating rhythm of its poetry and starts to discover the wealth of its imagery. It is precisely because the prose qualities of this story are quite obvious whereas its poetic qualities are not so easily noticeable that this study has emphasized the latter at the expense of the former. What is lost in this imbalanced approach is quickly regained in the enhanced aesthetic satisfaction that this study helps us to derive from the reading of the story.

It would seem that Achebe has consciously selected the beautiful medium of a prose-poem to narrate the far-from-beautiful, indeed the depressing and tragic story of Nwibe. The sad tale of Nwibe is told in a beautiful poetic form. Obviously Achebe's intention is ironic. This sty-listic irony is in perfect consonance with the central theme of the story, which is realized through a system of ironies. Just as the theme thrives on the ironic contrast that permits the mistaking of appearance for reality, so does the style derive its aesthetic forcefulness from the ironic contrast between content and form. Nwibe's story is ultimately a parable of the sad irony between a great expectation (Nwibe was to take the *ozo* title—the highest title in the land) and a sordid banal reality (Nwibe becomes a "madman"). The aesthetically pleasing poetry with which the sad irony of "The Madman" is narrated further emphasizes the sadness of the irony.

Finally, in raising the fundamental philosophical problem about the precarious existential situation of man in society; and in providing a moral perspective that places this story in the humanist tradition in literature; Achebe's story has revealed that, contrary to the opinion of Bernard Bergonzi (251–56), the genre of the short story has the capacity to deepen our understanding of the world and of one another.

NOTE

1. Emphasis in this and subsequent quotations in the rest of the chapter is supplied by me.

9

Fixions: A Return to Origins

INTRODUCTION

The return to origins in Taban lo Liyong's *Fixions*, being part of a general phenomenon in African prose fiction, can be fully appreciated only if we first understand the historical background, nature, and literary ramifications of the general phenomenon itself. Hence, the first part of this chapter proposes and substantiates the hypothesis that African fiction has completed its first full cycle in the search for a style. African writers began with a folklore-inspired prose that was basically phantasmagoric, then moved to realistic prose, and are now back to a fiction largely imitative of folklore.

THE STYLISTIC CYCLIC PROGRESSION: FROM FANTASY TO REALISM AND BACK TO FANTASY

A literary history of African prose fiction, as Lalage Bown correctly points out, should begin with the study of the pseudo-literary materials written by the Africans who first used English ("Development of African Prose-Writing" 33, 38).[1] Even though such materials, which include personal letters, diaries, biographies, legal documents, historical accounts, economic and scientific reports, and religious and political tracts, cannot strictly be classified as fictional literature, they often exhibit the stylistic qualities of creative prose. Consequently, they can be seen as dating the origin of prose fiction, and hence their prominence at the beginning of literary histories.[2] It is on this premise that Bown dates the history of African prose in English to over two centuries ago. ("Development of African Prose-Writing" 33). The modern history of African literary prose in English, however, began with Amos Tutuola and the appearance of his novel, *The Palm-Wine Drinkard*, in 1952.

However, Tutuola was not well received by fellow Africans, one of whom the critic O. R. Dathorne reports as having said that Tutuola had nothing to offer except "a good imagination and bad grammar" (*African Literature in the Twentieth Century* 94). Tutuola's rejection had a lot to do with the political climate of the fifties, which was the period of agitations for independence. At this time Africans were most anxious to prove to the colonial masters that they were quite capable of managing their own affairs, but Tutuola's tale and its linguistic medium, on the contrary, seemed to fellow Africans to paint the picture of Africa as a naive, primitive culture. His ungrammatical English, which could be interpreted uncharitably as an evidence of Africans' intellectual inferiority, added to the embarrassment of the day. Hence, while Western critics, mistaking Tutuola for a bold modernist experimentalist, were praising him, African intellectuals, regarding him a political liability, were doing their best to sweep him under the diplomatic carpet of the independence movement.

Africa at this time was clearly not ripe for either a folklore-inspired fiction that could attract the cultural stigma of primitivism or for a modernist fiction whose message would be lost in the ambiguity of stylistic experimentations. What was wanted was a realistic fiction whose unambiguous cultural message was a strong support for the political argument for independence. Hence, the publication of Chinua Achebe's *Things Fall Apart* six years after Tutuola's novel was greeted with enthusiastic approval.

Things Fall Apart was a novel that completely answered the needs of the moment. Its obvious linguistic competence and the uniqueness of the manner in which language was manipulated beyond the capabilities of any native English speaker to express the reality of an African culture not only erased any suggestions of intellectual inferiority unwarily implanted by Tutuola's novel, but also showed that Africans were highly ingenious. But above all, the novel had the proper politicocultural message for its time. Using the example of the Umuofia community, Achebe advertised the point that prior to the intrusion of the colonizers, Africa had well organized and prosperous societies with efficient economic, political, legal, and social systems. The implication of this kind of depiction was that since Africans were obviously a civilized people, Europeans had no business coming to Africa in the first place on their so-called mission of civilization. Consequently, Achebe's novel subtly questioned the claim of Europeans themselves to being civilized, since no truly civilized people would fail to realize that difference in culture did not amount to a lack of civilization. Thus, the novel's indictment of colonialism was further strengthened as the Europeans' genuine or pretended ignorance was presented as the justification for the destruction of African culture and the imposition of alien European culture.

Thus, Achebe's novel was a most welcome cultural weapon in the struggle for independence. However, its relevance would have been less obvious had its timely politicocultural message been clouded in folkloric fantasy or modernist ambiguity. It was therefore not surprising that the realistic mode of *Things Fall Apart*, rather than the folkloric fantasy of *The Palm-Wine Drinkard*, henceforth became the model for African prose fiction.

There was, of course, an additional reason for realism becoming the vogue in African fiction. When fiction writing started in Africa in the fifties, Africans were more familiar with the prose of nineteenth-century European realists than with the writings of the contemporary modernists even though the latter were dominant in Europe at the time. The school and university syllabi had introduced Africans mainly to the classics of the realist period of the European prose. This was inevitable because the classics of the realist period had fully established themselves while the prose of the modernist trend was still probing, still experimenting, still trying to find its feet. Besides, for some critics such as Ian Watt, the novel was necessarily realistic because its "formal realism" was what distinguished the novel from previous forms of prose writing (33–37). Thus, when Africans came to write novels they of necessity borrowed from their experience of known examples of that form, and these were mostly the nineteenth-century European realistic novels. These were the major reasons Achebe's realistic mode swiftly displaced Tutuola's folklore-inspired prose style barely six years after fiction writing commenced in Africa.

Luckily, however, after independence African realistic prose was very early infused with the spirit of criticism. Being among the most sensitive members of the society, African writers were quick to observe that the postindependence economic, social, and political affairs of Africa were being badly managed by the political, intellectual, and social elites, who subsequently became the targets of the writers' satires. Thus, if we were to identify the type of realism dominating African fiction, we should call it *critical realism*, to borrow a Russian term. The writers, in fact, became so critical that the most sensitive of their protagonists, finding life unbearable, either escaped into cynicism, as in the case of Teacher in *The Beautyful Ones Are Not Yet Born* and the major characters in

The Interpreters; or suffered madness or existential agony, as Baako in *Fragments* and Mugo in *A Grain of Wheat*; or risked the danger of action by seeking a revolutionary transformation of society, as Ofeyi in *Season of Anomy* and the communalist or proletarian characters in *Two Thousand Seasons, God's Bits of Wood, Petals of Blood,* and *Devil on the Cross.*

Thanks to the dynamism infused into African prose literature by this critical spirit, the novelists and short story writers soon began to find traditional realism too tame, too inadequate as a medium of expressing the depth of their disappointment and criticism. Thus, along with critical realistic prose works such as *A Man of The People, Mission to Kala, The River Between,* there also appeared novels in the spirit of socialist realism, such as *God's Bits of Wood, Petals of Blood, Season of Anomy,* and novels whose existential sensitivity was so heightened that they became almost surrealistic, as in the case of *Why Are We So Blest?, Fragments,* and *A Grain of Wheat.* Some writers did not even pretend to write realistic novels or stories anymore. Instead of verisimilitude and correspondence between the world of the novel on the one hand and objective reality on the other, these writers proposed a fiction that was larger than life. This fiction was created either by expanding the boundaries of existing art forms or by imitating the methods of African oral literature. Femi Osofisan, for example, had so expanded the boundary of satire that in the grotesque, absurd world of his novel, *Kolera Kolej,* everything was completely turned upside down. In this novel reason and logic had no place and that which was absurd had become the normal, the ordinary. Taban lo Liyong, on the other hand, synthesized the literary devices of African oral literature and Western modernism to create his world where even the most realistic of events was invested with an unreal atmosphere. Fantasy, for instance, dominates his *Fixions* and *The Uniformed Man.*

The back-to-origins literary movement, which was still tentative in the late sixties when it was first noticed, and christened *orature* by Ngugi wa Thiong'o ("Okot p'Bitek and writing in East Africa" 76), has become the dominant trend in the best novels of Africa since the late seventies.[3] Novels such as *Two Thousand Seasons, The Healers, Season of Anomy, Petals of Blood, Devil on the Cross,* and a host of others owe their freshness and aesthetic appeal to this tendency. It must be noted that the movement is equally vibrant in poetry, drama, and other fields of art, including film-making, music, drama, painting, and sculpture. Without this artistic journey back to source, it is unlikely that we would have been blessed with such compelling classics as Okot p'Bitek's *Song of Lawino* and Wole Soyinka's *Death and the King's Horsemen,* to mention just two examples. The movement was seen as a welcome development by African critics, as is evident in *Toward the Decoloni-*

zation of African Literature, one of whose central objectives was to urge African writers to return to African oral literature for creative inspiration (Chinweizu, Jemie and Madubuike 146, 290, 291).

It would thus seem that African-written prose fiction has completed its first full cycle in the search for a style. It has returned to Tutuola and his world of fantasy and myth. By now Africans are no longer ashamed of Tutuola, whose works are already recognized as classics. In fact, as far as lo Liyong is concerned, Tutuola is the best writer Africa has produced (*The Last Word* 157–170).

However, it would be erroneous to suggest that realism as a prose style in Africa is dead. No, indeed, the realistic novel will still continue to be written in Africa as in today's postmodernist Europe and America. It would be equally misleading to suggest that African prose fiction had at any time experienced a complete break with the oral tradition. The influence of folklore has always been evident even in the most realistic works by our writers. For example, Achebe's exploitation of Ibo proverbs and traditional philosophy and religious rituals are only a step removed from the mythical and fantasy world of Tutuola's novels. Achebe has written a most insightful interpretation about this world in an article titled "Work and Play in Tutuola's *The Palm-Wine Drinkard*." At times the realistic satire of T. M. Aluko completely emerses the reader in the fantasy world of folklore. In *One Man, One Matchet*, for instance, the Ipaja people believed that Chief Momo's corpse "had been sent by aeroplane to the white man's country where it was going to be kept in a special kind of prison for ghosts." Some, however, argued that it was not the whole of the chief's corpse that was transported but only "certain selected organs of the body, those connected with Momo's stubbornness and manliness," and that this was done to ensure that "the dead man would be truly dead, and that if and when he came back to earth under another name he would not be a menace again to Government" (112–13).

It is thus obvious that even our realists are deeply rooted in the fantastic, mythical, and mystical world of our oral tradition. This is why it is difficult to understand the skepticism of Gerald Moore in his essay "Amos Tutuola: A Nigerian Visionary" (187) and it is equally difficult to know why Charles R. Larson should have been so categorical in insisting that "Tutuola's books are far more like a fascinating cul-de-sac than the beginning of anything directly useful to other writers. The cul-de-sac is full of wonders, but it is nevertheless a dead end" (*The Emergence of African Fiction* 9).

To repeat Tutuola exactly is not what anybody would look forward to, but Tutuola has been repeated creatively by other writers in one form or another. The greatest of all those who have repeated him is the Ugandan writer, Taban lo Liyong.

TABAN LO LIYONG AND AMOS TUTUOLA

Basil Busacca accurately defines lo Liyong's uniqueness as an artist when he describes him as "an East African writer and critic who genuflects before no idols—European, Nigerian or local—and who proves that he is right to exercise the prerogative of genius" (quoted in Zell and Silver 153). This is also what Donald Carter in his review "Sympathy and Art" means when he speaks of the "unconventionality" of lo Liyong's artistic manner (141–42). It is important to stress, however, that it is not only "the prerogative of genius" that is at work, for lo Liyong's confidence stems from a thorough knowledge of both the European and the African literary traditions. His keen interest in the latter has produced the book *Eating Chiefs*, a collection of the tales of the Lwo people that is outstanding for its originality and poetry. Lo Liyong may have no "idols" but he does not hide his sympathies or the fact that he has a mentor, as his dedication in the epigraph preceding the story "Lexicographicide" shows: "For Amos Tutuola from whom I have learnt many important things, the greatest being that the most important virtue is courage" (*Fixions* 40).[4]

The courage mentioned here refers to the courage to be able to depart from the recognized beaten paths of European and African writings and return unabashedly to the less-cultivated modes of oral literature. It means in addition the courage not to copy blindly one's mentor (Tutuola in this case) or oral literary tradition itself, but to develop an independent, critical and creative approach to both. This is exactly the kind of approach that he has adopted with regard to Tutuola and to his native Lwo folk tradition. For him oral literature is only a source of inspiration to provoke original creation and that is why in the introduction to *Eating Chiefs* he urges other artists "to treat their tribal literature as raw material, or artistic forms for containing their views on the past and the present" (x–xi). He further insists in the introduction to his book of avant-garde poetry, *Frantz Fanon's Uneven Ribs*, that the original creation inspired by oral literature must be as "food worthy the nourishment and excitation of joyous wits;" and that in order to achieve this, the writer must aspire beyond the "hard uninteresting frames" of anthropologists towards an original and artistic self-expression (2). In *Eating Chiefs*, lo Liyong explains what has been his own guiding principle in this matter: "I have been not so much interested in collecting traditions, mythologies, or folk tales. Anthropologists have done that. My idea has been to create literary works from what anthropologists collected and recorded. It is my aim to induce creative writers to take off from where the anthropologists have stopped. Greek dramatists based their play on Greek mythology" (x).

It is therefore not surprising that even though lo Liyong has based his short stories on Tutuola's example and on Lwo tales, his creative originality is what comes out most strikingly. Even in "Tombe 'Gworong's Own Story" and "Lexicographicide"—two stories in *Fixions* (25–29, 39–45) that come closest to Tutuola's manner, we do not have the Tutuolan ghosts and spirits nor his semi-human and semi-supernatural characters on whom the actions of his parabolic tales usually depend. Instead, lo Liyong has appropriated only the Tutuolan fantasy to weave his own equally parabolic tales. An example is the way he uses the Tutuolan theme of the "complete gentleman."

In the Tutuolan story, a girl who has consistently refused all suitors on the ground that they were unsuitable finally experiences an overpowering attraction to a "complete gentleman"—meaning a man who is extremely handsome and suitable all round, whom she meets at the market. She doggedly follows the footsteps of this handsome stranger with the intention of claiming him for a husband in spite of the man's dissuasions and even as he leaves the market far behind and goes deeper into the bush of ghosts. Soon the handsome man begins gradually to reveal his true nature. Step by step he returns the various parts of his body, all of which he had borrowed for an outing. In the end the "complete gentleman" is completely dispossessed and returns to his original self—a mere human skull. The deceived girl is not only disappointed but has already been lured away to a spirit world from which escape seems impossible until the enterprising narrator-hero comes to her rescue.

This story is Tutuola's parable on the naivety, or perhaps the folly, of an idealistic young girl hoping to find in our imperfect world an ideal man for a husband. This tale is full of ghosts, dangerous encounters, and narrow escapes as the narrator successively turns himself into either a lizard, air, or bird to rescue a deceived girl, and it takes several episodes to narrate in *The Palm-Wine Drinkard*.[5] In "Tombe 'Gworong's Own Story," lo Liyong paraphrases it into just a paragraph (*Fixions* 29). His version teaches the same parabolic lesson as Tutuola's tale but, compared to the latter, it immediately reveals lo Liyong's own artistic originality. The story in lo Liyong's version has lost its scaring encounter between men and ghosts but has retained the elements of fantasy as witnessed by the mysterious rejuvenation of the private part of the butchered man. The horror in the Tutuolan version is translated into the shocking violence of the murder in lo Liyong's rendering, but there is the ironic twist at the end: the dead man nonetheless succeeds in consummating his marriage even after he is murdered. And this constitutes a punishment for the girl because she is taken in spite of everything by the man she abhors. Also significant is the fact that it is the deceitful man who faces the greater danger and not the idealistic girl. It is precisely here that lo Liyong goes beyond Tutuola in using the tale to infuse traditional morality. While the Tutuolan story seems to censure mainly the naive, idealistic girl for her folly, lo Liyong's version punishes both the girl for being too naive and the man for taking advantage of the girl's naivety by deceiving her. The girl suffers through her disappointment as well as through the fact that she is taken by the man she hates. The man, on the other hand, is killed by the girl he has deceived. The moral is that one should not only learn to avoid being deceived by mere appearances but should also desist from presenting false fronts with the intention to deceive.

The important thing to note is that this version has not only retained the essentials of Tutuola's story, but has further enriched the morals the parable is meant to teach. However partial one may be to the narrative flavor of Tutuola's style, one cannot but agree with Donald Carter when he says that lo Liyong "slips along" the "bush-path of narrative will" with "a greater (and slyer) sense of route and destination" than Tutuola, his mentor (142). The same brevity and creative ingenuity are displayed by lo Liyong in his other variation on this Tutuolan motif, which he presents in "Lexicographicide" (*Fixions* 44–45). Here, attention is focused on the moment of returning borrowed parts and is presented surrealistically in a dream by a seven-year-old would-be dictator boy.

Another one of Tutuola's themes that lo Liyong has handled with the same creative originality is the theme of the novel *Simbi and the Satyr of the Dark Jungle*. Simbi is a born-lucky girl who knows only wealth and happiness. In due course, however, Simbi goes out of her way to experience poverty, hardship, and misery. She undergoes serious hardships in the Path of Death and later in the Dark Jungle, but in the end she returns home a sadder and wiser person.

Taban lo Liyong's version on this theme is presented in the story "The Old Man of Usumbura And His Misery" (*Fixions* 1–10). The old man of Usumbura is born lucky like Simbi. He is so wealthy and so lucky that "all his life he had never known the pangs of sorrow or grief" (2). Just as Simbi has her poor friends, Rali and Sala, so also does the old man have his own poor friend, the "miserable old man of Kigali." The two friends are the antipodes of each other: one is the extreme of wealth, luck, and happiness, the other the extreme of poverty, ill-luck, and misery. In the same way that Simbi wants to taste the poverty and hardship always experienced by her friends, Rali and Sala, the happy old man of Usumbura soon grows bored with his happiness and sends his many children to bring him misery from his friend, the old man of Kigali. The latter gives the children a bundle of straw that he strictly enjoins them not to open on the way. Curiosity gets the better of the children and they disobey. As they discover that the bundle contains nothing, a quarrel develops among them in the process of allocating blame as to who is responsible for losing whatever the bundle must have originally contained. The quarrel escalates and before long, one hundred and fifty children of the chief have killed one another. The hundred and fifty-first child, who escapes to convey the news to the father, is struck dead by the father himself. The first blow is because the father is impatient for the child, who is out of breath, to tell his story. The second mortal blow comes before the old man knows of the fate of his children. It is from the disappointment of hearing that misery has escaped. Thus, the old man is left with no son, and even his sixty-five wives soon leave with all their daughters. The old man becomes a lonely, poor, miserable creature.

What is fascinating about this story is not merely the retelling of the Tutuolan theme of the overpowering force of the quest of man for knowledge even at great personal risks. What holds the reader's attention is the story's narrative style. The reader's attention is first captured by the extreme simplicity of the story itself and the way it is told. The plot is reduced to such a level of simplicity that a little child can comprehend it. This simplicity of plot is also matched by a simplicity of language: "There was an old man of Usumbura who was very rich.... There was another old man of Kigali who was very poor.... The rich happy old man of Usumbura and the poor miserable old man of Kigali were friends" (2–3).

The story gradually gathers its details in this simple fashion until it is fully told. But behind this deceptive simplicity is beautifully written poetry. The whole piece is conceived as a story narrated through a folk song, complete with repetitions, refrains, and flourishes. The way the story-song is presented presupposes an audience participation. It appears the story is so well known that when the narrator sings the first sentence, this sentence is taken up by the audience in an already transformed and abbreviated form that contains the essential meaning. In the process whole words and phrases are repeated, and this gives a definite rhythm to the passage. Monotony is avoided through the introduction of variations in wording and phrasing. The variations themselves serve to add new details to the story and thus advance the action of the story in the manner of the creative repetition, which Ruth Finnegan in *Oral Literature in Africa* says is characteristic of panegyric oral poetry (132). Nobody, for example, can read the following passages and remain indifferent to their poetic beauty:

There was an old man of Usumbura who was very rich. This old man of Usumbura. He was so rich he had eight thousand cows. This rich old man of Usumbura. With these cows he married for himself sixty-five wives. This old man of Usumbura. He was so healthy that he had three hundred children from these wives. Our healthy man of

Usumbura. He was so happy and successful that with industry his wealth increased manifoldly. He and all the members of his family were so lucky none of them ever felt sick. These lucky people of Usumbura. All his life he had never known the pangs of sorrow or grief. This lucky Usumburan. (2)

Now that there was no more misery to carry home, what were these boys to carry home to their father? These obedient boys of Usumbura. One brother's hands were already striking another for having opened the bundle. These useful hands we have. Another hit another on the head, another smote another, another speared another, another clubbed another, another speared another, another drank another's blood. These killers of their own brothers. (7)

Now with this simple and beautiful poetry goes a complexity of depth in meaning. This complexity is introduced through the several allusions, ironies, adages, and philosophical comments that abound in the story. Here, for instance, is an allusion to Tutuola's heroine, Simbi: "This happy man of Usumbura. He asked to be shown the nature of misery" (3). Another alludes to Charles Dickens's *Great Expectations* and the protagonist Pip: "These hot-headed sons of Usumbura would not like a delay. These children full of great expectations" (4). This one is to James Shirley's poem, "Death the Leveller": "Oh, the fatal end. Death, you have reaped a rich harvest. Death that levels all" (7). Here are some examples of irony: "These children who can see green at night" (6); "One brother's hands were already striking another for having opened the bundle. These useful hands we have" (7); "They abandoned their happy husband to his fate and went off to their several parents' homes. These good wives of Usumbura" (10). There are also some adages and philosophical comments: "The curiosity that killed that cat" (7); "Oh, human wisdom that always condemns those who are afflicted" (9); "Oh, the love that is intensified by the degradation of others. He was the only black sheep in this snow-white home. Give a dog a name and you hang him" (9).

The examples of these three stories surely reveal that in every case lo Liyong has set for himself a task much beyond the scope of the original task that was before Tutuola. Thus, the older writer has only provided a stepping stone for the younger artist's creative genius to take off. Taban lo Liyong's aim has never been to imitate Tutuola but to use the latter's achievements as a source of creative inspiration. This, as we can see, he has done extremely well.

LO LIYONG AND AFRICAN ORAL LITERATURE

The greatest source of influence on lo Liyong, however, is not Tutuola but African oral literary tradition, particularly the Lwo version of this tradition. A strict contrast is, of course, not intended here between

Tutuola's art on the one hand and oral literature on the other because both are actually complementary. What is being stressed is the degree of influence exerted separately on lo Liyong by the body of folktales lo Liyong has known independent of Tutuola. Tutuola has shown lo Liyong a creative approach to folk tradition but lo Liyong has on his own learnt many things from folklore.

One of the first things lo Liyong must have learnt is that a folktale is always told with a purpose and that it always has an addressee who is either explicitly stated or implied. These are precisely the conditions which govern lo Liyong's fiction. All of his stories in the tradition of folktale aim both to entertain and to teach. These two aims, as correctly pointed out by Ruth Finnegan with regard to folklore, are always combined even when it appears as if entertainment is the sole purpose (350–51). The entertainment is provided by the subject matter as well as by the various narrative devices employed in order to make the story interesting and beautiful. We shall examine these devices in due course, but it seems that even though folklore always entertains, its primary purpose nonetheless is to teach, to educate. Lo Liyong shares this view and affirms the primacy of the educational function of literature in the introduction to his second collection of short stories, *The Uniformed Man* (xiii–xiv).

Because those most in need of education are little children, the majority of the stories in *Fixions* address this class of society. Practically every story in this collection teaches a moral lesson. Some of these lessons are clearly spelled out, especially when a story is intended for children. This is, for example, the case with the piece that bears the long title, "Ododo Pa Apwoyo Gin Ki Lyech." In this story, Jumbe Elephant and Master Hare are close friends. The elephant is a hard worker while the hare is very lazy. During the planting season the elephant cultivates a large field of peas. The hare, on the other hand, roasts his peas, eats them, and pretends he has planted them. At harvest time the hare secretly steals from the farm of the elephant. He does this successfully for a time but is caught in the end. The story closes in this manner: "You see, if you do bad things, you may escape discovery once, but one day you will be caught. If you are caught, you will be punished. That is what my story about Master Hare and his friend Jumbe Elephant teaches us" (75).

When the moral of a story is not explicitly spelled out in this manner, it is usually through a simple parable that is easy enough to understand. This is what happens in the case of the two stories earlier discussed: the parable of the chief's daughter who would marry only a "complete gentleman" and that of the rich old man who wants to experience poverty and suffering. This is likewise the case in the story "Stare Decisis Deo," whose first title is most revealing: "Parable from Another Land."

This story, so simply written, is against racial discrimination in general and against American racism in particular; and it begins with a telling epigraph:

> Accept him.
> As he is.
> > So sang the Dove. (22)

This epigraph is later reinforced at the end of the story, which closes in this poetic manner:

> Everyday the Dove sings:
> > Accept them, as they are.
> > Accept them, as they are.
> > > as they are.
> > > as they are (24).

But there are also instances when the lessons or moral of a story is accessible to only a mature and experienced adult. In such cases, the author uses subtle irony and satire and at times even the complex method of the absurd, as shown in the next chapter. The stories "Fixions," "He and Him," "Sages and Wages," "A Traveller's Tale," and to some extent "Tombe 'Gworong's Own Story" all fall within this category. Also, behind those stories with obvious morals often lurk other meanings not easily comprehensible to children. For example, a child might not know the symbolism involved in making the song above come from a dove and not any other bird except it is explained that the dove is a symbol of peace, mutual respect, acceptance, compromise. Similarly, the child might think that the story about the old man of Usumbura is only about "the curiosity that killed the cat." It has to be explained to him that the story is primarily concerned with the indomitable quest of man for knowledge even at great personal risks. Thus, both a child and an adult can equally learn from lo Liyong's stories, and this is itself characteristic of folktales, which usually have different levels of meaning.

The immediate concern of folktales is about human society, human beings, and their actions; but quite often the characters in folktales are not human beings in human societies but animals in animal environments. These animals, according to Finnegan, "act like human characters, experiencing human emotions, and yet the fact that they are also animals is not altogether lost sight of" (346). This device, which in Europe is associated with the fables of Aesop, is one of the folkloric characteristics of lo Liyong's stories. Animals play the leading role in many of the stories in this collection. Apart from the fact that the song of the dove bears the burden of the moral in "Stare Decisis Deo," for instance, the only other characters in this story are animals: two "friends"—monkey and python. Similarly, all the characters in "Ododo Pa Apwoyo Gin Ki Lyech" are animals. In addition, the famous tortoise of African folklore narratives who, according to the findings of Finnegan, "now aspires to white collar status in Southern Nigeria and attends adult education classes" (345), has already graduated in this story by lo Liyong and is called, albeit with irony, "Master Knowall, Doctor Witch-Doctor, the Honourable Doctor Tortoise, M. D., D.W.D., etc." (67). Of course, it is obvious that here lo Liyong is satirizing the African man's inordinate love for titles, titles that often sound incongruous and absurd.

In "Tombe 'Gworong's Own Story" animals also feature prominently. Animals are, for instance, competing in a race, and the trickster, chameleon, outwits the fastest runner, the hare, to claim victory. In the same story, lo Liyong exploits the African belief in witchcraft and we see human beings undergoing transformation to become animals. This story, which could easily serve as the index to characterization in the stories of lo Liyong, has completely obliterated the boundaries between human beings and animals and even between men and inanimate things. This is to stress the symbolic significance of his characters, all of whom, whether humans or animals, animate or inanimate, serve to act out human existence. The use of these characters, as illustrated by the ironic treatment of "Master Knowall, Doctor Witch-Doctor, the Honourable Doctor Tortoise, M. D., D.W.D., etc." shows how lo Liyong often handles the original folkloric motifs with a touch of genius and transforms them into something "worthy the nourishment and excitation of joyous wits"—one might add, sophisticated and aesthetically discriminating wits.

The human characters who appear in lo Liyong's stories also follow the pattern of such characters in folktales. These characters are often one-dimensional and they represent a specific idea. The old man of Usumbura represents wealth and well-being untainted by the least degree of want, while the old man of Kigali represents abject poverty and misery. In addition, the old man of Usumbura is depicted as kings usually are in African folktales. Kings always possess "exaggerated wealth and power" (Finnegan 355). Because the one-dimensional characters in folktales are merely representational, they often have no personal names. Actually, absolutely none of the human characters in *Fixions* possesses a name. It is either "an old man of Usumbura" or "another old man of Kigali" ("The Old Man of Usumbura And His Misery"); "she" and "her daughter" ("Sages and Wages") or "he" the farmer and "him" the urban man ("He And Him"). Similarly, it is "the victim" ("Lexicographicide"), or "an Italo-American woman, a Negro bum, and an African student" ("A Traveller's Tale"), or "the President" ("Fixions").

The purpose of denying these characters' individuality by not giving them names is, of course, to endow them with a universal quality. Folktales always prefer to deal in universals rather than in particulars; and because of this, the individual characters and incidents themselves are not what matter but the general ideas they help to inculcate into the audience. The immediate characters, incidents, and environments are of the moment and they consequently change from one culture to another, but the morals they teach are to some extent independent of the medium through which they are expressed and are everlasting. To individualize these characters and make them multidimensional, therefore, may distract from the universal truths they are meant to communicate.

An essential quality of the creative imagination, to borrow Shakespeare's expression, is the ability to create "out of airy nothing" and to give the resultant creature "a local habitation and a name." The field of creative imagination where this quality is exploited the most is undoubtedly folklore. A highly fertile imagination is indispensable to folklore because just as the realistic novel depends on the verifiable, so does folklore depend on fantasy. When one listens to folktales, one must of necessity suspend disbelief, because the most unverifiable, the most fantastic, the most incredible thing is presented matter-of-factly. Spirits and ghosts interact with human beings, and the latter can also transform into spirits and ghosts in order to operate in the spirit world. Animals and even inanimate objects possess human qualities. And in making all these possible, folklore makes no apologies and, in fact, gives no allowance for disbelief.

The same suspension of disbelief is required of us as we read the stories of lo Liyong. In "Lexicographicide," for instance, we have a dream world where all that happens is not only incredible but absurd. A child of seven leaves school because he realizes that "being in school was a waste of time." This youth, who describes himself as "an intellectual intelligentsia—convertible" is soon revealed to have borrowed every little bit of his body in the manner of the skull who borrows human parts in Tutuola's "The Complete Gentleman." In another story, "The Old Man of Usumbura And His Misery," misery, an abstract idea, is transformed into a concrete material object to be carried by the children of the rich old man. There is also the story of how human beings change themselves into leopards in order to cannibalize on their neighbors in "Tombe 'Gworong's Own Story."

Even in instances when we are not dealing with pure fantasy, we must still stretch our imagination far, before belief is possible. This is because lo Liyong is fond of the folkloric exaggeration that is achieved through the use of the comparative or the superlative degree of comparison. The old man of Usumbura, for example, is extremely rich and happy while the old man of Kigali is extremely poor and miserable. The family of the rich old man of Usumbura, which numbers sixty-five wives, one hundred and fifty-one sons, and one hundred and forty nine daughters, were all so wealthy and lucky that not even a single one of them ever felt sick! Also Jumbe Elephant and Master Hare are not simply friends, but "two great friends."

Lo Liyong also creates his superlative degree of comparison by using the famous folkloric simple device of repeating the same word twice or thrice: "The tree trunks were big, very big, bigger than a man's chest" (54); "Jumbe Elephant's mother was called Min-Jumbe. She was very very old" (55); "We want to plant peas, peas, peas. You must eat plenty of peas so that you grow big, big, big, like your father" (55).

Noticeable in some of these exaggerations is the characteristic folkloric device of contrast. The contrast is always simple and for this reason very effective. The wealth and happiness of the old man of Usumbura, for instance, are contrasted with the poverty and misery of the old man of Kigali. Jumbe Elephant's hard work is compared to the laziness of Master Hare. The simplicity of the farmer is shown against the background of the oversophistication of the urban man in "He And Him" (*Fixions* 31–38). In each instance, the exaggeration either underscores the moral of the story, as in the tale of the elephant and the hare (which teaches that laziness does not pay), or it helps to sharpen the edge of the intended satire, as happens in the case of the farmer and the urban man. The urban man is so sophisticated that he departmentalizes practically everything, including space. His house is partitioned into tiny cubicles and we have not only the usual divisions for lounging, reading, dining, and sleeping but also separate cubicles individually for yawning, coughing, sneezing, and smoking. The *redutio ad absurdum* does not end here. When dining, there is a separate room for picking up the meat, another for chewing it, and a third for swallowing it. But the absurdity of this attitude of oversophistication, overdepartmentalization, which is being ridiculed comes out most clearly in the procedure for eating salad: "You eat the salad first and the dressing later" (36).

The stories of lo Liyong rarely have introductions. They begin straight with the action, and this accounts for their brevity and effectiveness. In at least two instances, however, his stories start with the famous folkloric beginning formula that always sets the action of the tale in some remote, unspecified time in the past. The story "Ododo pa Apwoyo Gin Ki Lyech," for instance, begins in this manner: "Long, long ago, when the world was very young, there lived two great friends" (53).

This formula is slightly modified in "The Old Man of Usumbura And His Misery," whose first sentence reads like this: "There was an old man of Usumbura who was very rich" (1).

Since folk narratives are usually set in some distant past, the narrator is in most cases precluded from being a witness or a participant in the action, which in any case might have taken place in an animal kingdom or in a spirit world. Thus, the third-person impersonal narrative is the traditional form in folklore. Tutuola's predominant use of the first-person narrator is the author's own peculiar style and was adopted probably to achieve intimacy and authenticity. In traditional folklore, however, the third-person narrative is the usual mode. Except for the occasion within the story, "Lexicographicide," when the first-person narrative is used as we read the personal notes of the character himself (42–45), all of the stories in *Fixions* are written in this folkloric third-person impersonal narrative.

Folklore is perhaps the most free of all forms of literature. Just as it recognizes no boundaries between the believable and the fantastic, between human beings, animals, and spirits, so it recognizes no limitation as to what it can treat as its subject. It has no shame and no taboos even though it is always moral. These qualities are also characteristic of the stories of lo Liyong, many of which treat violence and sex in a matter-of-fact manner. The treatment of childbirth, for instance, in "Sages and Wages" would be shocking and could appear callous to one who is not aware that the author is using the method of the absurd to depict the absurdity of a situation in which people actually profane the beliefs they supposedly hold sacred (*Fixions* 11–20). However, the parody of the American Declaration of Independence in the epigraph preceding the story already prepares one's mind for the shock to follow. Also, the prudish reader will be shocked by lo Liyong's story "A Traveller's Tale," which narrates the story of a sex-starved woman who "wanted to be raped" and "looked forward to it." This woman's desire is fulfilled in a most bizarre manner when she is publicly raped at a subway station overpass in New York. This woman's hypocrisy, which is the object of satire, reveals itself clearly in her complaints: "Why did he want to rape me? me, a mother of four?, and among all these people?" (51). The marriage of violence and sex in the stories of lo Liyong is typified by the already cited incident regarding the chief's daughter in "Tombe 'Gworong's Own Story." The daughter is in the end disappointed by her "complete gentleman," so she murders him and cuts him up into pieces, but before she succeeds in throwing away the pieces "the man part of the dead man . . . jumps and disappears right into her woman part." The moral behind this story has already been explained, and it is this that saves it from degenerating into mere pornography. Thus, even though lo Liyong recognizes no taboos and he treats sex and violence in a very frank manner, his stories none-theless remain highly moral in the same way as folklore maintains its morality.

His love of riddles and puzzles, no doubt, derives from his intimate acquaintance with folklore. Riddles and puzzles constitute a major genre in oral literature and they help to train the minds of the young. The puzzle associated with the straw, which symbolizes misery in "The Old Man of Usumbura And His Misery," comes most readily to mind. Also, as Donald Carter points out, the collection's title story, "Fixions" is itself a puzzle (142). Similarly, the meanings of some stories, such as "Sages and Wages" and "Lexicographicide," constitute puzzles.

Finally, following the example of folklore, the language of lo Liyong is for the most part simple, enriched with local imagery, and is poetic after the manner of folk songs. Simple words and constructions, as opposed to complex ones, predominate his sentences. Direct speech is cast in a very simple way: "When he arrived, Python called aloud to his mother like this: 'Mummy, mummy, bring some food. My friend, Mon-key, has arrived' " (22). The imagery in lo Liyong's stories are also simple and are drawn from the local cultural background. Monkey, for in-stance, thinks to himself: "I will eat to death" (22), and Jumbe Ele-phant's mother advises her son to eat and grow big so that he will have heavy steps that will be heard when he is still "a river away" (55). Some of the simple imagery are derived from modern reality. Python, we are told, coils himself into a heap "like tyres of different sizes" (24), and the skin on the body of Jumbe Elephant's mother is wrinkled "like a flat bicycle tube" (55). We should also note that these are simple similes. The use of imagery from modern cultural reality reflects the normal tendency of folklore to constantly update itself with regard to language and imagery so that successive generations will continue to understand and profit by it.

The poetic quality of lo Liyong's language has been examined while discussing the elements of folk song that make the story "The Old Man of Usumbura And His Misery" so rhythmical and poetic. Simple phras-ing, repetition and refrain were the elements noted. We might add here that after the old man has found his misery, the tone of the story changes very appropriately as the author introduces elements of folk elegy. The beginning exclamatory and mournful sound "Oh!" followed by a complaint—all of which is reminiscent of lamentations at burials—starts frequently to punctuate the narrative. On page 7, for instance, we read: "Oh, the fatal end. Death, you have reaped a rich harvest. Death that levels all. Alas, who will inform the rich man of Usumbura?" On page 8, we have: "Oh, the fatal messenger that should never arrive." And on page 9, we get this: "Oh, misery that curiosity brings."

If this elegaic "Oh" introduces an appropriate mournful tone to "The

Old Man of Usumbura And His Misery," the simple repetition of the song of the dove in "Stare Decisis Deo," which has earlier been quoted, adds beauty to the quiet command the dove issues. The simple simile and the onomatopoeic sounds in "Ododo pa Apwoyo Gin Ki Lyech" make the story more hilarious: "Then, he broke wind like this: 'Doo-oot,' just like the blowing of a trumpet or a school bugle" (69). Or "Jumbe closed his eyes tightly and swallowed like this: 'Boo-rooch!'" (70). Poetic beauty is further created through carefully and rhythmically balanced sentences such as this: "But once a boy is yours, foolish or clever, poor or rich, obedient or disobedient, you will keep him and help him" (70).

The frequent reoccurrence within a passage of words repeated either for emphasis or to create a superlative degree of comparison in the process of making an exaggeration also helps to give a passage a certain poetic cadence. The following repeated words and phrases, for instance, punctuate the first three pages of "Ododo pa Apwoyo Gin Ki Lyech": "long, long ago," "big, very big, bigger than," "rained, but rained hard," "very, very old," "grow big, big, big," "grows small-small-small-small" (54–56). Thus, the beauty of the imagery and poetry in lo Liyong's stories, as has been seen, is achieved mainly because the author strives to imitate the simplicity of the language of folk narratives and folk songs.

CONCLUSION

Two observations naturally emerge from the above discussion. The first is that literature is by and large governed by a politicoeconomic imperative. The necessity for the colonial subjects of Africa to send a clear pro-independence message to the world compelled their writers to shift from the ambiguity of folklore phantasmagoria to the clarity of the realistic style. Having regained a measure of economic, political, and cultural confidence, African writers have largely returned three decades after independence to the ambiguity of folkloric fantasy and myth-making. The second observation is that, judging from the example of lo Liyong, the return to origins movement in African literature is a most desirable trend, being aesthetically exciting and rewarding. He aptly points the direction the literary return to origins should take. His collection, *Fixions*, demonstrates the originality of a genius who has appropriated the devices of oral literature and has written wonderful short stories that at the same time qualify as folktales of the highest caliber.

NOTES

1. See also Lalage Bown's *Two Centuries of African English* and O. R. Dathorne's "African Writers of Eighteenth Century" for an elaborate discussion of this issue.

2. Rene Wellek and Austin Warren also hold Bown's view, as is evident in their *Theory of Literature* (21).

3. The critical study of the nature and aesthetic function of oral tradition within written literature also started around the late sixties. Bernth Lindfors's *Folklore in Nigerian Literature* is of special interest because it not only analyses the phenomenon but also evaluates other critics' attempts to grapple with it.

4. Taban lo Liyong's first collection of short stories, *Fixions*, was published in 1969 but references in this study are to the 1978 reprint.

5. Pages 17–31 in the 1977 Faber and Faber paperback edition.

10

Fixions: A Study in the Absurd

CHARACTERISTICS OF ABSURDIST AFRICAN LITERATURE

The absurd, both as an element of satire and as a style in its own right, has always been manifest in African literature both oral and written. However, in the effort to redirect the focus of African literature and criticism from Eurocentricism to one informed by African aesthetics, vocal African critics like Chinweizu, Onwuchekwa Jemie, and Ihechukwu Madubuike have persistently condemned the encouragement of modernist tendencies in African writing: "If African literature is not to become a transplanted fossil of European literature, it needs to burst out of the straightjacket of anglomodernist poetry and of the 'well made novel'" (239). Their advice to African critics is that the critics must "liberate themselves from their mesmerization with Europe and its critical canons" (302) and must stop encouraging "the manufacture of a still, pale, anemic, academic poetry, slavishly imitative of 20th-century European modernism, with its weak preciosity, ostentatious erudition, and dunghill piles of esoterica and obscure allusions, all totally cut off from the vital nourishment of our African traditions" (3).[1]

The antagonism of these critics against modernism appears to be based on seemingly incontrovertible evidence, provided by Chinweizu, the group's spokesman, in an essay titled "Prodigals, Come Home!":

There was a specific burden of tradition that Western modernism reacted against in its revolt. But however familiar we may be with all that; however familiar we may be with that tradition or with the various modernist revolts against it (Symbolism, Dadaism, Surrealism, Futurism, etc.) they are not part of *our* history. They do not belong to our *past*. (8)

However, the view Lewis Nkosi expressed on the matter in his book *Tasks and Masks* appears to me to be closer to the truth:

It is fairly obvious that a 'modernist' movement is now taking shape in Africa which may create links with modernist movements in other parts of the world, chiefly in Europe, in North and South America. Nevertheless, to see what is now occurring in African fiction merely as an extension of a development occurring somewhere else is seriously to misjudge the nature of the African phenomenon, its roots and its ideological compulsions. For one thing the modernist movement in Africa faces both ways at once; it faces forward to the latest innovations in fiction as well as back-ward to the roots of African tradition. Indeed, some of the experiments being carried out in African fiction owe nothing to European and American examples, but achieve their queer effects by returning us to African traditional sources and by exploiting certain properties of native language. (54)[2]

Modernism indisputably exists in African art and literature, but its historical causation, philosophical orientation, and stylistic characteristics are not the same as those of Western modernism. We are, for instance, familiar with the Western literature of the absurd, the purpose of which is to depict man as "a bewildered being in an incomprehensible universe" (Holman 3). For the absurdist in the West, man sees no purpose in life, and as Martin Esslin in *The Theatre of the Absurd* attests, man is "bewildered" because he has been "cut off from his religious, metaphysical, and transcendental roots," and as a result, he "is lost" and "all his actions [have] become senseless, absurd, useless" (5). As Esslin also reports, in 1942 Albert Camus, one of the chief theorists and practitioners of the tradition, "was calmly putting the question why, since life had lost all meaning, man should not seek escape in suicide" (5). Camus was indeed a major voice seeking a solution to absurdity, but it is significant that suicide was an answer he once seriously considered.

The root of the existential agony of the philosophers of the absurd lies in the spiritual depression existing at the time in the Euro-American world, a depression brought about by the lessons of history. By the forties, Western man had come to the realization that he was not advancing in civilization, but was actually getting more and more barbaric, more and more destructive, more and more incapable of learning from history. The numerous European wars had not taught him the way to avoid the first World War, nor had that war provided him with the wisdom to prevent Hitler and the incalculable carnage of the second World War. The economic depressions he could not prevent further undermined his faith in himself and in addition worsened his standard of living. With his self-assurance eroded, Western man inevitably plunged into an agonizing spiritual crisis characterized by pessimism and despair. This was the mood that gave rise to the literature of the absurd in Europe and America. The poetic, dramatic, and fictional manifestations of this literature are evident in the works of its most distinguished representatives: Samuel Beckett, Eugene Ionesco, Arthur Adamov, Jean Genet, Edward Albee, Joseph Heller, Thomas Pynchon, Kurt Vonnegut, Jr., John Barth, Harold Pinter, and others.

Contemporary African literature of the absurd, on the one hand, is undoubtedly a manifestation of the worldwide malaise dominating all spheres of modern life. The general dissatisfaction with politics as it is run the world over, the arms race that continues to produce sophisticated weapons with overkill capacities, the worldwide economic depression that daily erodes the quality of life, and the calm with which the world receives news of mounting crimes and violence are the factors that have combined to produce the pessimistic, cynical man of today for whom the absurd is an indisputable reality. These are also the factors that inspire absurdist literature. The malaise may not be as intense in Africa today as it was in Europe and North America, before, between, and after the world wars, but that perhaps in part explains why there are not as many absurdist artists and writers in Africa as in Europe and North America.

Apart from this general malaise, however, the African of today is a product of a specific historical and racial experience molded by slavery, colonization and neocolonialism. The African had expected that with independence and blackman ruling blackman, the quality of life would change drastically for the better. Expectations might have been naive, even utopian, but that is the reason dissatisfaction with postindependence reality is all the more intense. A country like Nigeria since independence has tried the parliamentary, the military, and the republican systems of government and has experienced in the process over nine officially acknowledged successful and attempted military coups d'état and a civil war. The high level of misgovernment attended by official corruption, misappropriation, and embezzlement, together with armed robbery, bank holdups, religious and student riots, and city traffic chaos all show that the reality of postindependence is a far cry from the utopian heaven it seemed to have promised. The degree of pessimism and cynicism this disparity between expectations and reality has engendered can be measured by the indifference of the average

Nigerian to matters of public good. This is a society where human corpses stay exposed in public places for days before individuals and government officials overcome their complacency and act.

It should therefore not surprise anybody that conditions such as prevail in Nigeria and in other African countries in varying degrees should produce writers with "pessimistic vision" (Nkosi 55) who feel that the most appropriate way to deal with "the widespread dislocation and loss of equilibrium in modern African society" (Nkosi 56) and with "the conditions and absurdities of neo-colonial Africa" (Chinweizu, "Beyond European Realism" 2) is through an absurd art. This is inevitable particularly when these writers are not only familiar with Western absurdist literature but also have an oral tradition in the absurd.[3] In fact, the world debt crisis of the late eighties and early nineties is actually creating more fertile ground for absurdist art and literature in Africa. Nigeria, for instance, is a country that is extremely rich in both natural and human resources, but in recent years it has been finding it increasingly impossible to provide the basic needs of her citizens. And this is not because it does not earn income, but because it spends the greater percentage of her billions of oil dollars in repaying and servicing both genuine and dubious debts owed to the industrialized nations of the so-called first world.

In any case, Amos Tutuola's fiction is a sure link between African oral and written literary traditions and it should reveal the connection, if any, between African folklore and African modern practice of the absurd. An examination of *The Palm-Wine Drinkard* (1952), for example, suggests that this novel is predicated on the assumption that the absurd is an acceptable mode of oral narration. Were it not true, it would have been impossible to accept a fantasy that it is conceivable for a man to love palm-wine to the extent that he would risk the safety, security, and comforting certainty of this familiar world to go into the mysterious and dangerous bush of ghosts in search of a dead palm-wine tapper. Here we have a man who so loves life and pleasure that he seeks to guarantee his pleasure by starting an undertaking that is sure not only to eliminate pleasure but endanger life itself. This undertaking is so fabulously absurd that nobody takes it as other than a mythical allegory, but it is important all the same to remind ourselves of this underlying absurdity.

But for this acceptance of the absurd, it would have been totally unimaginable to consider a situation in a Yoruba culture, in which the hero, a first male child, has not only raised "pleasure to the status of work" (Achebe, "Work and Play" 26), but is actually encouraged in this anticultural tendency by his father whose duty—his wealth notwithstanding—is to uphold tradition. Since all family responsibilities at a father's death devolve on the first male child, Yoruba culture uncompromisingly insists that the first child must be responsible. But here we have the case of a complete reversal that makes nonsense of tradition. To a Yoruba this is an absurd reversal of values. Absurdity also underscores the fantasy that suggests that a child could be conceived in and delivered from a swollen thumb rather than from a womb. Finally, if it were not for the assumption in *The Palm-Wine Drinkard* that the illogical and the absurd are native to oral narrative, nobody would accept the fact that a hero who possesses the magical power to transform himself into a boat or a bird would allow himself to be embarrassed on several occasions when this power is all he needs to find food or escape ordeals at the hands of enemies.

The underlying absurdity in the fantasy of Tutuola's novels would, of course, cease to matter if we abandoned literal interpretation for the more fruitful allegorical and mythical analysis of the sort that has been undertaken by numerous critics such as Chinua Achebe in "Works and Play in Tutuola's *The Palm-Wine Drinkard*" and John Coates in "The Inward Journey of the Palm-Wine Drinkard," just to mention two. All the same, it should not be forgotten that the literal understanding of a story always precedes its depth analysis. A thorough study of African oral literature will probably reveal that the style of the absurd is more prevalent than we indeed have suspected.

The Palm-Wine Drinkard, for instance, contains a story that is common to the folklore of many nationalities in Africa. This is the story about a girl who would marry only the ideal man—the "complete gentleman," as Tutuola puts it. This story, which reveals man's universal search for perfection, is narrated with absurdist details wherein shock, horror, and pornography are treated matter-of-factly. Tutuola's heroine pursues her "complete gentleman" to the bush of ghosts in a journey that is marked by increasingly terrifying episodes. In a characteristically absurdist fashion, the "complete gentleman," who is the most handsome man alive, is progressively dismembered as he returns borrowed human parts and organs, until final horror is attained and he becomes a mere skull. What is more significant is that all this is told in a straightforward, realistic language that does not suggest that anything is amiss. Yet all is amiss: the world has been turned upside down, evil has become more attractive than good, and human beings have been reduced to machines with spare parts. This motif, as we have seen in the preceding chapter, is also used by Taban lo Liyong in his absurdist short stories "Tombe 'Gworong's Own Story" and "Lexicographicide." Kole Omotoso's *The Combat* (1972) has also been recognized by many critics as an allegory reflecting the absurdity of the Nigerian fratricidal civil war of 1967–70 (Nicols 220, Dash 49–50, Oladitan 16). Similarly, Femi Osofisan's *Kolera Kolej* (1975) has been analyzed as an absurdist and sur-realist depiction of the postindependence deformed reality of Nigeria (Balogun, "Kolera Kolej: A Surrealistic Political Satire").

Contemporary African literature of the absurd, therefore, developed as a reaction to the general world malaise and the specific absurd con-ditions of modern Africa. European absurdist tradition and African oral absurdist literature have also played major roles in fostering its growth.

African absurdist literature, however, differs in style from the Eu-ropean tradition. The latter is characterized by "extreme forms of illogic, inconsistency, nightmarish fantasy," abandonment of "usual or rational devices and the use of nonrealistic form" (Holman 2–3) in the effort to create an "anti-style" that would present absurdity "in being" (Hinch-liffe 10) so that absurdity is reflected in absurd style. Except, perhaps, in a few instances such as is the case with two of lo Liyong's short stories, "Sages and Wages" and "Lexicographicide" (*Fixions* 11–20, 39–45), African absurdist literature in general does not aim at creating an "anti-style" to make absurd form reflect absurd content. Rather, follow-ing the example of African oral literature of the absurd as reflected in *The Palm-Wine Drinkard*, modern African absurdist writers use nor-mal, rational, and realistic devices combined with hyperbole, irony, and satire to convey the absurd. There is, of course, a basic use of fantasy, as in all absurdist traditions, because without suspension of disbelief absurdist literature is hardly possible. Other than this, the language of narration is realistic even though it is heightened by exaggeration and satiric irony. Femi Osofisan, for instance, presents in his *Kolera Kolej* (1975) a dream world where common sense has been totally displaced by illogical reasoning, a world ruled by an absurd logic involving the reversal of all standards of judgment, be they aesthetic or ethical, po-litical or social.

The country "Kolera Kolej" is ruled by a cabinet of ministers com-posed exclusively of professors, who show an amazingly high degree of ignorance and illiteracy. A professor of geophysical sciences, for ex-ample, cannot tell whether Holland is only "a town in Russia" or "a fishing company in Denmark" (*Kolera Kolej* 91). In this country, as-sassins are required to book appointments with their prospective vic-tims to arrange the date of assassination. Here it is also considered mean to be faithful to one's wife, and to be patriotic is to qualify for a traitor. These and many more are the characteristics of the absurd and surreal world of *Kolera Kolej*, where wanton murder is considered as normal. Nonetheless, all these absurdities are conveyed by Osofisan in a highly lucid and realistic language that at times reaches an enviable height of ironic lyricism, as in the following extract that vividly recalls T. S. Eliot's poem "The Love Song of J. Alfred Prufrock":

He was thinking: there is a warning of storm in the air: but they will tell us, there is a time for everything: perhaps even a protocol of passion, of token fury and patriotic curses: a time also like this moment, tense and stripped for harmattan, for the cracking lips of wanton flesh.

My heart is dry like the drought. (50)

Kole Omotoso, who in *The Combat* (1972) depicts a world which is no less absurd than that in *Kolera Kolej*, is even more realistic in his style. Unlike Osofisan, Omotoso does not plunge us immediately into an unrecognizable, absurd world. Rather, he guides us gently into a very real world where, however, the trivial leads imperceptibly into the tragic; where realism is gradually replaced by fantasy; and where logic unnoticeably yields to illogicality. The world of *The Combat* is the absurd world where it is possible for a child to have two biological fathers. It is a world where two "bosom friends" would engage in an internationally sponsored and refereed combat, a world where a person is treasured only after death.

In what we might therefore describe as its "unabsurdist" mode of presenting the absurd, African absurdist literature is not unique. It closely resembles the style of the American novelists of the absurd who, according to Charles B. Harris, use the traditional novelistic conventions of characterization, language, and plot in an ironic reflexive manner that employs burlesque and parody. Harris says that "the absurdist novel of the sixties in America is rarely so total in its commitment to absurdity as are the French plays, nor does it completely abandon the use of rational devices." He further states that American novelists of the absurd "seldom employ what Leslie Fieldler calls 'the fallacy of imitative form' by attempting to reproduce absurdity through an 'anti-style'.... American novelists of the absurd ... while they sometimes exaggerate reality, seldom feel the need to distort it beyond recognition" (20–25).

The most significant distinction between African literature of the absurd and its Euro-American counterpart, however, lies in the difference in their philosophical outlooks on life. Even though according to Harris, American absurdist novelists "do not insist that despair represents the only possible human response to life's absurdity," and even though these novelists in fact believe in the possibility of love as a way of coping with absurdity, it is significant that the same novelists do not have even the faith that the existentialists have in man in a world where there is no God: "To the contemporary novelists of the absurd ... man is far too puny and helpless for self-reliance" (Harris 31). The French Theater of the Absurd on its part is deeply steeped in despair and pessimism. Thus, whereas the European absurdist sees life as being absurd and meaningless, so absurd and meaningless, in fact, that he contemplates suicide as a solution, the absurdist in Africa is like the Afro-American outsider who does not accept "absurdity as being so normal that he believes in nothingness' (Lester 93). The African absurdist writer does not believe that life in itself is absurd, meaningless. As a matter of fact, life to him is quite meaningful; what can be absurd and meaningless are individuals and situations. The conditions, the instances, the personalities, and the attitudes that deprive life of this meaning that he values so much are the things he ridicules in his works by exposing the absurdity inherent in them. Ultimately, therefore, the absurd for the African fulfills the same purpose as satire—a way of correction. The African absurdist may have a pessimistic, cynical vision but he has not yet despaired.

The corrective objective of African absurdist literature on the one hand, and this literature's "realistic, unabsurdist" style on the other hand, obviously begs the question as to what constitutes the difference between satire and absurdist literature. There is in fact a close similarity between the aims and methods of both, but the distinction is also clear. Satire can indeed employ the absurd as one of its methods, but that which is satirized is not necessarily absurd. Objects of satire are usually human frailties and social imperfections. Jonathan Swift's aim in *Gulliver's Travels* was not to portray a world that was totally absurd, but to satirize imperfect—let's even say absurd—aspects of an otherwise sane world. Also, even though characterization in the novels of Chukwuemeka Ike is usually absurd in the process of satirizing Nigerian University intellectuals, the academic community that is the focus of his novels is never presented as being absurd in its entirety, nor are the stylistic devices in the novel, apart from characterization, pervaded with absurdity.

In the literature of the absurd, on the other hand, that which is depicted is always wholly absurd. The ironic realistic language of *Kolera Kolej* and *The Combat* does not for a moment deceive us into accepting any aspects of the worlds of these novels as being normal. On the contrary, the realism of the language only heightens by an ironic contrast the absurdity of the worlds of these novels. Using a calm, unruffled, realistic language to present absurdity as Osofisan and Omotoso have done is perhaps a more effective way of emphasizing absurdity than committing "the fallacy of imitative form" in an effort to make an absurdist style reflect absurd content in an "anti-style." Thus, satire is only partially absurdist—if at all—in content and form, whereas absurdist literature is totally absurdist in content and form even though the form may masquerade as realistic, "unabsurdist." A "realistic" language that heightens absurdity through the force of its ironic contrast is ultimately a shade different from the realistic language of the realistic novel.

We can therefore differentiate African literature of the absurd from European absurdist literature and from satire.

TABAN LO LIYONG: THE ABSURDIST

Taban lo Liyong is an exciting avant-garde writer who refuses to be tied to any traditional literary models. As already discussed in the preceding chapter, although lo Liyong acknowledges his indebtedness to both Tutuola and African oral literature from which he claims he draws inspiration, his attitude to these sources is not slavish but creative. Like most avant-garde artists, lo Liyong proceeds in his creative writing from the premise that literary models existing before him are no longer adequate to express the reality of his time. An artist who accepts without question existing artistic traditions is not likely to create anything new. The Italian Futurists, for instance, announced their appearance with a provocative manifesto that proclaimed: "We want to demolish museums, libraries, fight against moralism, feminism, and all opportunistic and utilitarian cowardices. . . . Set the library stacks on fire! Turn the canals in their course to flood the museum vaults!" (quoted in Howe 170–71).

The call to destroy museums and burn libraries was, of course, only a symbolic gesture on the part of the futurists who knew that nothing new could be created until the artists turned away from traditional models. This also was the point the Russian writer, Yevgeny Zamyatin, was making when in his essay "On Literature, Revolution, Entropy, and Other Matters," he said that "the formal character of a living literature is the same as its inner character: it denies what everyone knows and what I have known until this moment. It departs from the canonical tracks, from the broad highway. . . . Let yesterday's cart creak along the well-paved highways. The living have strength enough to cut away their yesterday" (111).

Among African writers, lo Liyong is perhaps the one who best understands the challenge of "a living literature." He perpetually experiments by synthesizing old and new methods with the hope of creating a style that is uniquely suited to his themes. In a story called "Sages and Wages," for example, he has at one point a sentence with an unusual syntax that has been equalled and surpassed by the American writer, Donald Barthelme, whose story titled "Sentence" is a one-sentence story covering eight pages. What is important, however, is that, given lo Liyong's independent approach to creative writing and his taste for avant-gardist experimentations, it is only to be expected that he would explore the exciting artistic possibilities of the mode of the absurd.[4]

Taban lo Liyong's collection of short stories, *Fixions*, can be rightly described as an "African Short Fiction of the Absurd." There is absurdity in the use of details. For instance, in a story with the intriguing title, "Lexicographicide," a character details his experience of being waylaid by robbers, who most politely demand to have:

> my coat and its pockets, my eyeglasses and handles (and case too, if I had any), my watch, and its winder, and straps, my shoes and the strings as well, my socks (the holes and smell too are good for them), my trousers (buttons and buttonholes included), the zip too was worth their trouble, if I had a belt, that was also one of their specialties, my shirt, tie, tie-pin, my vest, and my underwear. (43–44)

Hardly any reader can miss the absurdity in the act of robbers demanding, among other things, a victim's pair of socks solely because they covet the smell and the holes in the socks. An element that further heightens the absurdity is the contrast between the intention of the thieves and the language employed by them. It is highly unusual for thieves in the process of robbing a man of all that he possesses to speak in such a refined, delicate, and polite manner as would make one think they were gentlemen performing a service for which one should be grateful. The details of this waylaid character's dream, in which he is cannibalistically devoured by his creditors, further reveal greater absurdity. The passage recalls the shocking declaration by the narrator of "Tombe 'Gworong's Own Story," who says: "I am a Tombe 'Gworong—that is, of the tribe that eats people" (26). Later on in this latter story, we read about the overdemanding daughter of a chief who, like the heroine of Tutuola's tale, wants to marry only a perfect, ideal husband. As we already know from Tutuola's version, she finally finds a person "who fulfilled all her prescription of what her man should be," but when they were about to sleep and he strips, she discovers that he is as ordinary as the men she had rejected. In annoyance she "got out a knife and cut him to pieces. When she was going to throw the cut pieces away, the man part of the dead man jumped about dancing and singing a song, nodding his head. It finally jumped and disappeared right into her woman part" (29).

The absurdity in these passages and in those similar to them is not just in the shocking act of cannibalism itself but in the manner in which it is described. The act is presented in such a calm, deliberate manner as if there were nothing to it, as if it were the most mundane of things. Cannibalism is a total negation of human civilization, a negation of all that man stands for; and the ease with which it is accepted in these passages is absurd if only because such an acceptance is totally unthinkable.

Often the absurd is created through the use of exaggeration. In "Lexicographicide," for instance, we are informed that a child decided to leave school at the age of seven "on the ground that being in school was a waste of time" (40). In another story with the mouthful title "Ododo pa Apwoyo Gin Ki Lyech," a female character so much liked the food prepared by her host that "she ate, and ate, and ate, till she even ate one of her fingers" (61).

Sometimes, lo Liyong exploits human weaknesses to create an absurd story. For instance, man's habit of often going into extreme in his actions provides the occasion for the absurd and hilarious story titled "He and Him." Here the sophisticated urban white man with his tendency to overdepartmentalize life to a rigid and illogical extent is made the object of ridicule. In the story a farmer from the country is paying a visit to his friend in the city. The host is the typical affluent, sophisticated, departmentalizing urban white man, whose house is so full of amenities and conveniences that apart from the regular separate rooms for sleeping, dining, reading, lounging, and so forth, he also has separate cubicles: one for smoking, another for yawning, a third for sneezing, a fourth for coughing, and so on. The absurdity of the situation is further heightened by the fact that the town man rigidly enforces the use of these amenities. Once he commands his farmer friend, saying; "Yawn away all you like here, as freely as you like. In the future if you feel it coming, make a dash for this place. These amenities are here to be used, and must be used, otherwise how can we justify their existence?" (35–36). Thus, we can see that the departmentalizing white man (as indeed any other departmentalizing man, black or white) has not only created amenities for his convenience but has also made himself a slave to these amenities. This is what lo Liyong is attacking with his method of the absurd. This is what he is inviting the reader to laugh at.

In fact, while reading stories by lo Liyong one cannot help but laugh. One laughs, for example, when the folly of prejudice is ridiculed in the story "Stare Decisis Deo," which explores a motif common to the folklore of many African countries. This story depicts hypocrisy and racism using the form of a parable. On a Christmas day Monkey visits his friend, Python. The latter prepares a feast and invites his guest to eat. Monkey rushes at the food, being very hungry, but he is ordered to go back and wash his hands. Monkey complies but his host is not satisfied with the washed hands. Monkey rewashes his hands but his host still remains dissatisfied. This repeatedly goes on until Monkey takes a butcher knife and scrapes off the offending black skin in his hands. Monkey consequently returns to the table with his hands dripping blood, but Python finally dismisses him with racist arrogance, saying: "How can you be so uncultured? So unintelligent? Don't touch my food with your blood. I am no cannibal" (23).

A year passed and it is the turn of Python to pay a visit to his good friend Monkey on the Christmas day. Monkey prepares a delicious feast and invites his guest to table. Python starts to eat but Monkey does not like his guest's sitting posture and requests him to seat himself properly. Python tries again and again but repeatedly fails to satisfy his host. With a familiar racist condescension, Monkey orders Python to "get seated like other folks" and to learn "to sit properly inside a house" (24). In the process of sitting upright at table rather than coiling, Python's head pierces through the roof. Meanwhile Monkey eats the food alone, takes a cutlass and chops off seven feet from Python's tail. Significantly, during both of these Christmas visits, the peace-loving dove keeps singing to the hearing of both friends its words of wisdom:

> "Accept him,
> As he is.
> Accept him,
> As he is" (22, 23, 24).

But as we have seen, the friends ignored the song of the dove and the result, of course, is a vicious cycle of laughable absurdities expressed through prejudice and discrimination. The poetic beauty of this story, achieved mainly through the simple device of repetition and parallel syntactical constructions, is striking and it recalls the passage earlier quoted from Osofisan's *Kolera Kolej*. Just as in Osofisan's novel, the aesthetic satisfaction derived from the poetry ironically contrasts with the story's unpleasant subject matter. Thus, the exposed absurdity is further highlighted.

The title story in lo Liyong's collection, "Fixions" (78–81), also paints a picture wherein a president of an African country receives in his secret chambers an envoy of a foreign nation in the middle of the night. This president had earlier requested aid to build a road and a bridge to his home, and the envoy now comes to report that the money for the project has arrived. Thereupon, the president concludes arrangements for the money to be diverted into his personal bank account and he is overjoyed for, as he says, "It should earn me quite a bit of interest" (79). The envoy then proceeds in a studied fashion to inquire about the state of the president's national security. Thereafter the envoy discloses that a coup d'état is secretly being hatched by the leader of the opposition in collaboration with the deputy president, and that the plotters intend to kill the president. Before departing, the envoy succeeds in putting the president in a state of seething rage. The story ends as the president is about to unleash a blood-thirsty, insane revenge on the supposed plotters.

All along the story strongly suggests that actually there is nobody plotting a coup, that the calculated lie is told with the aim of destabilizing the African country. Furthermore, the reader is aware that the malicious envoy succeeds only because he is not dealing with an African leader of worth but with this greedy fool of a president, who appears to be even more gullible, more naive than a mere child. This president is presented to be indeed no better than an animated cartoon being manipulated according to the wishes of the foreign envoy, his master. When a person—the more so the president of a whole nation—becomes a mere puppet, his life loses meaning, it becomes absurd. This story is an obvious satire on certain African heads of state represented here by the president. Furthermore, the situation that makes the reign of such ignorant, unpatriotic characters as the president possible is exposed for its absurdity.

Humor derived from an absurd situation also pervades the story titled "A Traveller's Tale," which presents a comic incident as the answer to the rape-wish of a sexually starved housewife. This woman is so starved of sex "she wanted to be raped. She looked forward to it" (49). At long last she finds an obliging Negro bum who, with her full cooperation and participation, rapes her on the open platform of a subway station in Harlem, New York, in the full view of waiting passengers. As if this were not enough, the situation is made even more hilariously absurd by the appearance of an African student who helps to complete the job half-done by the hasty Negro-bum. She is again raped on the same subway platform, and once more with her full cooperation and participation. The humor and the absurdity of the story are further heightened as it ends with the woman's shameless hypocrisy: "Why did he want to rape me?, me a mother of four?, and among all these people?" (51).

Just as hilariously absurd is the story "Sages and Wages." The absurd epigraph, which is a parody of the American Declaration of Independence, sets the tone of the story right from the start:

> We hold these as truths, self-evident:
> A reader must not yawn
> During the yarn
> Without the loss (of his head)
> Or that, of the writer's.
> *The Lay of the Ancient Optics Grinder.* (12)

After this epigraph a reader who expects a logical, meaningful narration will be disappointed because, of all the stories in the collection, "Sages and Wages" is easily the most heavily loaded with all sorts of absurdities. There is lexical and semantic absurdity: "I am still seventeen years old compared to the captain who accomplished the same distance in fifty-four seconds when her age is already forty, T t tra, l ab ba cir stan cum ces phy graph hmn l you she that this in on at aton afin onat thishe." (15)

There is absurdity of illogical reasoning. Here, for instance, is a conclusion without a premise:

that javelin I threw this morning fell just four inches beyond the point I threw yesterday, it is therefore a fair calculation that tomorrow, everything being equal, I should be in a position to throw just one-half inch beyond this point and the day after another one-half of one-half inch will bring me to the same distance as our captain. (14–15)

There is also the absurdity that derives from an improbable exaggeration. In one instance, a character makes this fabulous claim: "Three miles I can now run in exactly one minute" (15); and in another instance, the character asserts: "We must remember that they are athletes, now athletes do not 'sleep': they are forever athletizing: awake or dreaming" (18–19).

We also find the absurdity emanating from incongruous human behavior. The character who at the end of the story impersonates Jesus Christ acts like a madman: "He, on his own accord, taking off his tunic and waving it about like a wand, and exposing his sides to everybody around said: 'She is not dead' " (18).

The greatest absurdity of all, however, is that this ten-page story, which mixes facts with fantasy, reality with dream, makes absolutely no sense. No matter how one reads it, the story yields no meaning, and one is forced to conclude that perhaps the author simply wants to create an absurd meaningless story using an absurd meaningless style. This obvious deviation from the usual mode of rendering absurdity in African absurdist literature shows that lo Liyong, if he so wishes, can successfully employ the European absurdist mode of "anti-style" to make form reflect content.

At every stage in this story, lo Liyong manages to amuse the reader, although the humor tends to be profane. A woman who is in birth-labor and shown bound to a pillar would frequently cry out to her mother: "Mama, choke me! Choke me! and her mother would be at it till the eyes of both mother and daughter were red. But she was stronger than her mother, and the latter ended up by relaxing her grip before the daughter was weakened enough or had the satisfaction from the choking" (13).

Humor in these stories serves two traditional purposes: namely, to sustain reader's interest and to heighten the effect of satire, especially when absurdity reflects human culpability. Making oneself the slave of one's creation becomes all the more ridiculous after reading "He and Him," just as racism and discrimination are more distasteful after going through "Stare Decisis Deo." Similarly, Africans who read "Fixions" will become more critical of their puppet heads of state in the same way as the readers of "A Traveller's Tale" will have a greater abhorrence for hypocrisy. Thus, like Omotoso and Osofisan, lo Liyong has remained faithful to the optimistic vision of African oral literature of the absurd by making the absurd serve a satiric end. His stories, whatever the level of their absurdity, are optimistic and are postulated on the belief that absurdity can ultimately be overcome. This belief makes the need for the writer to communicate his abhorrence of absurdity in such a way as to be understood by his readers a determinant factor in the mode of rendering absurdity. Using the method of anti-style might be more intriguing, more ingenious, but communication will be for that reason more hampered; and for the absurdist with a satiric objective, communication is not negotiable. Hence lo Liyong, again like Omotoso and Osofisan, for the greater part has followed the example of African oral absurdist tradition by not abandoning "usual or rational devices" in rendering absurdity. He rarely resorted to "the use of none realistic forms," rather he predominantly presented the absurd in a "realistic," "unabsurdist" style.

One of the qualities that distinguish lo Liyong from Omotoso and Osofisan as absurdist writers is the former's greater sense of humor, which makes his readers escape the depressing experience of unrelieved absurdity that, for the most part, attends the reading of the works of the latter two. This difference is partially explained by the fact that Omotoso and Osofisan patronize the genre of the novel, which is by nature cumulative in the way it creates impression through a prolonged process of amassing details. On the other hand, the short story that lo Liyong uses achieves its effect with epiphanic brevity. Even after this generic explanation has been given, lo Liyong still appears a more lively writer who is more at ease in his narration.

The other distinction between these writers is that, where Omotoso and Osofisan still conceal their art for the greater part, lo Liyong in his characteristic lively manner deliberately reveals his technique. He begins "He and Him," for instance, by saying: "A story doesn't have to have many characters in it. In this one, for example, we have two people, and we feel they are enough" (32). Generally, he loves to be playful with his readers and even to tease and puzzle them. The story, "Tombe 'Gworong's Own Story," for instance, begins with this announcement: "To understand this story there are three things you must know" (26). Thereafter, he gives a lengthy explanation of the "three things" in four paragraphs of three-and-a-half pages. Finally, he tells "the story," and this covers only a paragraph of six-and-a-half lines. The reader is not only amazed at the disproportion in size between "the introduction" and "the story" but is also puzzled by the discovery that what purports to be "the story" is in fact only a footnote summary of the moral of the first of the "three things" earlier advanced to aid the reader's understanding of "the story." Thus, lo Liyong has, it seems, written a story that is not a story.

On the one hand, this might be lo Liyong, the absurdist, commenting on the failure of art, on the pretension of art that claims to create illusion of reality. Taban lo Liyong might be saying that here we have the example of a story that has failed in its most basic task of telling a story. If art cannot fulfill its basic purpose, then it becomes redundant, its existence is absurd. On the other hand, it could well be that the exact contrary is the case, that lo Liyong is emphasizing the importance of art by revealing its inner complexities. It would appear that he has played a simple trick on his reader because each of the "three things" given to aid the reader's comprehension of "the story" is by itself a full story. In effect, we have not one story, but three stories. The reader, it would seem, is thus being tutored in the art of reading the short story, a genre that prides itself in its epigrammatic, allusive terseness that says so much in so few words. To fully understand a good story, a reader has to pay attention to all its details. Unless the reader does this, he might not understand "the story," as always happens at the first reading of "Tombe 'Gworong's Own Story." I am encouraged in this latter interpretation by one of the possible semantic readings of the already quoted epigraph to "Sages and Wages." This particular interpretation becomes obvious if we scrutinize the phrases I have emphasized in the following passage:

> We hold these as truths, self-evident:
> A *reader must not yawn*
> *During the yarn*
> *Without the loss* (of *his* head)
> *Or that, of the writer's.*

If a work is not read carefully both the reader and the writer have sustained losses, namely, the reader has failed to learn and/or be entertained and the writer has failed to teach and/or entertain. Lo Liyong especially stresses the need for the reader to pay careful attention to works of literature when in his preface to *The Uniformed Man* he says: "Let the office worker relax in the office. When he takes up your stories or poems, engage him intellectually so that, at least once, he is alive and awake.... The first sentence his eyes alight on should give him the realization that he is in a thick forest where hurrying will not do ... that the whole length of the landscape has its fascination in every inch of it and demands to be observed specially.... Neither is the traveller to think that he might be given another chance to tread the same path" (xii–xiv).

It is evident that lo Liyong has succeeded to a great extent in his absurdist experimentations. His stories have a unique freshness emanating from his dexterity in deploying elements of oral and written literature of Africa and Europe to enhance the quality of his avant-garde writing. His stories are exciting and aesthetically pleasing to read. Finally, he has succeeded in using the modernist art of the absurd to probe contemporary African reality without deviating from the principles of African traditional aesthetics, which demand of art purposefulness and committedness. His stories are understandable and purpose-directed; they present absurdity not as the summation of life but as a comment on negative aspects of life; and their objective is satiric, corrective.

NOTES

1. See Chapter 3 of *Toward the Decolonization of African Literature* for a more elaborate criticism of the modernist tendencies of the so-called Ibadan-Nsukka School of Nigerian Poetry. The co-authors' earlier attacks on this school appeared in *Okike* numbers 6, 7, 13, and 14.

2. I need to point out that Nkosi's understanding of modernism is a little broader than mine because he has treated as modernist works that I would have hesitated to classify as such. His position in this particular quotation, however, coincides with the views I had earlier expressed in "Modernism and African Literature," a paper presented at the conference of the Literary Society of Nigeria held in Benin, September 17–21, 1980; and which is now available in *Ife Studies in African Literature and the Arts*.

3. Contemporary African writers of the absurd discussed in this study have all had close acquaintance with world literatures. Taban lo Liyong, for instance, participated in the University of Iowa Writers Workshop, as also did Femi Osofisan, who studied in France and holds a Ph.D. in French. Kole Omotoso holds a Ph.D. in Arabic literature, obtained from the University of Edinburgh, Scotland, and has also attended the Iowa workshop.

4. The fact that *Fixions* (1969) was written before the rule of Idi Amin Dada, who gained worldwide notoriety for his absurd personality and the grotesque horror of his reign (1971–1979), is a further evidence that the absurdist vision has all along been part of African reality, although significantly intensified by postindependence disillusionment caused by politicians like Idi Amin.

11

The Uniformed Man: A Composed Short Story Cycle on the Theme of Violence

INTRODUCTION

One is easily tempted to dismiss Taban lo Liyong's second collection of short stories, *The Uniformed Man* (1971), as being inferior to his first, *Fixions* (1969). This temptation is invited, to begin with, by the un-impressive printing and cover design of the second book, published locally in Nairobi by the East African Literature Bureau. Moreover, in the preface to the collection, lo Liyong declares his belief in the primacy of content over form, saying that "the importance of thoughts, ideas, rather than of art should be our primary concern" and that "instead of writing a story solely for the purpose of emotive satisfaction we should strew every bit of the paper with thoughts which cannot be ignored for the story" (xiii). This idea is reiterated in *Thirteen Offensives Against Our Enemies* (1973), where lo Liyong claims that "we need utilitarian literature rather than sweet music" (118).

The attachment of greater importance to subject matter than style is, however, not a novel idea with lo Liyong, who in *The Last Word* (1969), published the same year as *Fixions*, argues that the entertain-ment aspect of traditional African literature "is merely the means of attaining the end, which is the imparting of knowledge" (68–69). It is obvious, therefore, that it is wrong to assume that in writing *The Uni-formed Man* lo Liyong has been less concerned with artistic excellence than when composing *Fixions*.[1] This wrong impression is created by Elizabeth Knight in her otherwise excellent study titled "Taban lo Liyong's Narrative Art," which has greatly underestimated the artistic quality of the stories collected in the *Uniformed Man*. Her view is that "Asu the Great" is "a very obscure" story (114), that generally, the stories are "rambling with a quite arbitrary selection of incidents," and that they contain anecdotes that "seem quite irrelevant" (110). She believes that "only in 'The Education of Taban lo Liyong' is there evidence of structuring" (110–11); but she claims that even here lo Liyong has overdone his "self assertion and become simply pompous" (115).

Knight will surely not be the only critic who will take lo Liyong's preface too literally, thinking that *The Uniformed Man* is a collection of fragmented stories haphazardly put together more for the ideas they express than for their artistic merits. The stories, it seems, are significant only for their ruggedness, disorder, myriad allusions, digressions, parentheses, authoral intrusions, incomplete narration, and other qualities that appear to suggest works over which the author has lost control. Beneath all these outward appearances, however, lies a conscious and meticulous artistic design that defies comprehension not only by the careless, inattentive reader but also by one unaware of contemporary narrative experimentations. Indeed, on closer examination, *The Uniformed Man* turns out to belong to that highest caliber of short story collections known as *short story cycles* that, in the words of Forest L. Ingram, reveal "unity of character, theme, setting and symbolism" as well as a pattern of "recurrence and development as an integrated movement" of stories "linked to each other in such a way as to maintain a balance between the individuality of each of the stories and the necessities of the larger unit" (14–15). The stories in a short story cycle are "so linked to each other by their author that the reader's successive experience on various levels of the pattern of the whole significantly modifies his experience of each of its component parts" (19).

In the light of lo Liyong's theory of reading, which we have come across while discussing "Tombe 'Gworong's Own Story" in the immediately preceding chapter—a theory that demands meticulous attention to every detail of a short story—it should not surprise us that lo Liyong would employ the complex design of the short story cycle in his second collection. For the rest of this chapter, we will be examining the thematic and stylistic elements that constitute *The Uniformed Man* into a short story cycle.

VIOLENCE AS A THEMATIC CYCLE

The seven stories in *The Uniformed Man* are a coordinated study in the cause and nature of violence as a pervasive reality of human existence. There is a deliberate plan in which our knowledge about the cause and nature of violence is gradually deepened by each successive story either by showing an increasingly intensified level of violence through a correspondingly intensified symbolism, or by demonstrating the pervasiveness of violence through an expanding variety of human participation. Also, each story is in itself a complete artistic unit that reveals three aspects of violence, namely, the personal, the societal and the universal.

The first story, a fable titled "A Prescription for Idleness" (1–4), for example, demonstrates the personal level of violence by portraying the vanity, pretentiousness and stupidity that led Earl Hasty Hare to inflict self-violence by amputating three of his legs so as to compete favorably with the deceitful Count Cuckle Cock for the love of the beautiful Miss Gazelle. The deprivation of freedom to animals who are imprisoned in a zoo shows the second level of violence: society's infringement on the rights of the individual. The zoo is an obvious symbol of prison and all forms of social coercion. The third level, the universal, is evident in the pervasiveness of the violence in the human–animal setting of the story. Human beings have imposed on the animals by enclosing them in a zoo; the animals deceive, cheat, and lie in their daily competition with resultant violence; and individual animals inflict violence directed against the self. The news of the escape of "one of the greatest bank robbers" (2) from prison not only explains Brother Tortoise's agitation over the loss of his own freedom but links the animal world to the human society, and also shows that violence is not restricted to any section of life, but is universal:

Breakfast over, Brother Tortoise sat down doing three things at once: sipping his black coffee, listening to the morning news broadcast over the transistor radio, and reading the morning paper. . . . He looked stirred up; and acted so. . . . He was excited. Excited so much, his drinking just involuntarily kept pace with his thinking. Sir, this also applied to the other zoo animals. We focused on Brother Tortoise because our sympathies are more with him. . . . The fact is . . . one of the greatest robbers had just escaped from prison. The desire for freedom animated the zoo animals. (1–2)

The story, like all the others following it, shows how people deal with violence. Some, like Earl Hasty Hare, not only accept the violence per-petrated on them (incarceration in prison or zoo) but, as Io Liyong points out in *Thirteen Offensives*, they, in the manner characteristic of the weak and the violated, further "flagellate themselves" (90). The ironic tone in the presentation of Hasty Hare shows that people like him deserve nothing but scorn. Others, like the introvert Brother Tor-toise, reject violation and cope with the inevitable by mental self-lib-eration and in the process create things of permanent value, such as the beautiful story of the love of County Cuckle Cock and Earl Hasty Hare for Miss Gazelle, recounted in the cell by Brother Tortoise. The men of action carry the principle of noncooperation with one's violators further than mental liberation, and the possible result is physical liberation. An example is the escape of the robber from prison, an escape that starts animals like Brother Tortoise thinking of their "animal condition." It also confirms lo Liyong's claim that "a virile human mind always finds ways out of prisons and dilemmas" (*Thirteen Offensives* 87).

The animal fable of "A Prescription for Idleness" is a deliberately mild introduction to the subject of violence that is brought closer home with intensification at all its levels in the next story, "Herolette" (5–15). Since lo Liyong wants our introduction to violence to be gradual and methodical, we are still made to tarry for a while in this second story in the folklore world of animated inanimate objects, such as the ladders that cry and chairs that are happy when sat upon. Violence expands from the personal level of the vengeful herolette to the societal level of cultural restrictions that lead to immorality in society and to sexual deprivations. The several females in this story who caught Taban in their sexual nets vividly recall the heroine of "A Traveller's Tale," who was so sexually starved "she wanted to be raped. She looked forward to it" (*Fixions*, 47–51). The universal nature of violence is suggested in the "Herolette" by the world war that was then taking its toll even in Africa.

This story further deepens our knowledge of violence as a universal phenomenon by showing that it is an inescapable, if unfortunate, aspect of human nature. Although the soldiers are a menace to the villagers whose girls and goats they kidnap, the children do not block the soldiers' route with their stone-rolling as an act of revenge, as one would have expected, but simply as a play, a wanton act apropos of nothing. That this is done by innocent children more deeply demonstrates the gratuitous nature of a great deal of human violence. The revenge of the herolette, the narrator says in the first line of the story, is also ill-motivated, "not right" (5). The motif of gratuitous violence receives further development in successive stories. Had Elizabeth Knight grasped the significance of the stone-rolling episode, for instance, she might not have judged it and others like it as being "quite irrelevant" (110).

Violence is also received differently in this story. There is acquiescence on the part of some, as demonstrated by the women who agree to be kept as mistresses by the soldiers who had kidnapped them. Also, the herolette who is so vengeful in nature surprisingly does not utter a word or hurl a stone during the robbery episode, a fact that confirms the inconsistency of human nature. But there is also active resistance to violence. Taban's father, we are told, would, for instance, not have allowed himself to be abused by the defecating herolette; the young Taban who recounts this story as an adult describes how he tried to escape what he thought was a kidnap attempt; and the villagers opposed the theft of their goats by soldiers.

Although we recognize the human implication of fables, we are more sensitive to the violence suffered by the human characters in "Herolette" than that experienced by the zoo animals in "A Prescription for Idleness," despite the comparably greater seriousness of the violence involved in the latter. It is therefore through the image or symbol with which it conveys violence that the second story expresses greater intensity in the development of the common theme of violence. This image receives further intensification in the third story—"The Education of Taban lo Liyong" (16–35). Intensification is achieved by conveying resistance against societal violence through the hypersensitive consciousness of the writer-protagonist. For lo Liyong, society's beliefs, laws, myths, and traditions amount to "sanctions and regulations" (*The Last Word* 67) that, together with social institutions such as the church and the school, perpetrate the worst type of violence on the individual. He says, "Everybody is caged in by institutions, layers and layers of them," that "the cages or curtains are many and concentric and imprison each man in the centre like a unicorn," and that "at the present moment school education is the most effective centre of induction and indoctrination into conformity and uniformity" ("Education of Taban" 26). Formal education is particularly obnoxious to him because "millions of youths and men are herded together in schools and universities to be imprisoned there" (26). He views school as "the place where the monster, Society, does its worst" (26–27), because it promotes what he calls, not the dehumanization of man, but the "mechanization of man" (*Thirteen Offensives* 101).

In this third story, there is a further amplification of the imagery of the zoo as prison because we are told that the society is full of "layers and layers" of coercive social institutions such as schools. The story cycle has thus progressed from the physical imprisonment in the zoo, the prison, to the greater form of imprisonment—mental imprisonment by schools and other social institutions. There is also a further development on the motif of robotism, which we have met in those characters like Earl Hasty Hare and the soldiers' mistresses, who not only abet the violence perpetrated on them but further aggravate it by self-inflicted violence. The society at large, as shown through the example of lo Liyong's fellow students, accepts mental imprisonment. This motif will receive more elaboration and development in subsequent stories; but for now, the universality of violence is also stressed, firstly, by shifting the setting of the story from Africa to the United States, and secondly, by using a multiplicity of examples of violence. Professor Panfacade, for example, seems to enjoy torturing his students. Doctors, we are also told, "bless diseases, otherwise they would be unemployed" (16). We are similarly reminded of "the Red Indians, the natives of America for whom there will never be an independence celebration" (18). There is also an African-American girl who denies her heritage because of Africa's violent history of slavery, colonialism, and neocolonialism and who sees the term "Negress" as a "black badge of damnation" (18). The author-narrator who is the protagonist is aggravated by the shame of not being able to answer his professor's question and, in consequence, violently attacks everybody and everything—fellow students, his professors, social institutions, and the society at large. This is an extremely realistic portrayal and it underscores the basic selfishness of human nature, a trait that is often responsible for violence. The violent refusal of Taban, the hero, to accept any forms of violence draws its strength from his intellectual freedom, a trait we have observed in Brother Tortoise in the first story. Taban has what he calls "the eleventh commandment": "Thou shalt not restrain anybody—not even thyself" (33). Thus, this story combines in its major character the two categories of those characters who resist violence: one through mental action and the other through physical action.

The fourth story, "Project X" (36), is like the calm before the storm of the fifth story, "Asu the Great" (37–49). It is what is called the "minimal story" by critics of avant-garde literature; it is so brief that it is only a plan for a story but, amazingly, it is a complete story with all the ingredients of violence available in the other stories. In fact, it has more major characters than the preceding stories—eight in all: two enemies, a boy and a girl, a criminal and a policeman, and a would-be robber and a banker. Once again, it is the principle of multiplicity of characters that reveals the pervasion of violence beyond the individual level (two enemies), beyond the societal (a criminal and a policeman) to the universal (the situation between any pair of characters as projected in the story-plan holds true anywhere in the world). Vigilance—the informed level of intellectual alertness against, in this case, violence—is recommended as a way of coping with impending violence. The idea that violence is "impending" is significant in this story because nothing has happened and yet all may happen. This prepares us for the worst, which actually takes place in the next story. What "Project X" seems to be saying is that there is a permanent state of violence in the world in which even the loverboy lies in wait for the beautiful girl. This is a further broadening of the symbolic imagery of violence. Grouping lovers together with enemies, criminal and policeman, robber and banker also introduces a new dimension into our understanding of the nature of violence—that it is actually there where you least expect it.

Violence erupts into political murder in the fifth story, "Asu the Great." After a prolonged attempt at escape, which symbolizes the individual's refusal to abet violence on the part of Asu, the latter is caught by the king, who stands for the destructive, violent forces of coercive social institutions. That this murderous king is described as "a bloodthirsty brute of a child" (42) is meant both to stress the particularity of an obnoxious individual who clearly resembles Idi Amin and to underscore the universality of this type of violence by recalling the gratuitous violence of the "innocent" children rolling a stone to obstruct traffic in the second story of the cycle, "Herolette." We should also recall the further development of the theme of gratuitous violence in the third story where we met Professor Panfacade, who, for no obvious reason, loves to torture his students. In the present story, the motif of gratuitous violence is further developed through proliferation of the characters involved in violence. The narrator says, "That day, I chased Lancheek. Never mind the reason, probably there was none" (42). The quarrel between Asu and a fellow pupil that results in the epic chase that at once stands for the pursuit of Asu by the fellow pupil and the later hunt by his murderer, the King of Buranda—this quarrel also begins gratuitously: "One day, a boy hit Asuba. Asu hit back" (39). The idea of the universality of violence and political murder is reinforced through biblical allusions (Pharaoh, Christ, Gabriel, Moses, and Lucifer, 39, 41, 43, 44) and historical references (The Roman arena with gladiators and lions, 40).

The story is a complex one for it is an anecdote built on paradoxes. Asu, who is killed, actually never dies because he is indeed the narrator who tells us the story. The story in which Mr. Monkey outwits Mr. Shark illustrates how Asu in the end outwits his pursuer, the king. The survival of Asu is not to be taken literally, for he is physically dead. However, he is—according to the narrator—of the prudent few like Jesus, Seneca, Byron, and David Campbell who "choose the manner of the[ir] death" (41). Like these personalities, Asu has challenged evil and violence and has paid the supreme price. Asu outwits death by surviving through his intellectual and moral superiority over his murderer. The author identifies with these qualities as well as with the fact that Asu is a man of action who accomplished his goal: "He did his deeds; he died by the deeds" (49). The author has not only imbibed Asu's philosophy but also completely identifies with him, and hence throughout the story the author-narrator constantly interchanges his and Asu's identities until they finally merge. Thus, even though Asu is dead, he is still alive because the narrator, his double, is alive. Although we saw in the first story the infectiousness of the example of those who physically or mentally resist violence, this story brings the theme to a new understanding through the use of the technique of the double. Violence is ultimately futile because it not only breeds resistance but also because it is morally defeated even when it seems to have won the day. As we have seen, Asu is still alive in spite of the king's violence because this violence only succeeded in creating Asu's double.

The description of Asu's murderer as "a bloodthirsty brute of a child" is also significant from another angle. The characters associated with violence in all the stories we have discussed so far show a gallery of persons who successively show greater age. In the first story we have animals whom we generally rate lower than man in intelligence. The second story has a preschool-age herolette, while the third has an undergraduate as hero. The fourth uses a variety of adults but here we already notice a tendency to return to characters of lesser maturity by including a girl and a boy. This tendency is pronounced in "Asu the Great," the fifth story, by not only centering more attention on the young Asu as opposed to the mature Asu, but also by linking even the king with the child. In the next two stories this tendency will continue, for while there will be adult characters in each story, the victim of violence will be children. The victim in the sixth story is an infant, while in the last story it is a child victimized by a man who is but a robot. Thus, we have a circular progression in characterization in terms of age and maturity. This is undoubtedly meant to portray the unfortunate circular (complete) embrace of the world by violence.

The sixth story, "It is Swallowing" (50–57), is not only more tragic than all the preceding stories so far but also achieves a further intensification in the symbolization of violence. At the personal level we observe a terrorizing father and husband called "the commander-in-chief" (50). The societal level is marked by the unanimity of parents and society in compelling a recalcitrant young girl to marry according to traditional customs and against her wishes. The universal level of violence is revealed in the action of the society confronted by famine and hunger: "There were thefts; there were robberies; there were murders in attacks and defence: man killed animal man; few fathers knew they had sons, to say nothing of daughters" (54). In order to prevent us thinking these atrocities are unique to this society, the narrator stresses its universal quality: "Morals, mores, taboos, and all forms of social control work when we can still be reasonable. But, as man must eat, when famine enters through the main gate, all forms of social control dissolve into nothingness; their original quality" (54).

All the stories examined so far have identified the source of violence with man's selfishness and his innate quality, which sometimes propels him into gratuitous acts of violence. This story exhibits these traditional causes as well but goes further to broaden our perception by extending the cause of violence beyond man into nature, which is symbolized by the python that swallowed a hunger-emaciated, eleven-month-old boy.

At the height of the famine the boy is deposited in a path amidst tall grasses by the mother who climbs a nearby fig tree to pluck its fruits to alleviate their hunger.

This unfortunate mother is portrayed as an example of how to intellectually cope with violence. As a young girl coerced by society into obeying inhumane traditional marriage customs, she had presented a constant, informed opposition that distinguished her from the robot: "She was she. Had an independent mind" (50, 51, 52). She is later forced into conformity but is not broken: "She maintained she was right" (52). When she falls victim again, this time to cruel nature represented by the python, the narrator sympathizes with her as the target of the violence of cosmic irony. It appears fate has singled her out for misfortunes. The ending of the story seems to suggest that the way to fight this type of violence is to use the intellectual weapon of irony.

The seventh and final story, "The Uniformed Man" (58–67), rounds up the story cycle with the worst type of violence imaginable: the callous cold-blooded murder of one's child. The three levels of violence—personal, social, and universal, which also operate separately and individually in the story—all combine to create a powerful symbolism critical of society and human nature in the central episode. Society, which we are again told is "intellectually and physiologically cramping" (59), has managed to transform man with the aid of its coercive institutions into an unfeeling "bundle," a robot that mechanically and methodically murders his own child without any degree of self-awareness or guilt. The selection of the imagery of the soldier to represent socially conditioned robotism is an appropriate one for the army demonstrates man's condonment and formalization of violence. The soldier also symbolizes the ultimate stage of growth of all those characters in the preceding stories who accept and abet the violence inflicted on them and who sometimes even go further to perpetrate self-violence. The soldier appears to be a man who has not yet passed middle age, but his robotism reduces him in maturity below the level of even the animals in the first story, "A Prescription for Idleness."

Thus, characterization in terms of revealing violence through protagonists with varying degrees of maturity and humaneness shows a circular construction running through the story cycle. We move from the animal to the preschool boy, to the college student, to the politician, then back again to the preschool age, and, finally, to a robot. As far as the dimension and the degree of intensity of violence is concerned, however, each successive story in the cycle shows an intensification in an upward, perpendicular direction. A somewhat similar intensification in a perpendicular pattern is noticeable in the abstract objects with which violence has been symbolized: imprisonment, revenge, mental enslavement through education, enmity, political murder, cosmic irony, and robotism. Each story reveals negative character(s) who abet(s) violence and positive character(s) who resist(s) violence and resistance always has three aspects. First, there is some level of defeat: the animals are caged in the zoo, the herolette's revenge is ineffective, Taban is shamed in class and still has to do Dr. Panfacade's examination, Asu is murdered, the young girl is compelled to marry against her wishes and the python later swallows her child, the robot soldier kills the child he ostensibly wants to save. Second, there is physical action to resist violence; and third, this action demonstrates intellectual victory over violence: the robber escapes prison and Brother Tortoise recalls the love story of the Hare and the Cock for Miss Gazelle as a way of dealing with imprisonment; the herolette defecates to avenge a supposed offense and villagers prevent soldiers from stealing their property; Taban successfully resists mental enslavement in Dr. Panfacade's class; Asu, though murdered, intellectually survives in the paradoxical manner already explained; although compelled to marry against her wishes the heroine of "It is Swallowing" refuses to surrender her principles; and, finally, the narrator's satirical irony which reveals the robotism of the "mechanized" soldier registers the intellectual and moral victory of all those who resist social or mental enslavement.

It is obvious from the stories in this cycle that Taban lo Liyong has no illusions about human nature. Man, he correctly observes, "is not axiomatically human" and one cannot but also agree with him when he says, "Pity, humanism, reverence for human life are not inherent in man: these are acquired characteristics" (*Thirteen Offensives*, 101). Human acts of gratuitous violence, the violence induced by selfishness, and the role of society in promoting robotism through mental enslavement—all of which are shown in this story cycle—reflect lo Liyong's attempt to make us realize how much we have failed to transform ourselves from the "animal man" to the humane man. This is not pessimism but realism. If strong emphasis is laid throughout this cycle on the negative role of social institutions such as education, marriage, religion, and the army in promoting mental enslavement, robotism, and violence, we should not be misled into thinking that lo Liyong is advocating nihilist individualism and anarchy. Clearly, lo Liyong's objective is to alert us to the imperfections and negative characteristics of the institutions we operate so that we can better be able to organize a more humane, less violent society. This is a timely warning for Africa, his immediate audience, where violence has become a common feature thanks to the aberrations of some of its leaders and the inhumanity of apartheid. It is similarly a timely warning for the world at large engulfed as it is in daily regional violence, any of which, unfortunately, might develop someday into the holocaust of a third world war in spite of the periodic rapprochement of the super powers (which are short-lived in any case) and in spite of, or perhaps because of, the even less frequent redrawing of the political map of the world.

NOTE

1. In fact, lo Liyong has confirmed in a private correspondence to the author (August, 1990) that both *Fixions* and *The Uniformed Man* were originally submitted as one text.

12

The Uniformed Man: A Reconstructivist and Metafictional Parody of Modernism

While discussing in the preceding chapter the broadening perspective in the treatment of the theme of violence by the stories constituting *The Uniformed Man* into a short story cycle, we have, among other things, examined characterization, symbolism, and the use of cyclic and perpendicular constructs. In this chapter, we will take a close look at the elements of iconoclastic experimentation in the collection. There is a sense in which the violence of theme is matched by the violence of style, and hence, *The Uniformed Man* causes discomfort to readers who cannot appreciate works other than those in the traditional realistic style. Taban lo Liyong disturbs and disorients this class of readers with his confident assertive ego, his absolutely frank treatment of subject matter, his impious irreverence to established religious beliefs, philosophies, literary luminaries, critics and the establishment, his ironic parody of ostentatious modernist erudition, and with his liberal use of intrusive and digressive narrative technique, which produces collages and fragments rather than smooth chronological narration.

Taban, a graduate of the University of Iowa Writers Workshop, admits in his book of essays, *The Last Word*, that his works are "arbitrary or nonconformist," but then he challengingly asks, "So what? Isn't each writer an arbitrary maker, ordering or reordering the world? Isn't each reader a naturalized subject who submits to each author's dictatorship at his own peril and continues the relationship as long as it is mutually beneficial?" (8). Moreover, lo Liyong believes that "writers are to be more knowledgeable than the readers and should be ahead in intellectual leadership" (79). A reading of his books of essays, poetry collections, and prose works will convince even the most biased reader that he is either a genius or one who has worked exceptionally hard to maintain intellectual leadership of his audience. His erudition has given his writings a confident, proud ego that Peter Nazareth grudgingly agreed is "an egoism of the enlightened individual" (38). This admission notwithstanding, Nazareth so dislikes lo Liyong's ego, which he likened to the ego of a god, that he falsified evidence to belittle him. In his essay "Bibliyongraphy, or Six Tabans in Search of an Author," Nazareth claimed that lo Liyong, in replying to a critic's comments on his first two books in the *Times Literary Supplement*, says "out of nowhere" that "Friedrich Nietzsche is my greatest European hero. Followed by Karl Marx. Then, Adolph Hitler," and that "Taban sees no need to explain the relevance of these people to his essay since it goes without saying that what is important to Taban is of importance to the readers" (39).

The falsification in this biased comment becomes obvious when compared to the actual statement made by lo Liyong:

Friedrich Nietzsche is my greatest European hero. Followed by Karl Marx. Then Adolph Hitler. For, between the three of them African independence was born. This was a side effect, of course, but no matter. . . .

Nietzsche indoctrinated Germans with the philosophy of the master race, all blonde and blue. And Hitler bought it and fulfilled his destiny by bringing to reality frail Nietzsche's dream. In the course of the fulfilment of his destiny, Hitler sunk Europe into expensive wars and the colonial nations found it cheaper to give up the colonies. Furthermore, these wars brought together Africans from all parts of the continent and they forged a community of blackness. And most important of all, the whiteman's image of himself as God or superman was shattered when he trembled and died like everybody else in the battle front. So, thanks to Hitler, the white man was cut to his human size.

Karl Marx says the common lot of the workers is oppression by exploitation. The Communist International united the black workers and white workers in Europe and America. (*Thirteen Offensives* 116–17)

The openness and frankness obvious in the above quotation is characteristic of lo Liyong, whose ego is boosted, rather than humbled, by a critic's falsification of facts. Moreover, he is aware of the advantage of knowing one's worth, for he quotes Jorge Luis Borges' statement to the effect that "Kipling could have been a greater writer if he had known how great he was" (*Thirteen Offensives* 90). The same frankness is evident in his attitude to African and Western writers and critics. For example, he easily dismissed Chinua Achebe and Wole Soyinka, saying Cyprian Ekwensi and Amos Tutuola are more relevant (*The Last Word*

169). He severely criticizes Negritudist philosophy on every occasion and denies that philosophy's claim of a unique humanity for the black people. "Humanity," he says, "is a quality common to the downtrodden and those who side with them" (*Thirteen Offensives* 103). Furthermore, he believes that "if Europe and America are defeated some day, Europeans and Americans will be the most humanistic peoples on earth" (97). And in his characteristic frankness, he declares without apology that "Black Africa can only become strong, stronger, if we declare that our ultimate aim is world domination. The weak flagellate themselves; the strong flagellate other people. So having a turn at imperialism is good for the nerves, the hide, and the mind" (90–91).

This type of frankness that disturbs the emotion is the hallmark of *The Uniformed Man*. As we have seen in the preceding chapter, lo Liyong has an unflattering assessment of human nature ("man is not exiomatically human"), society, its leaders, and its institutions—all of which have made it possible for violence to remain a permanent, inevitable feature of human existence. This frankness is also there in his treatment of sex. Even when he describes the sex act with graphic vividness, he remains either frank and moral as in his folklore-inspired stories that we have earlier seen, or casual and ironic as in his experimental stories. He is never pornographic. The frankness, casualness, and irony with which lo Liyong, for instance, describes in the story, "Herolette" (13–15), his sexual experiences as a young boy or man trapped by a series of African and European sexually starved girls or women, would not surprise readers familiar with the treatment of sex in modernist and postmodernist Western fiction. In Ronald Sukenick's "The Death of the Novel," for example, sex is not only casually and frankly discussed but presented in a mood of cynicism and artistic self-conscious exhibitionism critical of public taste:

Meanwhile my chief concern is whether I'm going to be able to sell this unprecedented example of formlessness. How can you sell a current in a river? Maybe I better put my editor into it, he's a terrific editor, maybe that'll do the trick. A few more plugs like that and he won't be able to afford not to publish it. Or how about a little sex, that's the ticket. That's what this needs. A little sex. Okay, a little sex. (*The Death of the Novel and Other Stories* 49)

And true to his promise, there was more than enough of open sex in the rest of the story. There is good reason to compare lo Liyong with contemporary Western avant-garde writers. It is not simply because he studied at the University of Iowa Writers Workshop in the sixties, although that is highly significant, but because he consciously promotes a philosophy of "Synthesism":

John Pepper Clark is simply adopting [a] Greek technique for use on a work in hand. There is no harm in that. In fact, we need more Greek, English, etc., ways of doing things adopted by Africans. . . . It is ridiculous to bar an African from adopting foreign techniques. . . . It is not so much the technique as the personal style the artist has, his personal mark with which he stamps his works which is important. (*The Last Word* 53; see also 70, 132)

   In defending Clark, lo Liyong is indirectly defending himself, for his works reveal a consciousness of the techniques of avant-garde experimentations in Western fiction. These techniques, however, are distinctly stamped with his synthesizing personal mark in *The Uniformed Man*. He has moved far ahead of Raymond Federman who, according to Thomas LeClair, proposed that new fiction be "deliberately illogical, irrational, unrealistic, non sequitur, and incoherent," and has gone into what LeClair describes as "the next stage forward, synthesizing experimental forms, employing technical innovations to defamiliarize the materials of realistic fiction and not just the literary text" (LeClair 260). LeClair might equally have been describing the method and objective of lo Liyong in his fiction when he defined the style of American reconstructivist "avant-garde of mastery" whose "intent is transformation—of the work and of the reader, who is solicited, confuted, and released into a new system of ideas" (262).
   Like the reconstructivists, lo Liyong keeps "disorienting and reorienting" his reader in order "to first disturb, then revise the reader's notion of his culture" (265). For example, he is anxious for the African to lose his Negritudist misconception of innate humanity, and hence he shows in *The Uniformed Man* that all human beings are essentially violent and selfish in nature. The only way Africans can come to grips with the violence of which they have been victims throughout the modern history of slavery, colonialism, and neocolonialism is to understand it. The African must also be freed from his slavish attachment to what lo Liyong calls African "medieval past" (*Thirteen Offensives* 80), as well as from acquired Western philosophies, beliefs, and myths, if he is to compete successfully in the modern world of advanced technology. It is for this reason that *The Uniformed Man* is full of irreverence, especially toward European classical philosophers and major characters in Christian mythology. To begin with, he insists in the title story, "The Uniformed Man," that "the gods were imaginary, in the first place" and "have remained imaginary ever since" (58). In "It is Swallowing" the myth of the immaculate conception is ridiculed (55) and Jesus is presented as a bastard (53). Similarly, Christ is described as a sexually impotent man in "The Education of Taban lo Liyong" (22) and Christ's famous sayings are ironically and critically twisted around. In "The Education of Taban lo Liyong," for instance, we read: "Dirty hands do

not harm us as much as what comes from inside a man" (43); and elsewhere, we are told: "Blessed are the poor if they work hard to get rich" (*Thirteen Offensives* 91).

His attitude toward Christianity is the iconoclastic posture of a messiah and not the impiety of an innately irreverent nature, for he tells us that once "when I toured Europe I saw the spires, I saw massive crosses and other symbols in front and inside the churches. These cried out for my spiritual responses, stimulated me, and I gave of whatever piety I had" (*The Last Word* 51). His attitude is ideologically and politically motivated, for he also says that "the good news Jesus of Nazareth brought had been used by his priests to trample down on the black man" (*Thirteen Offensives* 118). Earlier he had explained:

Christianity is "the servant" religion, as Friedrich Nietzsche spent all his life telling the world. When it was introduced into Africa, the bulk of the population was serving one king or one war-leader or another; so Christianity was quickly embraced because it sang the same humility, the same self-negation, the same lack of ambition for things that really matter because they were difficult to attain; it is the religion of despair, the special diet of the weak. (*Thirteen Offensives* 81–82)

Lo Liyong sums up the ideological impulse for his Christian impiety this way: "Whoever gives man dignity is called Messiah. In that context, Nkrumah, our Redeemer, Our Osagyefo, is greater than Christ" (*The Last Word* 13). Thus, he is not merely making a gratuitous modernist exhibitionist gesture by his irreverence but seriously cultivating a style to serve an ideological goal.

Jack Hicks in his book *In the Singer's Temple* explains the characteristics of the type of fiction known as *metafiction*. This kind of fiction, he observes, is both metaphysical and *meta*fictional. It is metaphysical because it is primarily interested in the world of ideas and it is *meta*fictional in the sense that it is an experimental literature that attempts to extend its former possibilities by transcending its essentially mimetic status (18–19). This definition definitely makes *The Uniformed Man* a metafiction in both senses. Our discussion of the collection so far reveals lo Liyong as a philosophically concerned metafictionist and we shall soon begin to examine in detail his experimental use of the mode of parody to transcend not just the mimetic boundaries of realistic fiction but also the limitations of avant-garde modernist narration.

In practically every page of *The Uniformed Man*, lo Liyong is constantly holding conversation with, and taking to task, classical philosophers such as Plato, Aristotle, Socrates, Locke, Buddha, and Christ. His witty aphorisms and epigrams scattered all over the collection reflect his philosophical turn of mind and reveal his spirited ongoing argument with past philosophers. In one place he says, "Nature withstands patiently; man rushes, slips and falls. Ubi Sunt?" (24) In another place, he remarks, "The truth is: nobody is a failure if he does not regret" (33). Also he says, "You are no sooner born than you are approaching death" (41). His observation on another occasion is that "you may not be able to satisfy others. But if you satisfy yourself, you have administered to the need of at least one person" (56). His philosophical remarks also include this comment: "An alcoholic and a prostitute travel fast in the path of pleasure, so says Aristotle. Add to that a rider: the prostitute will derive catharsis and a purgation of the over-riding emotions" (64). A final illustration makes the following claims:

If you want to have conscience, learn a lot of prohibitive things which are contrary to the ways of nature. Sure enough you will find yourself following nature and being remonstrated by previous "learning" for your waywardness. That is what they call conscience—learning the unnatural and the impossible and failing as surely as could be predicted, then blaming yourself for the failure. (28)

The philosophical impact of these quotations are fully comprehended only in their integrated contexts. The last quotation, for instance, continues an interesting philosophical argument about the nature of art involving Horace, Castelvetro, Sir Philip Sidney, Wild Wilde, Plato, Shakespeare, and Teiresias.

Peter Nazareth complains that lo Liyong's "literary echoes do not reverbrate with meaning" as do those of other writers such as T. S. Eliot (39). What Nazareth fails to observe is that while lo Liyong delights in the use of modernist and postmodernist techniques, he is most of the time parodying these same techniques. This is quite obvious in *The Uniformed Man*, because he reveals his ironic attitude to the techniques he uses in at least two ways.

First of all, he overuses the techniques of experimental modernist fiction and purposely beats them to death. For example, myriad appearances in the text of literary, philosophical, and political allusions are used to parody the ostentatious erudition of the modernists. Also, he overuses parenthetical and direct digressions some of which are epical in their extensiveness. Here also is the reason for the superfluity in the use of the collage technique. There is no single story in the collection that is narrated in a sequential, chronological, uninterrupted manner. A typical story no sooner begins than it is interrupted by a seemingly unrelated digression that is followed by yet many more seemingly unrelated digressions. In the end, however, the story turns out a united whole with every one of the digressive fragments playing a vital role in advancing the central thesis of the story. If we understand, for example, that the first story, "A Prescription For Idleness," is about different levels of violence and how people cope with them, then we can appreciate the relevance of the love story of the Hare and the Cock for Miss Gazelle, which is recounted by Brother Tortoise, a story that at first appears quite irrelevant. It has already been explained that zoo and prison are obvious symbols of violence; that while some, like the robber who breaks jail, resist violence through physical action, others cope with it intellectually, as does Brother Tortoise with his escapist love story. Still a third group is like the despicable Cock who not only accepts the violence visited on him from the outside but also actually inflicts violence upon himself out of stupidity and greed and because of the deceit and selfishness that exist in every society.

There is, however, a subtle problem here: critics who fail to perceive the relevance of the fragments to the whole believe that lo Liyong has lost control over his stories. But those who do recognize the unity between the parts of the fragmented story are apt to forget that the reason for the overwhelming use of the digressive fragments is to parody the modernist technique of the collage.

The second way by which we know that lo Liyong is parodying his modernist technique is his use of footnotes, N. B.s, and explanatory parenthetical digressions that further playfully confuse the reader rather than shed more light on the point in question. A typical example is the footnote on "Mount Abora" on page 21. Other times, as in the last but one paragraph of the story, "Herolette," the summary is in fact the beginning of a new digression from the story. This method has been canonized in *Fixions* in the story titled "Tombe 'Gworong's Own Story." Also the technique of the "minimal story" is reduced to absurdity in the do-it-yourself story "Project X," where we have only the skeletal plan for a story rather than the story itself. This is a deliberate overextension of the practice of involving the reader in the creative process.

Lo Liyong's relationship with his reader reveals an instance of the convergence or synthesis of two different literary sources. He avails himself of the advantage of the rapport between audience and raconteur typical of oral performance by establishing familiarity with his reader, whom he often addresses directly as "Madam" and "Sir" in "A Prescription for Idleness." He frequently interrupts his story to address the reader with asides such as these: "I will research into that" (17). "I wonder if some critics will be so unfair to me as the barbarous *Quarterly* was to Keats. . . . It would be good to find out" (23). "Unlike other authors, I show you where my sympathies lie" (43). "(We don't know many curses, if you know any choice ones, indulge yourself)" (56).

Sometimes, he moves from the folkloric respectful author-reader familiarity to the parody of modernist disrespectful overfamiliarity. Such is the case when he uses expletives in "The Education of Taban lo Liyong" (35) and in "The Uniformed Man" (64), among others. It is similarly the case in "Asu the Great" when he commands the reader, saying: "Do this for me, will you? Say A aloud. Now say B" (41). He is purposely taunting and trying the reader's patience in "The Uniformed Man," where he devotes an inordinate amount of space describing the obvious mechanism of bicycles (60–61). Until the reader realizes he is being called upon by this seemingly insulting description to draw similarities between the inhuman mechanism of the bicycle and the robotism of the soldier, the reader feels his intelligence is being insulted. Also, often lo Liyong carries on self-editing in the process of telling his story, and this is not agreeable to some readers who feel they are being taken for a ride. In one instance, Taban edits his text in this fashion: "The trucks were many; I have already said that" (9). On another occasion, he writes, "Then there was, there were, those vying sisters— Martha and Mary" (22). In yet a third place, Taban corrects his sentence in this manner: "It was good he lost it—the sight—I mean, afterwards" (64).

Lo Liyong's self-consciousness as an artist is also a product of both his modernist consciousness and attachment to folklore. To the extent that he is conscious of the creative process and wants to deliver his text as effectively as possible, he is like the self-conscious oral raconteur. When, however, lo Liyong purposely reveals his technique as narrator, as he often does, he is like a modernist.

Nazareth says that "Taban the folklorist is genuinely creative" (35, 45). In the effort to achieve a beautiful narration, lo Liyong borrows heavily from folklore. Elizabeth Knight has correctly observed that he does not only borrow from folklore and give his fables modern setting, but also parodies the folklore-borrowed techniques (104, 105, 108). His fables usually exhibit a folkloric mixture of reality and fantasy and often have morals. These are pointed and obvious in *Fixions* but less so in *The Uniformed Man*. As in *Fixions*, the poetic beauty of *The Uniformed Man* has a largely folkloric origin. The use of a song-like poetic refrain is partly what makes "Asu the Great" such an aesthetically pleasing story. The refrain also serves as a motif for the chase and the escape from violence. The folkloric formula that he calls the "progression-and-repetition motif" (*Thirteen Offensives* 114; *The Last Word* 74) and that Nazareth defines as "call-and-response, chanting pattern" (45) and Knight describes as "one line of advancement of the story followed by one line of recapitulation" (105), has frequently been used to achieve a beautiful poetic rhythm. It is, however, not as elaborately employed in *The Uniformed Man* as in *Fixions*.

Folklore personification is also used to advantage in "Herolette," where we meet ladders that experience pains and cry: "Also a ladder on top of a man's head is a very uncomfortable experience, both to the man who owns the head and to the ladder. It is painful for a ladder to hit something. Secret: ladders cry when they break; so be careful with them next time" (6). Indeed, this sounds like an elderly person narrating a folktale to young children. It is the same in the following passage where chairs experience happiness: "A chair is good for sitting on; a chair is happy if sat upon, a chair clamours for the warmth of human buttocks; it is the nature of chairs to welcome buttocks; buttocks search for chairs; buttocks are good judges of seats; buttocks wear out trousers in order to communicate with seats directly; seats and buttocks are friends; bare buttocks and bare chairs are lovers" (7).

Lo Liyong's rhythmic prose is also a result of the use of traditional poetic devices of repetition, alliteration, imagery, and beautiful phrasing. None, for instance, can remain impassive to the beauty of a phrasing like this, the irony notwithstanding: "But changed to an angel, his thoughts would have been full only of nectar, ambrosia and glory unimaginable" (7). Brother Tortoise, we are told, "shares scales with snakes and crocodiles; legs with lizards and cats; shells with armadilloes and snails" (2). And here is how the stone-rolling episode is vividly described: "We rushed to the road and rolled it away. Then he would get it, carry it to the road. We took it out. He did it again, we repeated ours. He did; we did. Did, did" (12). Another example goes this way: "The Lord is good. He permitted Asuban to do his deeds. He did the deeds; he died by the deeds" (49). In the following sentences the meaning in a reading text is metaphorically called "food" and the printed text "plates": "I have reached a point of knowing certain things so thoroughly that when I read or re-read the same article, I derive no meaning from it.... I have already eaten the food and derived nourishment from it. The plates are of no value now" (32).

His love for wordplay, already remarked by critics (Knight 106; Nazareth 36, 37, 41), is in abundant evidence in *The Uniformed Man*. A good example is the use of "swallowing" in the story "It is Swallowing" (57). Another example is the following passage from "Asu the Great":

> Don't-this, Asuban.
> Don't that, Asuban.
> Don't.
> Asuban Don'ted.
> Asuban-Do never came. (42)

There are also neologisms such as "girlknappers" (9), "theologiphiles" (21) and "quelqueschoses" (64). Acholi and Swahili words like "panyakoo," "posho," "waragi," and "nguli" are freely used (11, 23). Latin and French are also incorporated into the text of some stories (4, 21–22, 24, 32, 51, 52). Colloquial speech is also mixed with standard English usage, sometimes to the extent of incomprehensibility, as in some pages in "Asu the Great." If we consider all of what lo Liyong manages to say in a story, we will begin to appreciate the amazing brevity of his style. Thoughts rush, stumbling one upon another, and this speed is often reflected in the fast tempo of his sentences, which are sometimes left uncompleted. Some of the quotations above well illustrate this.

It is inconceivable how any critic could have come up with the verdict that lo Liyong is ideologically irrelevant as a spokesman for the Third World peoples and that he is an artistic failure, as did Nazareth (48, 49). We may dislike his ego, which sometimes leads him to making himself his own subject matter, as in "The Education of Taban lo Liyong" and partially in "Herolette," "Asu the Great," and "The Uniformed Man," but we must remember that there is nothing strange in autobiographical fiction. Moreover, in the late sixties and early seventies when *The Uniformed Man* was written, it was the habit among avant-garde artists (in whose midst we must locate lo Liyong) to "take themselves directly as their major characters and work their own interiors— in confessions, analysis, fantasy—as subject matter" (Hicks 7).

He does not pamper the people of the Third World, just as he does not condone the weaknesses of the people of the developed nations. Rather, he uses his art to challenge the former to match the achievements of the latter. Lo Liyong believes in the unity of all men: "In the final analysis," he says, "society is also one" (*The Uniformed Man* xv) and he sees the differences in human beings as only a matter of "difference in degree," for as he points out, "A reliable balance sheet of innate qualities of the Blacks and the Whites and the Yellows has not yet been drawn up. For all practical purposes, there are no differences in them" (*Thirteen Offensives* 82). This is why he applies the same rule to all human beings and believes that the Third World has the capacity to catch up with the developed nations.

Lo Liyong is thus relevant, but he may be difficult to read. He believes that a work of literature should engage the reader intellectually, an engagement that should be uniquely pleasurable provided the reader is patient and the writer has done his homework (*The Uniformed Man* xiii–xiv). Our own homework in understanding lo Liyong consists in realizing how his synthesis of the techniques of folklore and modernism produces a strangely realistic fiction, for the achievement of lo Liyong is that he has defictionalized fiction and, by so doing, renewed it. Reading *The Uniformed Man*, everything looks so simple, so ordinary, that one wonders if this is fiction. But it is fiction in which there is a great deal of art and a distinct lo Liyong stamp. An arbitrary stamp, perhaps, but "art is arbitrary" as he points out. "Anybody can begin his own style. Having begun it arbitrarily, if he persists to produce in that particular mode, he can enlarge and elevate it to something permanent, to something other artists will come to learn and copy, to something the critics will catch up with and appreciate" (*The Last Word* 163).

The Uniformed Man proves Taban lo Liyong right. We are at last beginning to understand his collection's highly sophisticated reconstructivist strategy of reconstituting the minds of its readers in the areas of ideas and modes of literary art. Its metaphysical tendency, exemplified in the intense preoccupation with existing philosophical ideas that are invariably questioned, makes it a valuable contribution to twentieth-century African thought. Its metafictional quality, evident in the parodic style that tries to challenge the prevalent modernist mode of fiction, also makes *The Uniformed Man* a significant development in literary art. It is evident that the collection will cease to be an annoying puzzle to readers and become an interesting reading only if we grasp the metafictional orientation of its reconstructivist and parodic style. Unless critics understand this, they will continue to misinterpret the collection's intentionally exhibitionist overflogging of the devices of the minimal story, allusion, digression, collage, the footnote that playfully confuses rather than clarifies, wordplay, the preponderance of the first-person protagonist-narrator who self-consciously discusses his own style of narration, and other prevalent modernist devices that were threatening to become rigid canons of modern fiction.

13

Conclusion: The Challenges of the African Short Story

The foregoing general and close-up examination of African short stories will have achieved its primary purpose even if all it succeeds in doing is establishing the point that the African short story, by the extent, seriousness, and relevance of its thematic preoccupations as well as by the aesthetic interests of its artistic methods, is a major contributor to the making of the African tradition in literature and that, consequently, it deserves greater attention from the critics than it is currently receiving. The tasks before the critics are many. In order to gain knowledge of the peculiar thematic and artistic traits of individual short story writers, the critics have to undertake a systematic and comprehensive study of every important African short story writer. If our knowledge of African short stories as a significant body of literature is to be complete, critics must also provide answers to several questions.

What, for instance, are the regional and linguistic influences on the art of the African short story, since stories are written in different geographical and cultural zones and in diverse indigenous and European languages? What roles does the folktale play in molding the short story tradition in the various regions and languages? How does the short story tradition in a given European country affect the shaping of an African tradition in the genre in a former colony? In what respects are the short stories from anglophone and francophone African countries comparable? Do stories from anglophone countries necessarily have more elements in common between them than those they share with stories from francophone, lusophone, or Arabic African countries? What is the relationship between the formal short story, the folktale, and the children's story as practiced in Africa? How do African stories compare with stories from Asian, American, and European countries?

Critics of African literature need to supply the answers to these and other questions. They also need to provide comprehensive bibliographical listings of all the stories published in both the indigenous and European languages as well as the critical studies on them.

Publishers on their part need to know that shying away from publishing short stories and critical studies on the genre is financially counterproductive. The more they relegate the genre to the background, the less the profit that will accrue to them from the grudging investment they have made in its publication. On the other hand, the mere fact of investing generously on short story publishing is itself an advertisement and promotion for the genre and, consequently, the more the profit publishers will reap from the venture. Given the several activities competing for an individual's attention in our busy world today, the short story, with its advantage of providing maximum aesthetic pleasure within minimum time, has the potential to win more readers than the time-consuming genre of the novel, which is at the moment the favorite of publishers. Apart from bringing out short story collections and anthologies, well-known publishing houses should venture out into magazine and journal publishing whose aim will be to market top-quality short stories, poems, and excerpts from forthcoming novels by the best from among the older and younger generation writers. The greatest harm today is being done by the newspapers that publish anything under the rubric "short story," thus providing wrong models for aspiring writers. Newspapers will in fact gain in circulation if their editors begin to care more about the quality of the short stories they publish.

The pervasive ignorance of what constitutes a good short story is a direct result of the neglect of the genre by teachers and those who formulate the curricula for schools and tertiary institutions. And this is paradoxical because the short story is most ideal to introduce pupils and students to the elements of prose fiction. In fact, some of the finest and aesthetically pleasing writings in prose fiction are in the form of the short story. Writers find it a most pliable genre and hence the short story has become a regular school of prose craftsmanship and experimentation that pioneers new themes and new prose styles. In the hands of talented writers, the short story becomes the ideal medium to make a quick statement about a contemporary situation that is captured as a moment of history. Its ephemeral and contemporary significance can be carefully balanced against its permanent and more treasured universal value, using the mediating measure of an appropriate art form.

This is how classics like Chinua Achebe's "The Madman" and "Civil Peace," Taban lo Liyong's "Fixions" and "He and Him," Alex la Guma's "A Matter of Taste," Leonard Kibera's "Spider's Webs," Dambudzo Marechera's "Protista," Mango Tshabangu's "Thoughts in a Train," Ama Ata Aidoo's "Certain Winds From the South," Abioseh Nicol's "The Truly Married Woman," and many others are made. That is also what makes African short stories as a body fully representative of African prose fiction as a whole. There is no theme or style that is typical of the African novel, for instance, which is not available in the African short story. An introduction to African prose fiction at the secondary school and even during the first year of university can therefore be taught with an exclusive selection of appropriate short stories that would show the variety of prose themes and styles.

For all these reasons, it is obvious that accomplished African writers can no longer afford to abandon short story writing mostly to the incompetent hands of beginners as if it were only an apprentice genre. Similarly, critics of African literature ought to wake up to their hitherto abandoned responsibility with regard to identifying the contributions of African writers to the world development of the genre of the short story. This, of course, presupposes a thorough knowledge on the part of the critics of the developments in the genre in Africa, as well as an awareness of its history and contemporary practice in other literatures.

Works Cited

PRIMARY SOURCE

Single Author Short Stories and Collections

Achebe, Chinua. "In a Village Church." *Girls at War and Other Stories*. London: Heinemann, 1972. 74–77.

———. "Polar Undergraduate." *Girls at War and Other Stories*. London: Heinemann, 1972. 48–51.

———. *Girls at War and Other Stories*. 2d ed. London: Heinemann, 1977.

———. "The Madman." *Girls at War and Other Stories*. London: Heinemann, 1977. 1–10.

Aidoo, Ama Ata. *No Sweetness Here*. London: Longman, 1972.

Aidoo, Kofi. *Saworbeng*. Tema: Ghana Publishing Corporation, 1977.

Aniebo, I.N.C. *Of Wives, Talismans and the Dead*. London: Heinemann, 1983.

Easmon, R. Sarif. *The Feud*. Harlow, Essex: Longman, 1981.

Ekwensi, Cyprian. *Lokotown and Other Stories*. 1966. London: Heinemann, 1975.

———. *Restless City and Christmas Gold*. London: Heinemann, 1975.

Gordimer, Nadine. *Some Monday For Sure*. London: Heinemann, 1976.

Head, Bessie. *The Collector of Treasures*. London: Heinemann, 1977.

la Guma, Alex. *A Walk in the Night*. 1962. Reprint. London: Heinemann, 1968.

lo Liyong, Taban. *Fixions and Other Stories*. London: Heinemann, 1969.

———. *The Uniformed Man*. Nairobi: East African Lit. Bureau, 1971.

Omotoso, Kole. *Miracles and Other Stories*. 2d ed. Ibadan: Onibonoje, 1978.

Ousmane, Sembene. *Tribal Scars*. Trans. Len Ortzen. London: Heinemann, 1974.

Paton, Alan. *Debbie Go Home*. Harmondsworth, England: Penguin, 1979.

Themba, Can. *The Will To Die*. London: Heinemann, 1978.

Tshabangu, Mango. "Thoughts In A Train." *Africa South: Contemporary Writings*. Ed. Mothobi Mutloatse. London: Heinemann, 1981. 156–58.

wa Thiong'o, Ngugi. *Secret Lives*. London: Heinemann, 1975.

Zeleza, Paul. *Night of Darkness and Other Stories*. Limbe, Malawi: Popular Publications, 1976.

Multiple Author Anthologies

Achebe, Chinua, and C. L. Innes, eds. *African Short Stories*. London: Heinemann, 1985.

Denny, Neville, ed. *Pan African Short Stories*. London: Nelson, 1967.

Gray, Stephen, ed. *On the Edge of the World*. Johannesburg: Ad. Donker, 1974.

Komey, Ellis Ayitey, and Ezekiel Mphahlele, eds. *Modern African Stories*. London: Faber and Faber, 1977.

Larson, Charles R., ed. *Modern African Stories*. Glasgow: Fontana-Collins, 1970.

———. *More Modern African Stories*. Glasgow: Fontana-Collins, 1975.

Liswaniso, Mufalo, ed. *Voices of Zambia*. Lusaka: National Ed. Co. of Zambia, 1971.

Mutloatse, Mothobi, ed. *Africa South: Contemporary Writings*. London: Heinemann, 1981.

Nolen, Barbra, ed. *More Voices of Africa*. Glasgow: Fontana-Collins, 1975.

Obiechina, Emmanuel N., ed. *African Creations*. Enugu: Fourth Dimension, 1985.

Rive, Richard, ed. *Quartet: New Voices from South Africa*. London: Heinemann, 1977.

Scanlon, Paul A., ed. *Stories from Central and Southern Africa*. London: Heinemann, 1983.

SECONDARY SOURCES

Books

Abrams, M. H. *A Glossary of Literary Terms*. 3d ed. New York: Rinehart and Winston, 1971.

Achebe, Chinua. *Things Fall Apart*. London: Heinemann, 1958; New York: Astor-Honor, 1959.

Aluko, T. M. *One Man, One Matchet*. London: Heinemann, 1964.

Balogun, F. Odun. "The Soviet-Russian Short Story: 1950s–1970s." Ph.D. dissertation, University of Illinois, Urbana, 1977.

Beckson, Karl, and Arthur Ganz. *Literary Terms: A Dictionary*. New York: Farrar, 1975.

Beier, Ulli, ed. *Introduction to African Literature*. London: Longman, 1967.

Bellamy, Joe David. *Superfiction or The American Story Transformed*. New York: Vintage, 1975.

Bergonzi, Bernard. *The Situation of the Novel*. Harmondsworth, England: Pelican, 1972.

Bown, Lalage. *Two Centuries of African English*. London: Heinemann, 1973.

Burnett, Hallie. *On Writing the Short Story*. New York: Harper, 1983.

Chinweizu, Onwuchekwa Jemie, and Ihechukwu Madubuike. *Toward the Decolonization of African Literature*. Enugu: Fourth Dimension, 1980.

Darthorne, O. R. *African Literature in the Twentieth Century*. London: Heinemann, 1976.

Davidson, Edward H., ed. *Selected Writings of Edgar Allen Poe*. Boston: Houghton, 1956.

Emenyonu, Ernest. *Cyprian Ekwensi*. London: Evans, 1974.

Esslin, Martin. *The Theatre of the Absurd*. New York: Anchor, 1969.

Fagunwa, D. O. *The Forest of a Thousand Daemons*. Trans. Wole Soyinka. London: Nelson, 1968.

Finnegan, Ruth. *Oral Literature in Africa*. Nairobi: Oxford University Press, 1976.

Harris, Charles B. *Contemporary American Novelists of the Absurd*. New Haven, Conn.: College and University Press, 1971.

Hicks, Jack. *In the Singer's Temple*. Chapel Hill: University of North Carolina Press, 1981.

Hinchliffe, Arnold P. *The Absurd*. London: Methuen, 1969.

Holman, Hugh C. *A Handbook to Literature*. 4th ed. Indianapolis: Bobbs, 1980.

Howe, Irving, ed. *The Idea of the Modern in Literature and the Arts*. New York: Horizon, 1976.

Ingram, Forest L. *Representative Short Story Cycles of the Twentieth Century*. The Hague, Paris: Mouton, 1971.

Killam, G. D. *The Writings of Chinua Achebe*. London: Heinemann, 1969.

Larson, Charles R. *The Emergence of African Fiction*. Bloomington: Indiana University Press, 1972.

Lindfors, Bernth. *Folklore in Nigerian Literature*. New York: African Publishing, 1973.

lo Liyong, Taban. *The Last Word*. Nairobi: East African Publishing House, 1969.

———. *Eating Chiefs*. London: Heinemann, 1970.

———. *Meditations of Taban lo Liyong*. London: Rex Collins, 1970.

———. *Thirteen Offensives Against Our Enemies*. Nairobi: East African Lit. Bureau, 1973.

———. *Ballads of Underdevelopment*. Nairobi: East African Lit. Bureau, 1976.

———. ed. *Popular Culture of East Africa*. Nairobi: Longman, 1972.

Lukàcs, Georg. *Solzhenitsyn*. Trans. William David Graf. Cambridge: Massachusetts Institute of Technology Press, 1971.

Mvungi, Martha. *Three Solid Stories*. London: Heinemann, 1975.

Nichols, Lee. *Conversations With African Writers*. Washington, D.C.: Voice of America, 1981.

Nkosi, Lewis. *Tasks and Masks*. Harlow, Essex: Longman, 1981.

Omotoso, Kole. *The Combat*. London: Heinemann, 1972.

Osofisan, Femi. *Kolera Kolej*. Ibadan: New Horn, 1975.

Pearson, Norman Holmes, ed. *The Complete Novels and Selected Tales of Nathaniel Hawthorne*. New York: Modern Library, 1965.

Petersen, K. H., and Ann Rutherford, eds. *Cowries and Kobos*. Mundelstrup, Denmark: Dangaroo Press, 1981.

Ravenscroft, Arthur. *Chinua Achebe*. Harlow, Essex: Longman, 1977.

Stevick, Philip. *Anti-Story*. New York: Free Press; London: Collier, 1971.

Sukenick, Ronald. *The Death of the Novel*. New York: Dial Press, 1969.

Tutuola, Amos. *The Palm-Wine Drinkard*. London: Faber and Faber, 1953.

———. *Simbi and the Satyr of the Dark Jungle*. London: Faber and Faber, 1955.

Watt, Ian. *The Rise of the Novel*. Harmondsworth, England: Penguin, 1977.

Wellek, Rene, and Austin Warren. *Theory of Literature*. New York: Harcourt, 1956.

Wren, Robert M. *Achebe's World: The Historical and Cultural Context of the Novels of Chinua Achebe*. Harlow, Essex: Longman, 1981.

Zell, Hans, and Helene Silver, eds. and comps. *A Readers' Guide to African Literature*. London: Heinemann, 1977.

Articles, Reviews, Poems and Stories

Achebe, Chinua. "Work and Play in Tutuola's *The Palm-Wine Drinkard*." *Okike* 14 (1980): 25–33.

———. Introduction of *African Short Stories*. Ed. Chinua Achebe and C. L. Innes. London: Heinemann, 1985. ix–x.

Balogun, F. Odun. "Kolera Kolej: A Surrealistic Political Satire." *Africana Journal* 12, no. 4 (1981): 323–32.

———. "Modernism and African Literature." *Ife Studies in African Literature and the Arts* 1 (1982): 57–70.

———. "Achebe's The Madman: A Poetic Realisation of Irony." *Okike* 23 (1983): 72–79.

———. "Girls at War and Other Stories: A Failure of the Elites in Moral Leadership." Paper presented at ALA Conference held at the University of Illinois, Urbana-Champaign. April 6–9, 1983.

———. "Characteristics of Absurdist African Literature: Taban lo Liyong's Fixions—A Study in the Absurd." *African Studies Review* 27, no. 1 (1984): 41–55.

———. "Russian and Nigerian Literatures: Short Stories by Chekhov and Achebe." *Comparative Literature Studies* 21, no. 4 (1984): 483–96.

———. "Taban lo Liyong's Fixions and the Folk Tradition." In *Studies in the African Novel*. Ed. S. O. Asein and A. O. Ashaolu. Ibadan: University Press, 1986. 165–81.

———. "Nigeran Folktales and Children Stories of Chinua Achebe." *Multicultural Children's Literature* 4 no. 4 (1988): 50–69.

Barthelme, Donald. "Sentence." In *Superfiction or The American Story Transformed*. Ed. Joe David Bellamy. New York: Vintage, 1975. 213–20.

Bell, Elizabeth. "Fixions: Axept Him As He Is—The Short Stories of Taban lo Liyong." Paper presented at ALA Conference held at the University of Illinois, Urbana-Champaign, April 6–9, 1983.

Bown, Lalage. "The Development of African Prose-Writing in English: A Perspective." *Perspectives on African Literature*. Ed. Christopher Heywood. London: Heinemann, 1975. 33–48.

Carter, Donald. "Sympathy and Art: Novels and Short Stories." Review of *Fixions*, by Taban lo Liyong. *African Literature Today* 5 (1977): 141–42.

Chinweizu. "Prodigals, Come Home!" *Okike* 4 (1973): 1–12.

———. "Beyond European Realism." *Okike* 14 (1980): 1–24.

Chinweizu, Onwuchekwa Jemie, and Ihechukwu Madubuike. "Towards the Decolonization of African Literature." *Okike* 6 (1974): 11–27; 7 (1975): 65–81.

———. "The Leeds-Ibadan Connection: The Scandal of Modern African Literature." *Okike* 13 (1978): 37–46.

———. "Soyinka's Neo-Tarzanism: A Reply." *Okike* 14 (1979): 43–51.

Chukwuma, Helen O. "The Prose of Neglect." Paper presented at Third Ibadan Annual African Literature Conference. July 10–14, 1978.

Coates, John. "The Inward Journey of the Palm-Wine Drinkard." *African Literature Today* 11 (1980): 122–29.

Dash, Cheryl M. L. "Introduction to the Prose Fiction of Kole Omotoso." *World Literature Written in English* 16, no. 1 (1977): 39–53.

Dathorne, O. R. "African Writers of the Eighteen Century." *Introduction to African Literature.* Ed. Ulli Beier. London: Longman, 1979. 234–40.

Denny, Neville. Introduction of *Pan African Short Stories.* Ed. Denny. London: Nelson, 1965. ix–xvi.

Eastman, Carol M. "Taban lo Liyong's Cultural Synthesism in Socioliterary Perspective." Paper presented at ALA Conference held at the University of Illinois, Urbana-Champaign. April 6–9, 1983.

Echeruo, M.J.C. Introduction of *The Sacrificial Egg and Other Stories.* By Chinua Achebe. Onitsha: Etudo, 1962. 3–6.

Eliot, T. S. "The Love Song of J. Alfred Prufrock." *The American Tradition in Literature.* Ed. Sculley Bradley, et al. 4th ed. Vol. 2. New York: Grosset, 1974. 1174–78.

Fatton, Kathleen B. "A Walk in the Night Revisited." Paper presented at ALA Conference held at the University of Illinois, Urbana-Champaign. April 6–9, 1983.

Gordimer, Nadine. Introduction of *Some Monday For Sure.* By Gordimer. London: Heinemann, 1976. xi–xiii.

Gray, Stephen. Introduction of *One the Edge of the World.* Ed. Gray. Johannesburg: Ad. Donker, 1974. 9–11.

Julien, Aileen. "Of Traditional Tales and Short Stories." *Toward Defining the African Aesthetic.* Ed. Lemuel A. Johnson, et al. Washington D.C.: Three Continents Press, 1982. 82–94.

Knight, Elizabeth. "Taban lo Liyong's Narrative Art." *African Literature Today* 12 (1982): 104–17.

Komey, E. A., and E. Mphahlele. Introduction of *Modern African Stories.* Ed. Komey and Mphahlele. London: Faber and Faber, 1964. 9–12.

Larson, Charles R. Introduction of *Modern African Stories.* Ed. Larson. Glasgow: Fontana, 1970. 7–12.

———. Introduction of *More Modern African Stories.* Ed. Larson. Glasgow: Fontana, 1975. 7–12.

LeClair, Thomas. "Avant-garde Mastery." *TriQuarterly* 53 (1982): 259–67.

Lester, Julius. "The Outsider in European and Afro-American Literatures." *Okike* 10 (1976): 83–94.

lo Liyong, Taban. Preface to *The Uniformed Man.* By lo Liyong. Nairobi: East African Literature Bureau, 1971. ix–xviii.

Moore, Gerald. "Amos Tutuola: A Nigerian Visionary." *Introduction to African Literature.* Ed. Ulli Beier. London: Longman, 1979. 189–97.

Moore, Jack B. Review of *The Feud,* by R. Sarif Easmon. *African Literature Today* 14 (1984): 152–54.

Nazareth, Peter. "Bibliyongraphy, or Six Tabans in Search of an Author." *English Studies in Africa* 21, no. 1 (1978): 33–49.

Nkosi, Lewis. "Obituary—An Introduction." *The Will to Die.* By Can Themba. Ed. Donald Stuart and Roy Holland. London: Heinemann, 1978. vii–xi.

Nnolim, Charles. "The Critic of African Literature: The Challenge of the 80s." *Afa: Journal of Creative Writing* (of the Imo Poetry Club) 1 (1982?): 51–56.

——. "The Short Story as Genre: A Study in Basic Distinctions, Plus Teaching Notes on Three World Classics." Paper presented at 13th Annual Conference of Nigeria English Studies Association. University of Calabar, September 26–30, 1989.

Noss, Philip A. "Creation and the Ghaya Tale." *Artist and Audience: African Literature as a Shared Experience.* Ed. Richard K. Priebe and Thomas A. Hale. Washington, D.C.: Three Continents Press, 1979. 3–30.

Nwankwo, Chimalum. "Ngugi's Short Stories: A Socio-Political Window on Post-Independence Kenya." Paper presented at ALA Conference held at the University of Illinois, Urbana-Champaign. April 6–9, 1983.

Obiechina, Emmanuel. Preface to *African Creations.* Ed. Obiechina. Enugu: Fourth Dimension, 1985. vii–viii.

Oladitan, Olalere. "The Nigerian Crisis in the Nigerian Novel." *New West African Literature.* Ed. Kolawole Ogungbesan. London: Heinemann, 1979. 10–20.

Parker, Carolyn A. "The Advice of Elders, A Broken Leg, and a Swahili Proverb Story." *Artist and Audience.* Ed. Priebe and Hale. Washington, D.C.: Three Continents Press, 1979. 49–59.

Poggioli, Renato. "Storytelling in a Double Key." *Anton Chekhov's Short Stories.* Ed. Ralph E. Matlaw. New York: Norton, 1979. 307–28.

Scanlon, Paul A. Introduction of *Stories From Central and Southern Africa.* Ed. Scanlon. London: Heinemann, 1983. 1–12.

wa Thiong'o, Ngugi. "Okot P'Bitek and Writing in East Africa." *Homecoming.* New York: Lawrence Hill, 1973. 67–77.

Zamyatin, Yevgeny. "On Literature, Revolution, Entropy, and Other Matters." *A Soviet Heretic: Essays by Yevgeny Zamyatin.* Ed. and Trans. Mirra Ginsburg. Chicago: University of Chicago Press, 1970. 107–12.

Index of Short Stories

General Index

Abrahams, Lionel, 13, 42

Abrams, M. H., 38, 51, 82, 90

absurd, literature of the: African and American novels, 137; Camus, Albert, and, 132; characteristics of African, 133–34, 137–38, 145; characteristics of Western, 132–33, 137–38; *The Combat* (Omotoso), 137; Esslin, Martin, and, 132; *Kolera Kolej* (Osofisan), 136–37; lo Liyong, Taban, and Omotoso, Kole, and Osofisan, Femi, contrasted as writers in tradition of, 145; lo Liyong's, Taban, use of, 122, 139–49; *The Palm-Wine Drinkard's* (Tutuola) link with, 134–35; philosophical and stylistic differences between African and Western, 137–38, 145; purpose of African, 144; purpose of Western, 132; root of African, 133–34, 136; root of Nigerian, 133–34; root of Western, 132–33; satire and, 138–39; *The Theatre of the Absurd* (Esslin), 132

absurdist elements in *Fixions*: exaggeration, 141, 143, 144; factual details, 140–41; humor, 141–44; lexical and semantic absurdities, 143–44; neocolonial realities of Africa, 142–43

Achebe, Chinua, 19, 23, 43, 44–45; *Anthills of the Savannah*, 60; artistic style, 57–58, 60–62, 81–96, 102–10; and folklore, 35 n.3; *No Longer at Ease*, 79 n.1; poetic realisation of irony, 91–95, 101–9; presentation of the elites, 66–76, 98–99; as short story writer, 5, 7, 28, 29, 30, 31; themes, 57–60, 112–13; themes in *Girls at War and Other Stories*, 65–80; themes in "The Madman," 97–102; *Things Fall Apart*, 67, 69, 97, 112–13; and Tutuola, 78–79; on Tutuola's *The Palm-Wine Drinkard*, 63 n.1, 135

Achebe, Chinua, and lo Liyong, Taban, 57, 63 n.1; ideological similarities and differences, 59–60; as

ABOUT THE AUTHOR

F. ODUN BALOGUN holds a Ph.D. from the University of Illinois, Urbana and is a visiting professor of literature at George Mason University in Fairfax, Virginia. Through the support of a Social Science Research Council Fellowship, he is working on a book examining the extent and significance of Marxist aesthetics in socialist African literature. He plans to bring out *Structurally Adjusted Lives*—a series of short stories reflecting the experiences of Nigerians during the economic revisions of the current Structural Adjustment Program. His articles have appeared in a variety of journals, including *African Literature Today*, *African Studies Review*, *Presence Africaine*, *Comparative Literature Studies*, and *Black American Literature Forum*. Another book, *The Apprentice and Other Stories*, is scheduled for publication in Nigeria.